FACING KIRINYAGA

Dedication

To Denise, with love

FACING KIRINYAGA

*A social history of forest commons
in southern Mount Kenya*

ALFONSO PETER CASTRO

**Practical
ACTION
PUBLISHING**

INTERMEDIATE TECHNOLOGY PUBLICATIONS 1995

Practical Action Publishing Ltd
25 Albert Street, Rugby, CV21 2SD, Warwickshire, UK
www.practicalactionpublishing.com

© Alfonso Peter Castro 1995

First published 1995
Reprinted 2005

ISBN 13 Paperback: 9781853392535
ISBN Library Ebook: 9781780444918
Book DOI: https://doi.org/10.3362/9781780444918

A catalogue record for this book is available from the British Library.

The authors, contributors and/or editors have asserted their rights under the
Copyright Designs and Patents Act 1988 to be identified as authors of their
respective contributions.

Since 1974, Practical Action Publishing has published and disseminated books and
information in support of international development work throughout the world.
Practical Action Publishing is a trading name of Practical Action Publishing Ltd
(Company Reg. No. 01159018), the wholly owned publishing company of Practical
Action. Practical Action Publishing trades only in support of its parent charity
objectives and any profits are covenanted back to Practical Action (Charity Reg. No.
247257, Group VAT Registration No. 880 9924 76).

Typeset by Dorwyn Ltd, Rowlands Castle, Hants

Reasonable efforts have been made to publish reliable data and information, but the
author and publisher cannot assume responsibility for the validity of all materials or
for the consequences of their use.

The manufacturer's authorised representative in the EU for product safety is
Lightning Source France, 1 Av. Johannes Gutenberg, 78310 Maurepas, France.
compliance@lightningsource.fr

Contents

List of Maps, Tables and Figures

Preface

THE IDEA FOR this book came from conversations in the early 1980s with elderly Gikuyu men and women in Kirinyaga district, Kenya. I was carrying out anthropology fieldwork on deforestation along the crowded southern slopes of Mount Kenya. This linkage between anthropology and forestry may strike some readers as odd, but it is by no means so. Forest resources are integral parts of livelihoods throughout sub-Saharan Africa (and many other parts of the world), supplying timber, fuel, food, fodder, and other vital products, as well as contributing to the environmental stability of local production systems. Trees often possess spiritual, folklore, or other cultural significance for communities. The use and management of forest resources are embedded in a complex array of micro- and macro-level institutions ranging from individual households to global markets. Since the late 1970s anthropologists and other social scientists such as David Brokensha, Marilyn Hoskins, Ramachandra Guha, Michael Dove, John Raintree, Nancy Lee Peluso, Bernard Riley, Donald Messerschmidt, and many others have contributed innovative social perspectives to the realm of forestry.

One afternoon at the beginning of fieldwork my young assistants, Cyrus Kibingo and George Muriithi, and I encountered an old man near Kangaita Tea Factory in northern Kirinyaga. We were not too far away from the central government's forest reserve on Mount Kenya. The elder expressed surprised to see a *muthungu* (white man) walking in the midst of farmland. Despite the area's considerable beauty, it was seldom visited by tourists. He was impressed to hear that I had travelled on foot from Kagumo market, several kilometres down the slopes. Many of the local people believed that whites were incapable of walking long distances. The origin of this belief was easily explained. In the countryside they rarely saw a *muthungu* outside of a motor vehicle. The old man asked what we were doing, and he expressed approval to learn about our study of forestry matters. He told us that he could remember when the land we were standing on was thickly wooded, adding a fascinating bit of information: 'The land was claimed by the whites, but it was owned by Gikuyus.' The old man stated that the British seized control over the forest but eventually gave it back to the Africans. None of us had any idea what he was talking about. Cyrus and George were from other parts of the district and unfamiliar with the Kangaita area's history. I was unaware of any scholarly literature about such a dispute. We asked if this conflict took place during the Mau Mau War. 'No, earlier', but he could not recall exactly when. The conversation turned to other subjects, and we soon departed. I remained intrigued by the old man's story. In the course of other interviews elderly people provided similarly tantalizing yet sketchy accounts, often about forests now owned by the central government or the local country council. Because my research design concentrated on contemporary wood scarcity, though, I initially assigned a low priority to uncovering the mysterious conflicts (if indeed any mystery existed).

Another incident reinforced my sense of ignorance about the historical context of local tree management. Scattered throughout Kirinyaga were small stands of trees, often with a dense understorey of shrubs and other plants. I knew from interviews and the writings of Jomo Kenyatta and others that the trees were the remnants of the area's sacred groves. They were the places of worship before widespread conversion to Christianity in the twentieth century. An elderly informant insisted that I take photographs of a well-known grove near his home. On the appointed day Cyrus and I walked to the site. Cyrus was shocked to see that the bushes covering the grove's most prominent tree had been cleared away. Maize already grew close to the grove, so I assumed that the household was continuing the process of encroaching on the formerly sacred site. The needs of today, I reckoned, were more pressing than ancient customs. Cyrus required much coaxing to stand in front of the immense tree to provide a sense of scale for the photographs. He was worried about the tree's long association with the supernatural. We ended up talking to two old men on the path, who briefly described the tree's significance. Although surprised by the clearing, one of them pointed out, 'The owner of the land can do whatever he likes with the tree.' Upon reaching the informant's home, we excitedly told him about the clearing of the bush, certain that the event was filled with lessons about contemporary cultural change. Yes, he knew about the bush being cleared. He had asked the landowner, a friend, to do it so I could take a good picture! So much for my assumptions. Yet, I was left with the question of what exactly happened to the sacred groves following the onset of colonial rule?

It became increasingly apparent in the course of fieldwork that the past had much relevance for understanding present-day problems. Women, particularly from land-poor and landless households, often attributed the origins of wood fuel scarcity, for example, to the colonial-initiated land tenure reform of the 1950s. Other issues arose as well. Elderly people mentioned government-initiated tree planting dating back to the 1920s. The large-scale wattle (*Acacia mearnsii*) programme of the colonial era had been well documented by Michael Cowen and Gavin Kitching, but men and women in Kirinyaga recalled other afforestation efforts. They remembered compulsory tree planting on hillsides and along ridges. Some of them also described the tree nurseries that operated throughout the district during the 1940s. A few of the elders discussed the role of the Mount Kenya forest in the Mau Mau War, as well as the widespread deforestation that occurred during the counter-insurgency campaign.

My appreciation of the history of local forestry increased when I visited the national and district archives. The colonial records provided substantial insights, albeit from very different perspectives from the district interviews. Especially useful were a handful of files from the Embu archives (Kirinyaga was part of Embu district for most of the colonial era). Let me emphasize the word 'handful', for the district clerk allowed me to borrow a stack of files. Another field assistant, John Githuri Gichobi, and I transported the dusty records back to Kerugoya via *matatu*, the ever-crowded local cars and small trucks that ply the country roads. One file in particular proved helpful for sorting out the mysterious forest conflict near Kangaita. It was entitled 'Land Commission', and contained a detailed account of how the people of Embu appealed to the Kenya Land Commission during the early 1930s for the return of the Mount Kenya forest. The forest had been appropriated during the early years of colonial rule. The file also included a strange and protracted saga about the return of a patch of forest called Nyagithuci — the very place the old man had described.

I decided to limit this book to issues concerning the management and use of common property forests, groves, and trees. Until recently, the social history of Kenya's woodland was virtually ignored. Fortunately, publications by David Brokensha, David Anderson, Bernard Riley, Holly Dublin, Peter Dewees, and others have been important in illuminating some of the long-standing relationships between Kenyans and their forest resources. Still, there is much work to be done to provide a full accounting. I intend to incorporate my research on household tree planting in Kirinyaga into a broader study of the historical changes in the district's farming systems. It seems a much more appropriate setting for the topic.

For those unfamiliar with the literature on the Gikuyu, the title of this book derives from Jomo Kenyatta's 1938 classic *Facing Mount Kenya*. *Kirinyaga* is the Gikuyu term for Mount Kenya. I will follow Kenyatta's lead in referring to the *Agikuyu* (*Mugikuyu*, sing.) as Gikuyu, instead of the anglicized spelling of 'Kikuyu'.

At the publisher's request, I have eliminated nearly all of the references from government documents, including those from the Kenya National Archives and the Embu District Archives. Chapter 1 contains a brief description about the sources used, including colonial documents. Readers interested in particular sources may want to consult my writings in journals and edited volumes where parts of this book appeared originally in somewhat different versions (see the Acknowledgements). I also invite readers to write to me for further information.

Acknowledgements

I am grateful for the help that I received over the years. Many people and institutions contributed directly and indirectly to this study; indeed, it seems a considerable task to identify them all. Let me apologize in advance for any oversights!

A special thanks is owed to David Brokensha, a wonderful teacher and a good friend. His generous support and constant inspiration proved instrumental in completing this study.

In Kenya I must thank: my field assistants Cyrus Kibingo, George Muriithi, and John Githuri Gichobi; the staff and students of the Kerugoya School for the Deaf, particularly John Murigo, Annie Maina, Sister Firmina, Joe Morrissey, and James Molloy; the Office of the President; the University of Nairobi, Institute for Development Studies; the Kenya National Archives; district officials in Kirinyaga and Embu; the Kirinyaga and Embu County Councils; staff members of the Forest Department in Kirinyaga; the staffs of Kangaita and Kimunye tea factories; Albert Gichoki; Laban Kago; Susan Wangithi; Musa Njairu; and Anne and Pat Fleuret. Of course I also owe a tremendous debt of gratitude to the many people in Kirinyaga — women and men, old and young — who shared their knowledge and experiences.

Other people provided invaluable support and guidance. Charles Erasmus, Bernard Riley, and Manuel Carlos stimulated my interest in rural development when I was a student at the University of California, Santa Barbara (UCSB). Fellow UCSB alumni Enos Njeru, Miriam Chaiken, Tom Conelly, Thomas Hakansson, Randy Luce, and Elaine Barnard offered cheerful encouragement. My knowledge of community forestry has benefitted from discussions with Marilyn Hoskins, Mike Arnold, Michael Horowitz, John Miskell, C. Chandrasekharan, Richard Tucker, Mafa Chipeta, Michael Dove, Robin Levingston, and Ken MacDicken. Mike Warren invited my participation in the Indigenous Knowledge Series. Corwen McCutcheon gave important editorial assistance.

Colleagues at Syracuse University and neighbouring State University of New York, College of Environmental Science and Forestry provided encouragement, especially John Townsend, Doug Armstrong, Barbara Grosh, Michael Freedman, Carol Carpenter, Hans Buechler, Allen Drew, Charlie Hall, and Maggie

Shannon. My classes on social forestry and international development served as a forum for discussing many of the ideas in this book. Several students merit special mention: Bill Waters, Kreg Ettenger, Kathryn Stam, Kathleen Skoczen, Phillip Eskali, Jim Uhlig, Todd Nachowitz, Susan Hamilton, Sharad Karmacharya, Nate Appleton, Elliot Senekane, Mariel Durckheim, Myrna Hall, Aarti Saihjee, Greg MacKenzie, Beth Wolgemuth, Walter Aikman, Landis Hudson, Andre Rego, Elizabeth Kilmarx, Elena Quintana, Anne Marie McShea, Andrea Finger-Stich, Bhuvana Rao, Shana Udvardy, Anne Draddy, Teresa Hubley, Luciana Porter, James Gliet, Raymundo Cota, Zhiqiang Kong, and Jennifer Astone.

The National Science Foundation, the Intercultural Studies Foundation, the University of California, Santa Barbara, and the Appleby-Mosher Fund at Syracuse University gave financial assistance. Responsibility for the contents of this book, including opinions and errors, is mine alone.

I especially acknowledge the warm support of my family: my wife Denise and children Camille and David, as well as my parents Carmen and the late Alfonso Castro, sisters Tamara and Karen, and brother Robert.

Finally, parts of this book originally appeared as journal articles and chapters in edited volumes. I am grateful for permission to use copyrighted materials from:

Southern Mount Kenya and Colonial Forest Conflicts. In: J. Richards and R. Tucker (eds), *World Deforestation in the Twentieth Century*, Duke University Press, Durham, 1988, 33–55, 266–71.

Sacred Groves and Social Change in Kirinyaga, Kenya. In: M. Chaiken and A. Fleuret (eds), *Social Change and Applied Anthropology*, Westview Press, Boulder, 1990, pp. 277–90.

Indigenous Kikuyu Agroforestry: A Case Study of Kirinyaga, Kenya. *Human Ecology*, Vol. 19, No. 1, 1991, pp 1–19.

Njukiine Forest: Transformation of a Common-Property Resource. *Forest and Conservation History*, Vol. 34, No. 4, 1988, pp 160–68.

The Southern Mount Kenya Forest Since Independence: A Social Analysis of Resource Competition. *World Development*, Vol. 19, No. 12, 1991, pp 1695–1704.

Kikuyu Agroforestry: An Historical Analysis. *Agriculture, Ecosystems and Environment*, No. 46, 1993, pp 45–54.

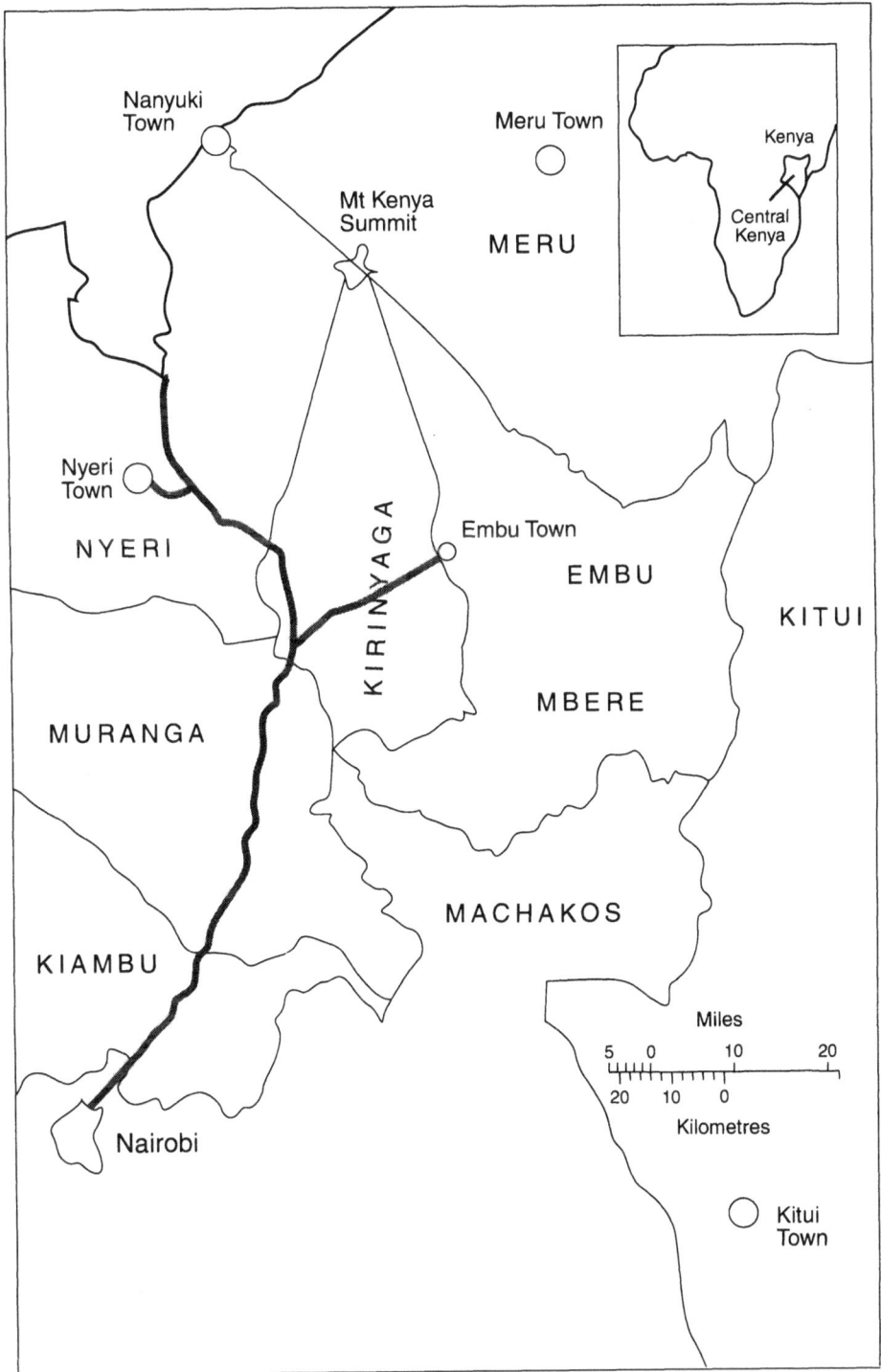

1. *Central Kenya (Adapted from Riley and Brokensha, 1988)*

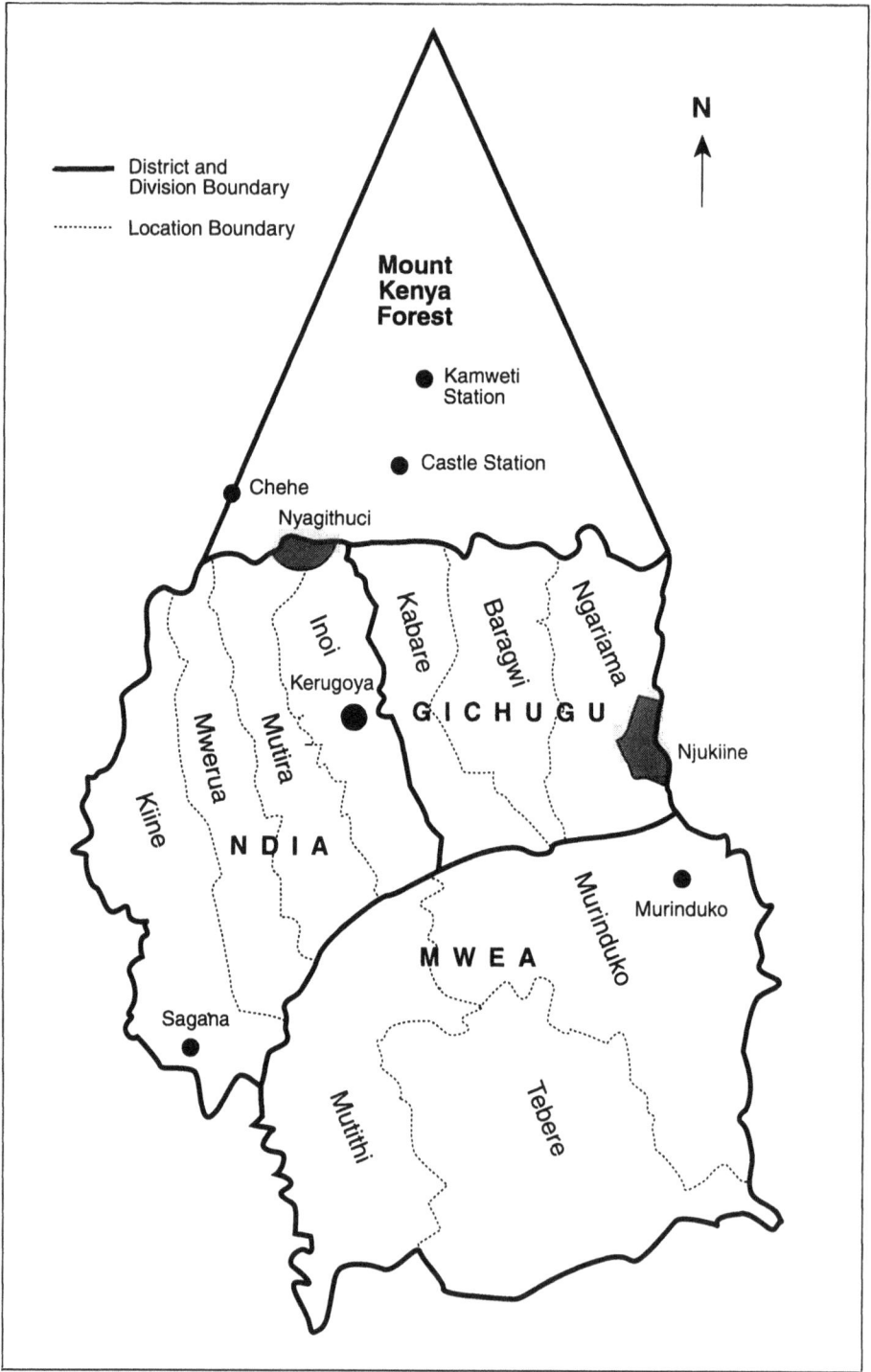

2. *Kirinyaga District (Adapted from* Kirinyaga District, *1980)*

1. Contested commons

THIS BOOK PRESENTS a social history of common property forest management and related political conflicts in a rural district along the southern slopes of Mount Kenya. Its purpose is to contribute to ongoing debates about how to manage forest resources on a sustainable basis. The study will analyse changes in the use and management of three forest resources in Kirinyaga, Kenya: the vast Mount Kenya forest; patches of woodland such as Njukiine forest; and sacred groves. At the beginning of the twentieth century the Ndia and Gichugu Gikuyu lived in small, independent communities, and they managed these forests through customary controls. In the colonial era each of the forests was taken over for different reasons by the British administration or its local authorities. Although the three types of forest resources still existed in 1988, when this study ends, their respective fates over the years reveal a considerable amount about local social change and the limits of state forestry.

The transition from local to government control and its impact on forest access, exploitation, and management are vital issues for understanding contemporary forest use patterns. In developing countries such as Kenya, where the system of public administration was inherited from colonial rule, knowledge of this past is indispensable for comprehending the traditions of state forest management and local attitudes about it. By becoming aware of the wealth of experience already available in terms of community and government forest management, we can better examine and consider the options and proposals that we have today.

As will be seen, a complex combination of factors — cultural beliefs and values, local social relations, economic concerns, and population pressures — governed indigenous use and management of forest resources. Trees were a vital part of pre-colonial Gikuyu livelihood, yet they conflicted with the need for agricultural land. The people of Ndia and Gichugu attempted to reconcile competing pressures for removing and retaining trees through a range of communal and farm-level strategies. Controls on clearing were part of the communal property rights regime and embedded in religious beliefs and custom. These controls were not aimed at reversing deforestation, but mitigating its impact by incorporating valued woodland and trees into local socio-cultural and household production systems.

Colonialism led to the dismantling and unravelling of these arrangements. State forestry devised in Europe and refined in India and South Africa was imposed by colonial authorities on Mount Kenya and, eventually, other forests. Based on bureaucratic control by technically trained experts, it denigrated and disregarded local forest users (cf. Fortmann and Fairfax 1989). The Forest Department became one of the most unpopular agencies during the colonial era. There is a long history of local resistance to state forestry in Kirinyaga. Yet, the department and local communities eventually reached accommodation on certain aspects of forest use and management. The structure of state forestry established in colonial times remained essentially intact after independence in 1963. Forest degradation and state-local conflicts during the 1980s revealed the limitations of government custodial management.

Internal socio-cultural and political change set in motion by colonialism also eroded the communal controls that maintained sacred groves and other small forests. The introduction of new religions, political organization, labour

1

migration, and socio-economic differentiation generated deep social fissures among the people of Ndia and Gichugu. The influx of Gikuyu immigrants from Kiambu and Nyeri during the 1930s and 1940s helped undermine the combination of local authority and low population density that maintained small wooded commons. Years of negotiation led to innovative arrangements that combined customary rights with state management of sacred groves and other small forests, though the Forest Department eventually gained exclusive control of the latter. Thus, a case study of Kirinyaga offers significant insights into the cultural, socio-economic, and political dynamics of common property resource management.

Common property resources and regimes

We live in what Harold Brookfield (1988) calls 'the New Great Age of Clearance'. What is being cleared? Forests and woodland, especially in the tropics. Carolyn Merchant (1992: 21) points out that tropical forests 'are disappearing at the rate of 100 acres a minute or more and the rate of destruction is increasing'. Although rain forests have received most of the attention, deforestation is also taking place in sub-humid and dry forests. Yet, many aspects about forest degradation remain poorly understood. Michael Williams (1989: 186) observes: 'The subject is bedeviled by a lack of objective data, and consequently, by claim and counterclaim.' There is much disagreement, for example, about the definition of deforestation and the rates of forest clearance (for example, see Myers 1984; Jacobs 1988; Williams 1989; Barraclough and Ghimire 1990; Kummer 1992). Nevertheless, few would disagree that tropical forest clearance is widespread, serious, and accelerating (see Caufield 1985; Gregersen *et al.* 1989; Houghton 1993).

However, Donald Messerschmidt (1993) warns us to beware of exaggerated claims about the inability of rural people to manage their forest resources. Similarly, Robert Chambers (1991) writes: 'A common belief is while professionals take a long-term view of sustainability, poor rural people live 'hand to mouth' and take a short-term view. Often, the opposite is true.' This book is concerned with contrasting the resource management regimes of rural people and those of professional foresters. It also deals with the uses and abuses of state conservation policies, both in the colonial and post-colonial eras. Through the study of the various forest commons in Kirinyaga, insights can be gained about how to promote sustainable land use in Africa and elsewhere.

Scholarly interest in common property resources and their management goes back a long time. Aristotle reflected on the care of the commons over two thousand years ago (McCay and Acheson 1987: 2). Garrett Hardin (1985: 90) claims that William Forster Lloyd, an Oxford political economy professor, articulated the basic principles for analysing common property in 1832. Hardin's own 1968 article on 'The Tragedy of the Commons', however, catalysed contemporary research on common property systems. In the quarter century since its publication the study of common property has emerged as a diverse field linking academics, technical specialists, community activists, planners, government officials, and international development organizations (see Ciriacy-Wantrup and Bishop 1975; Hardin and Baden 1977; National Research Council 1986; McCay and Acheson 1987; Berkes 1989; Bromley and Cernea 1989; Cernea 1989; Feeney *et al.* 1990; *The Ecologist* 1992; Messerschmidt 1993). The International Association for the Study of Common Property was formed in 1989, and its annual conference and *CPR Digest* serve as important channels for the world-wide exchange of information on the topic. Research on common property forestry resources, for example, has been promoted by such agencies as the Ford Foundation, the World Bank, the Food and Agriculture Organization, and the United Nations Research Institute for Social Development.

Ironically, the purpose of Hardin's 1968 article was to provoke thinking about carrying capacity and socially limiting population growth. He used the metaphor of severe overgrazing by herders in communal pasture to illustrate the clash between unregulated individual freedom to reproduce and collective survival. In subsequent works, though, Hardin (1985; Hardin and Baden 1977) applied his analysis to common property resources in general. The heart of his argument is that the commons represent an incentive and distribution system that inevitably results in environmental degradation. This outcome occurs because the commons are characterized by free and unmanaged access. Everyone has the ability to use the commons, but no one has an obligation to take care of. In such societies, Hardin (1985: 90) contends, .people live by the principle: 'to each according to his needs'. When conditions arise for individuals to maximize their use of the commons, they do so, passing on the costs to the resource and to society as a whole. The result will always be severe resource overexploitation and the collapse of the society that depends on it. Hardin (1985: 93) writes: 'To repeat, the system of the commons ends in disaster even if every member understands the situation completely.' The only way to avoid this situation is to delegate responsibility for the commons to individuals (privatize) or bureaucrats (socialize). Hardin (1985: 97) expressed many reservations about the latter strategy, but he claims that it nevertheless allows resources 'to escape the tragic fate of the unmanaged commons'.

In a recent article George Woodwell (1993: 12–13) argues that Hardin 'recognized correctly' the problem and solution to deforestation and resource mismanagement. Woodwell is not alone. A review article on the concept of common property observed that Hardin's interpretation 'has been accorded by some the status of scientific law' (Feeney *et al.* 1990: 2). According to some accounts, his ideas about resource management have become widely accepted in international development, shaping policies, programmes, and projects (McCay and Acheson 1987; Bromley and Cernea 1989). Yet, when such widespread influence is attributed to Hardin, I always recall a comment he made when I met him years ago at the University of California, Santa Barbara. Hardin joked that he was 'the man who invented over-population'. His point was that ideas about rural people misusing resources and exceeding their carrying capacity existed long before he proposed them. Indeed, such notions have been an integral part of the gospel of conservation that shaped the development of state forestry (see Fortmann and Fairfax 1989; Adams 1990; Guha 1990; Merchant 1992).   New interpretations of common property have emerged in recent years (National Research Council 1986; Oakerson 1986; McCay and Acheson 1987; Berkes 1989; Bromley and Cernea 1989; Feeney *et al.* 1990; Ostrom 1990; Thomson 1992; Messerschmidt 1993). Analysts are careful to distinguish between common property resources and their various sorts of property-rights managerial regimes. A common property or 'common pool' resource can be defined as one in which exclusion is difficult given existing technology and joint-use is separable. Although this book is concerned with forests, other sorts of common property resources include range, fisheries, and underground and surface water. The separable quality of common pool resources means that each user is capable of subtracting from the welfare of the rest of the group. Thus, there is always a potential for divergence between individual and collective interests. A decisive element is the sort of property-rights regime and its institutional arrangements. Four categories of property-rights regimes for holding common pool resources can be distinguished: open access, private property, communal property, and state property (see Feeney *et al.* 1990: 4). This typology is useful for identifying the forest management regimes in twentieth-century Kirinyaga and key issues about them.

Open access refers to the lack of well-defined property rights. Hardin (1985) claimed that African commons were typically open-access, a belief shared by colonial administrations and their successors. Considerable evidence exists demonstrating the fallacy of this assumption (Shepherd 1993). The belief that Kirinyaga's forests and woodland were open-access resources not only led to long-standing conflicts between the indigenous people and the colonial state, but also between local lineages and Gikuyu immigrants from neighbouring districts.

Private property involves exclusive yet transferable rights to land by an individual or group such as a corporation. This type of resource management regime was absent among the Ndia and Gichugu peoples prior to the 1950s, when the colonial government implemented land tenure reform as a counter-insurgency and economic measure. A significant debate within the early British administration in Kenya involved whether to convert the Mount Kenya forest into private property for the benefit of European settlers. The resolution of this debate had much significance for the nature of commercial forestry development on Mount Kenya.

Land rights in a communal property regime are vested in an identifiable group or community of interdependent users. Both formal and informal institutional arrangements regulate resource use among members while excluding outsiders. This sort of regime was pervasive in pre-colonial Kirinyaga. The patrilineage (*mbari*) and clan (*muhiriga*) were the traditional landholding groups, but rights of commonality extended to non-kin neighbours for certain uses of forests and woodland. Control over certain sacred groves were vested in the generation-set (*rika*), localized sodalities that cut across descent groups. Religious beliefs and customs were important elements in the management of local forest commons. It will be argued that the indigenous communal property regime offered a sophisticated, utilitarian, and durable mechanism for managing forestry and agricultural resources. This is not to invoke what Roy Ellen (1993) calls 'the myth of primitive environmental wisdom': the notion that tribal people lived in perfect harmony with nature. The cultural landscape of pre-colonial Kirinyaga was not static. Deforestation took place as population increased and agriculture expanded. However, the communal property regime based on kinship, neighbourhood relations, and religious customs imposed controls and obligations on land clearing and forest use to conserve certain woodland and trees.

State property regimes assign land rights exclusively to the government, including both central and local administrations. As in other regimes, the state as controller establishes its own institutional arrangements and working rules for determining land access and use. While communal property regimes often explain their resource control in religious and social terms, states justify their management through the ideology of science, commerce, and development (Merchant 1992; Simmons 1993). In the context of forests the predominant state property regime consists of centralized and custodial bureaucracy. Although state forest agencies nominally seek to serve the common good, they are often viewed by local communities as being anti-social because they criminalize traditional land use (Fortmann and Fairfax 1989; Guha 1990; Peluso 1992). The notion that state forestry offered a superior model for resource management served as the rationale for the colonial appropriation of Mount Kenya, and it was invoked many times in negotiations about smaller forests in the region. The issue of the appropriateness of custodial forest management will be questioned throughout. Indeed, as will be shown in Chapter 8, much contemporary forest degradation arises from official mismanagement and state-sanctioned development activities.

Kirinyaga offers an ideal situation for studying common property regimes. Although the smallest district in rural Kenya, it possesses a range of forest resources: a vast montane hardwood forest, small humid and sub-humid woodland, and scattered groves. Its Ki-Ndia- and Ki-Gichugu-speaking Gikuyu peoples remain very dependent upon forest products for fuel, building materials, and other items. As in other parts of the Kenyan highlands, there are intense land pressures. The population has more than quadrupled since the 1920s, rising to over 400 000. In some places the population density exceeds 500 people per km². Yet, one-fourth of the district consists of government forests. Understanding the merits and limitations of local and state forestry management in Kirinyaga will furnish significant insights for land use elsewhere in the country and the tropics in general.

Forest conflicts

The world's forests have long been both the source and site of conflicts between local communities and outsiders, including nation-states and large-scale commercial interests. In medieval Europe, for example: 'Most movements of rebellion against authority included among their reasons, demands concerning the use of the forest' (Bechmann 1990: 257). Capitalist and state expansion, whether in Europe, the Americas, Asia, Africa, or Oceania, led to conflicts over forest ownership and use, as well as the control of forest-dwelling populations (see Tucker and Richards 1983; Little and Horowitz 1987; Richards and Tucker 1988; Anderson and Huber 1988; Hecht and Cockburn 1989; Guha 1990; Bodley 1990; Martin 1991; Peluso 1992). Ramachandra Guha (1990: 186) writes regarding the Himalayan region of India: 'The social idiom of protest in Uttarakhand bears a striking resemblance to the conflicts over forest rights that were an important feature of the transition to industrial capitalism in Europe.' Nancy Lee Peluso (1992) describes 'forest-based cultures of resistance' generated by state resource appropriation. The ongoing struggle of indigenous peoples and other forest-dwelling populations to have their land rights respected and outside encroachment stopped has been described in an insightful and often passionate manner by a number of authors (see, for example, Denslow and Padoch 1988; Gradwohl and Greenberg 1988; Colchester 1992; *Cultural Survival Quarterly* 1993).

Resistance and violence are integral parts of the forest history of twentieth-century Kirinyaga. Studies of colonial land alienation in Kenya have usually centered on issues and conflicts generated by European settlement (for example, see Sorrenson 1968; Leo 1984). Yet, large tracts of land were also appropriated as Crown Forests. By the late 1930s over 13 000 km² had been designated as government reserves. This forest had been used or occupied to varying extents by local people. Its loss often resulted in bitter and protracted controversies similar to those caused by land alienation for white settlement. The threat of forest alienation was also used by colonial authorities in negotiations about the management of small forest patches. This book aims at uncovering the process of colonial forest alienation in southern Mount Kenya, as well as the local responses to it. As will be seen, resistance took many forms over time, from individual acts of defiance such as unauthorized wood collection, to protests through state-sanctioned means, and rebellion as part of the Mau Mau movement. Much of this political activity was connected to wider processes of social and economic change, including labour migration, urbanization, and local cash-cropping, which go beyond the scope of the present study. Thus, I have not attempted to analyse the entirety of Kirinyaga colonial and recent politics, but only those aspects connected to the management or use of the forest commons.

The present study does not examine all state forestry efforts and related conflicts in Kirinyaga. There have been farm-based afforestation interventions in the district since the early years of British rule. These were run in the colonial era by the field administration, the Department of Agriculture, and the local native council. Since independence, the Rural Afforestation Extension Scheme in the Forest Department has carried out such work. In many ways the circumstances of farm-based tree growing differ from those involved in the forest commons and must be treated separately (see Castro 1983, 1993, forthcoming).

Methods and sources

Different sources have been used to reconstruct the history of forest commons in Kirinyaga. Research was carried out in Kenya from May 1982 to March 1983, with brief revisits in late 1983 and 1988. Cyrus Kibingo, John Githuri Gichobi, and George Muriithi served as research assistants during different phases of the ethnographic research. Formal and informal interviews were carried out with forestry officials and staff, other government officers, owners and employees of several small-scale forest-based enterprises, forest users such as groups of women collecting fuelwood, and local households. Fieldwork included numerous trips on paths, trails, and roads inside the Mount Kenya reserve bordering Ndia and Gichugu divisions in Kirinyaga, plus visits to smaller forests such as Njukiine and Murinduko.

Six types of written sources were consulted: (i) European accounts at the time of initial contact; (ii) colonial reports and other documents from the Kenya National Archives, Embu District Archives, and the Embu County Council; (iii) Colonial Office records (CO 533 series from 1905 to 1938) available at Syracuse University; (iv) the testimony presented at the Kenya Land Commission in 1932; (v) descriptions from other parts of central Kenya; and (vi) contemporary published and unpublished government documents, including the minutes from the Kirinyaga County Council and annual reports from the Kirinyaga district commissioner, the Kenya Tea Development Authority, the Forest Department, and other agencies.

A number of colonial documents were consulted from the Kenya National Archives: provincial and district record books; annual and miscellaneous reports from Kenya Province, Kikuyu Province, Central Province, Embu district, Fort Hall district, Kerugoya sub-district, Ndia division, Nyeri district; the minutes of the South Nyeri Local Native Council; and daily correspondence files on forestry, agriculture, land tenure, female circumcision, the Kerugoya Dried Vegetable Project, and other topics. The Embu District Archives included daily correspondence files on the Kenya Land Commission, tree planting, saw mills, pit-sawyers, soil conservation, coffee growing, and different aspects of the Mau

Mau counter-insurgency campaign, plus various reports on forestry. The minutes of the Embu Local Native Council from 1925 to 1962 were seen at the Embu County Council's offices (these are also available in the Kenya National Archives).

All of the sources required careful sifting, cross-checking, and analysis. Some writers, for example, were clearly misinformed or biased in their depictions or interpretations. Other accounts were set apart by their descriptive excellence. None of the elders interviewed during the 1980s had been adults in the pre-colonial era, but they were familiar with many aspects of local custom and history. In particular, they had first-hand knowledge of the common property resource regime that existed before land privatization and the expansion of cash-cropping in the 1950s.

Outline of the book

Chapter 2 presents an ecological and historical sketch of Kirinyaga. It emphasizes the attributes of the physical environment because the subsequent chapters dwell heavily on the social aspects of resource management. However, it also contains a chronology of administrative changes and key historical events that the reader may wish to use later in the book.

Indigenous forest management and agroforestry are covered in Chapter 3. As Gill Shepherd (1993: 99) points out, the linking of forestry to agriculture is especially important: 'By and large, the tenure and authority regimes which once governed the successful use of forests are also those that govern the use of farmland and other local resources.' Chapter 3 argues that indigenous land tenure, religious beliefs, and farming practices contributed to the conservation of forests and trees. Although social controls were placed on felling trees, the purpose was to mitigate the impact of deforestation, not to halt it. The pre-colonial Gikuyu sought to incorporate valued woodland and trees into local socio-cultural and household production systems. The next five chapters examine specifically the management of Mount Kenya. The colonial conquest is analysed in Chapter 4, including the debate among the British as to whether to turn the mountain over to prospective timber entrepreneurs or the Forest Department. The eviction of the Ndia and Gichugu peoples from the forest is also described. The next chapter records the handling of local grievances about the forest appropriation through the Local Native Council and the Kenya Land Commission in the 1930s. Chapter 5 also examines the conflicts arising over the handing back of Nyagithuci tract as part of the commission's settlement. The Nyagithuci affair is particularly revealing about the assumptions held about the Gikuyu by British officials, as well as conflicts over land policy between different levels in the colonial administrative hierarchy.

The management and industrial use of the southern Mount Kenya reserve are covered in Chapter 6. As will be seen, timber development never attained the levels envisaged by early white entrepreneurs. Pit-sawyers, mainly immigrant Gikuyus, actually carried out much of the timber production on the southern slopes. Numerous conflicts eventually arose about the Forest Department's unwillingness to increase pit-sawing licences. Chapter 7 explores the relationship between the anti-colonial Mau Mau movement and the forest. It also analyses the impact of warfare on state management, plus the acceleration of plantation forestry development in the last years of colonial rule. Changes and continuity in state forestry in the first quarter century after independence in 1963 are traced in

Chapter 8. Small-scale forest users continued to be seen as the major threats to the reserve. Yet, the most important sources of forest degradation in the 1980s appeared to be official mismanagement and tea development.

Chapters 9 and 10 deal with smaller tracts of wooded commons in Kirinyaga. The former uses sacred groves as a window for understanding socio-economic and cultural change among the people of Kirinyaga. Such trees were once key cultural institutions associated with rites and ceremonies that fostered a sense of community among scattered homesteads. The decline in their religious and social value during the twentieth century derived from, and was indicative of, emerging social divisions among the people of Kirinyaga. Chapter 10 analyses changes in the management of Njukiine and other small forests. Gikuyu immigrants and internal social divisions contributed to the downfall of the traditional communal property regimes. Colonial efforts to take control over the forests were resisted by the Embu Local Native Council, a district-wide body set up as part of indirect rule. Between 1941 and 1952 the council operated an innovative programme for managing local forests. Financial difficulties as a result of the Mau Mau War led to the transfer of the wooded trustlands to Forest Department control. Their fate since independence as production and protection forests is covered as well. The final chapter explores the implications of Kirinyaga's forest history in terms of common property resources.

2. Kirinyaga: the ecological and historical setting

R.E. MOREAU (1944: 62) complained half a century ago about the paucity of information on the ecology of southern Mount Kenya. This theme was largely repeated at a 1989 international workshop on 'Ecology and Socio-Economy of the Mount Kenya Area' (Winiger et al. 1990). This chapter aims at providing a succinct overview of the land and people on the mountain's southern slopes in Kirinyaga district. The purpose is to establish an ecological and historical context for understanding changes in the use and management of forest resources during the twentieth century. As will be seen in the opening part of the chapter, the district is characterized by a pronounced environmental gradient based on elevation, climate, and vegetation. Over a relatively short distance Kirinyaga offers a striking contrast from glaciers to moist tropical forests to semi-arid savannah. The area contains some of the most productive farmland in the country because of fertile soils and favourable rainfall. The implications of ecological zoning for past and present local land use are explored. The second part of the chapter examines the settlement of Kirinyaga, from the ancestral migration of Thagicu-speakers to the movement of Europeans and Asians into the region during the twentieth century. It also presents a chronology of key historical events in the colonial and independence eras related to forestry management in the area.

Contemporary boundaries

Kirinyaga covers 1437 km² on the eastern edge of Central Province. From the summit of Mount Kenya, its boundary radiates southwards at an acute angle through moors and forests until reaching farmland, where a series of streams and other landmarks serves as dividing lines. Kirinyaga borders Nyeri and Murang'a districts on the west, Embu district on the east and south, and Machakos district on its southernmost tip. Kerugoya, the district headquarters, is located about 130 km north-east of Nairobi.

According to recent official statistics, one-quarter of Kirinyaga is categorized as national parkland (46 km²) and government forest reserve (308 km²) on the upper slopes of Mount Kenya. Its farmland is divided into three administrative divisions: Ndia, Gichugu, and Mwea (see Table 2.1). Ndia and Gichugu are situated in the high rainfall areas north of the Sagana-Embu road. They have been the thickly populated heartland of Kirinyaga since pre-colonial times. By the mid-1980s population densities exceeded 400 per km² for Gichugu and 370 per km² for Ndia. Mwea Division, with all the land south of the road, is generally drier and less fertile. Its population density exceeded 140 per km² in 1984. Southern Kirinyaga came under permanent settlement only in the twentieth century, having previously served as a communal grazing ground. Perhaps more than half of Mwea's residents originate from outside the district (Mutahi 1983: 28). The divisions are further partitioned into 10 locations and 76 sublocations (see Table 2.1).

The land

The district's name derives from the Gikuyu word for Mount Kenya (5199 m above sea level), on whose slopes it is situated. Located immediately south of the equator, this extinct volcano is the second highest mountain in Africa. From a

Table 2.1:　Kirinyaga district: divisions, locations, and populations, 1979

Division/location	Area (km²)	Population
Ndia Division:		
Kiine	114	31 820
Mwerua	82	24 242
Mutira	64	27 493
Inoi	74	40 381
Total	334	123 936
Gichuqu Division:		
Kabare	58	27 862
Baragwi	68	30 410
Ngariama	87	28 169
Total	213	86 441
Mwea Division:		
Tebere	175	38 279
Murinduko	218	20 603
Mutithi	187	22 172
Total	580	81 054
Kirinyaga District Total	1 127	291 431

Source: Kenya Population Census, 1979, Central Bureau of Statistics, Nairobi.

distance, however, the massif's height is less impressive than its gentle gradient. Indeed, the rise to the summit is so gradual that the three snow-capped peaks appear 'dwarfed by their own immense pedestal' (Huxley 1931: 171). According to Gikuyu traditions, Mount Kenya is the resting place of Ngai (also known as Murungu), the supreme deity. The notion that it is an intimate part of creation is appropriate because of the mountain's pervasive influence on local ecology and land use.

The upper two-thirds of the district consists of a series of ridges radiating southwards from the summit. They are separated by valleys and a dense network of streams whose waters originate in highland tarns, moors, and forests. Moving down the mountain, the ridges broaden, and the streams merge into the district's major rivers, including the Sagana (Tana), Ragati, Thiba, Nyamindi, and Rubingazi. Several of the waterways have been tapped for irrigation or domestic water-supply projects. All of the rivers drain into the Tana. There are wetlands of varying size scattered throughout the district. The ridges eventually give way to the Mwea plains, an undulating prairie which is part of Kenya's extensive upland plateau. A few hills of granitic origin lightly contrast with Mount Kenya's gentle slope. The most prominent hills are Kamurdwana (1890 m) in northern Ndia and Murinduko (1440 m) in north-eastern Mwea.

The summit is blanketed by rock outcroppings, scree, glaciers, and snowfields. Much of the ridge country, however, possesses deep, well-drained, reddish and chocolate loams and clays derived from soft volcanic tuffs (Jaetzold and Schmidt 1983). The water-storage capacity of some of the volcanic soils exceeds 300 mm. The loams and clays of the ridge country are generally very fertile and able to sustain intensive cultivation. Other types of soil are found in the district as well. Moderately fertile black cotton clays cover extensive areas in Mwea (Moris 1973). Pockets of low soil fertility occur in southern Kirinyaga, where sandy loams and quartz-laden gravels predominate.

Seasons

The flow of agricultural and non-farm activities in Kirinyaga, both past and present, revolves around the cycle of seasons. The district has a bimodal climate typical of most of Kenya east of the Rift Valley. Shifting trade winds associated with the intertropical convergence zone (ITCZ), a trough of low pressure, set the seasonal patterns in motion. As the ITCZ follows the zenith position of the sun across the equator towards the June and December solstices, it divides the year into two wet and two dry seasons.

December to early March is a dry and warm season known locally as *thano*. There is often a lack of cloud cover, though skies are sometimes hazy due to blowing dust and smoke from fields being prepared for cultivation. Mount Kenya's peaks are frequently visible at this time of year, an indicator of the air's dryness. The summit is mostly clouded over the rest of the year. Temperatures reach their annual extremes in January and February, characterized by warm afternoons and cool early mornings. The heat and absence of clouds raise evapotranspiration to its highest annual rate (Veen 1973).

South-easterly winds blow inland from the Indian Ocean in March, bringing moisture and cloudy skies. Heavy rains usually begin in late March and last through May. About half of the year's rainfall occurs during this period, traditionally known as the '*njahi* rains' (*mbura ya njahi*), referring to the lablab bean sown at the start of the season. People also call it the 'maize rains', (*mbura ya mbembe*), connoting the contemporary pre-eminence of this grain in local farming systems. Another widely used term is the 'long rains' (*mbura nene*). It is the main food production season in most of the district.

The movement of the intertropical convergence zone into the northern hemisphere brings another dry interval between June and September, known locally as *gathano*. Mists and light drizzle are common, especially in July and August. Even in the Mwea lowlands, where orographic clouding has little impact, overcast skies predominate. It is the coolest time of year. Because of the cool, cloudy weather, evapotranspiration falls to its lowest annual level season. By September the days warm and the mists dissipate as the ITCZ once again approaches. Heavy showers resume in October and November, typically supplying one-third to two-fifths of the year's total rainfall. This wet season is called the 'short rains' (*mbura nini*) or 'millet rains' (*mbura ya mwere*). It supports a second crop of maize and beans in the district's midlands and lowlands. North-eastern trade winds return in December, and the cycle of seasons continues.

For reasons that are not fully understood, the ITCZ is irregular in movement and effect (Nicholson 1985). As a result, there is variation in the onset, duration, and intensity of the rainy seasons, particularly in the lowlands. The region regularly experiences runs of above- and below-average rainfall (see Moris 1973). According to L.G. Ogallo (1990: 138), rainfall records from Meru between 1931 and 1989 do not indicate any sustained shifts in seasonal or annual rainfall characteristics. Studies of the Lewis Glacier near the summit, however, show a steady decrease in its volume, area, and length since the turn of the century (Ogallo 1990: 139). Quite clearly, additional research is needed to clarify current trends. Kirinyaga is less vulnerable to drought than much of central Kenya because of orographic rainfall and, since the 1950s, increasing use of irrigation.

Microclimates

A pronounced climatic moisture gradient occurs along the mountain slopes and plains, affecting potential land use. Mean temperatures decrease as one travels from the lowlands to the summit. A comparison of the annual maximum and minimum mean temperatures from three sites at different elevations in the district is illustrative: Mwea Experimental Station (1158 m in altitude), 28°C and 20°C; Kerugoya (1570 m), 24°C and 18°C; and Castle forest station (2040 m), 19°C and 10°C (Kirinyaga District 1980; Jaetzold and Schmidt 1983). The summit is cold enough year-round to maintain glaciers and snowfields.

There is a significant difference in rainfall between the lowland plains and highland slopes. Southern Kirinyaga is the driest part of the district, averaging less than 1000 mm per year (see Table 2.2). The lowland wet seasons are highly variable, experiencing on a regular basis poorly distributed or inadequate rainfall for crop growth (Moris 1973). In addition, Mwea has the highest local evaporation rates because of its frequent lack of cloud cover and warm temperatures (Veen 1973).

Table 2.2:   Agro-ecological zones in Kirinyaga district

Agro-ecological zone	Altitude in m	Annual mean temperature in °C	Annual average rainfall in mm
Rocks and glaciers, and tropical alpine moor and heatherlands	Above 3200	2.0–10.0	Below 18 000
Forest zones	1700–3200	10.0–16.0	1800–2550
Tea–dairy zone	1760–2130	17.8–14.5	1700–2150
Coffee–tea zone	1520–1820	19.3–17.5	1400–1700
Main coffee zone	1400–1580	20.1–19.0	1200–1500
Marginal coffee zone	1310–1400	20.6–20.1	1100–1250
Sunflower–maize zone	1280–1340	20.9–20.1	950–1200
Cotton zone	1220–1280	21.2–20.9	900–1200
Marginal cotton zone	1090–1220	22.0–21.2	800– 950
Lower midland livestock–millet zone	Small transitional strip		

Source: Adapted from Jaetzold and Schmidt 1983.

The amount and reliability of rainfall, as well as the length of growing seasons, steadily increase as one moves northwards and upwards until approximately the 2500 m contour. This orographic rainfall is induced by the cooling of moist air as it rises on the windward slopes. Kamweti forest station, at 2438 m in altitude, is probably the wettest place in the district, averaging 2550 mm per year (Jaetzold and Schmidt 1983). Above that elevation rainfall decreases as the moisture-depleted air quickly blows over the peaks to the lee of the mountain. There is a marked rain-shadow effect on the northern and western sides of the mountain.

Agro-ecological zones

The Ministry of Agriculture's *Farm Management Handbook of Kenya* provides a useful profile of the climatic moisture gradient in Kirinyaga (see Table 2.2). The classification of zones is based on the probability of meeting temperature and soil moisture requirements under rainfed conditions for leading cash and food crops (Jaetzold and Schmidt 1983). The very cool and steep tropical alpine zones consist of the land above the 3200 m contour. In the 1940s the alpine slopes were incorporated into Mount Kenya National Park. The forest zones are comprised of the state forest reserve. Set aside by the colonial administration in 1910 for indigenous and plantation forests, much of the southern portion of this land is probably capable of sustaining intensive cultivation. There is a lack of water stress in the roughly 15 km belt from the 2500 m contour to the 1600 m contour, despite decreasing rainfall, because of the volcanic soils' high water storage capacity and low evaporation due to frequent cloud cover (Jaetzold and Schmidt 1983). Whether population and commercial pressures for farmland outweigh forestry and watershed needs for maintaining the reserve is a major topic of debate in Kenya (see Chapter 8).

The distribution of agro-ecological zones among the administrative divisions is summarized in Table 2.3. Tea and coffee are the most valuable cash crops in contemporary Kirinyaga, and the best growing zones are located almost entirely in Ndia and Gichugu. Prior to the introduction of coffee and tea in the 1950s, these zones supported (and continue to support) intensive cultivation of grains, pulses, and other cultigens. An early colonial officer wrote about the heartland of Ndia and Gichugu, 'The country . . . is very rich and fertile . . . Famine and drought are unknown' (Dickson 1903: 38). Three decades later, at the Kenya Land Commission, an official stated that in Ndia 'the crops never fail altogether', apart from a 'very occasional famine'. The region was regarded as a breadbasket by neighbouring peoples and passing caravans, who regularly obtained food from it (Crawshay 1902; Arkell-Hardwick 1903; Ambler 1988). At the time Mwea primarily served as a seasonal pasture for cattle owned by upland-dwelling Ndia and Gichugu Gikuyu (Moris 1973).

The lowlands are classified as particularly good for growing cotton. For a variety of reasons, however, the crop has not prospered locally since its introduction in the 1930s. The widespread adoption of oxen ploughs during the 1930s and 1940s opened much of Mwea to grain and pulse production (Moris 1973). Despite erratic wet seasons, southern Kirinyaga continues to be a major centre of rainfed cultivation. There has also been increasing use of irrigation to overcome agro-climatic constraints. The Mwea irrigation scheme, begun in the 1950s, covers over 6000 hectares (Chambers and Moris 1973). The Kibirigwe scheme, started in the early 1980, supplies water to over 150 hectares in south-western Ndia. In recent years a growing number of lowland households have invested in

Table 2.3: Distribution of farmland by agro-ecological zone and division in Kirinyaga district

Agro-ecological zone	Area in km²				
	Ndia	Gichugu	Mwea	Total	%Total
Tea–dairy zone	10	28	0	38	4.0
Coffee–tea zone	55	69	0	124	13.0
Main coffee zone	72	51	0	123	12.9
Marginal coffee zone	70	28	4	102	10.7
Sunflower–maize zone	21	0	42	63	6.6
Cotton zone	41	0	117	158	16.5
Marginal cotton zone	6	0	332	338	35.5
Marginal cotton to lower midland livestock–millet zone	0	0	9	9	0.9
Total farmland	275	176	504	955	100.0

Source: Adapted from Jaetzold and Schmidt 1983.

irrigation equipment, especially for commercial production of French beans. The harnessing of local water resources is likely to continue, resulting in increased competition among the various users.

Quite clearly, the potential use of land for agriculture varies widely over short distances because of differences in climate, soil, terrain, and other variables affecting growing conditions. People have long adapted to the gradient of agro-economic potential by having multiple farm plots in a range of micro-environments, including different rainfall regimes, relief, and soil types. Official rural development policies, particularly tenure reform, have attempted to eradicate land fragmentation (Shipton 1988; Haugerud 1989). The cultivation of scattered plots, however, remains a viable strategy of risk aversion for many families.

Kirinyaga has very favourable agro-climatic conditions by Kenyan standards. More than 90 per cent of its agricultural land is classified in the *Statistical Abstract* as high potential, with mean annual rainfall exceeding 857.5 mm. Nationally, only 13 per cent of agricultural land falls into the high-potential category. Nevertheless, the district has a steep environmental gradient, affecting land use potential.

Vegetation and land use

The flora of Kirinyaga reflects several features of the intrinsic environment, including local topography and climate. It is also the product of human intervention, both deliberate and unintended. There is a marked gradient in vegetation along the slopes and plains. For analytical purposes five broad zones can be identified: the alpine zone; bamboo thicket; moist montane forest; agricultural land; and sub-humid woodland and grassland. These zones to varying extents correspond to the agro-ecological zone classification.

The vegetation of the alpine zone has been well documented in recent years (see Beck *et al.* 1990; Hedberg 1990; Scheibe and Beck 1990). The zone is characterized by a transition of plant communities adapted to the cold temperatures, frequent mists, the relatively dry to boggy conditions, and the steep terrain. The sparse vegetation near the summit is dominated by groundsel (*Senecio keniophytum*), lobelia (*Lobelia telekii*), and a comparatively dry tussock grassland. On the wetter alpine slopes and valleys these are supplanted by plant communities typified by giant groundsel (*Dendrosenecio keniodendron*), cabbage groundsel (*Dendrosenecio brassica*), lobelia (*Lobelia keniensis*), and tree heaths (*Philippia keniensis, P. excelsa*). The lower part of the zone largely consists of open moorland with tussock grasses and heath (*Ericaceous sp.*). Before the appropriation of Mount Kenya by the colonial government, a few people from Kirinyaga regularly ventured up the alpine slopes to collect medicinal plants (Stigand 1913: 260). Okiek (Dorobo) hunters also used to roam the moors in search of elephant and other animals which occasionally emerged from the forest (Mackinder 1900). Nowadays the area is visited by tourists who enter the park through tracks located in other districts. Increasing populations of hyrax and rats, supported by scavenging the trash left behind by tourists, sometimes heavily browse the rosette shrubs and other plants when other food is unavailable (Beck *et al.* 1990: 46). Otherwise, the flora of the alpine zone appears to have been little modified by human activities.

Open moorland gives way around 3200 m to dense stands of bamboo (*Arundinaria alpina*) in the upper forest zone. In the pre-colonial era bamboo (known locally as *murangi*) was harvested by the Ndia and Gichugu for poles, quivers, and other uses. Its availability in local markets was known over a wide area. As early as 1900, colonial officials went to Kagio to buy bamboo and timber for Kitui station in Kamba country. This involved a one-way trip of over 120 km. There are scattered podo (*Podocarpus latifolus, P. falcatus*) and other large trees in this zone as well (Young 1990; Beentje 1990a). Podo (*muthengera*) is one of the county's few indigenous conifers. It is a highly valued for its timber and other uses. Below 2500 m in altitude the bamboo thicket yields to other, much more diverse, vegetation.

The forests of Mount Kenya have received less attention from researchers than the alpine zone (Winiger and Rheker 1990). In the 1990s there remains much work to be done on vegetation analysis and forest management. Remarkably, after eight decades of state management of the Mount Kenya forest, systematic studies have yet to be conducted on its sustained yield capacity (Beentje 1990a: 50). Recent work by the National Museums of Kenya, the University of Nairobi, and other bodies promise to increase understanding about the composition and ecological processes of the forest (see Winiger *et al.* 1990).

H.J. Beentje (1990a, 1990b) identifies several forest types for southern Mount Kenya: mixed *Podocarpus latifolus* forest; primary and secondary *Ocotea* forest; and *Albizia-Neoboutonia-Polyscias* forest. These categories represent different points along a continuum of species, rather than sharply distinguished communities. Their composition and distribution have long been influenced by human activities. Local use of the forest extends back to the earliest period of human occupation. State control of Mount Kenya began in 1910, and the central government retained jurisdiction over it after independence in 1963.

The mixed *Podocarpus latifolus* forest is situated in the transition between the bamboo belt and the *Ocotea* forest. It is also found on south-western slopes

(Hutchins 1907). Tree species include podo, a commercially important softwood, and *Nuxia congesta* (*muchorowe*). The *Ocotea* forest is mainly located on the southern and south-eastern slopes receiving the heaviest rainfall. The name derives from *Ocotea usambarensis* (East African Camphor, *muthaiti*), an economically valuable hardwood timber species. It grows to an exceptional height (50 m) and girth, with large spreading limbs. Other trees associated with the primary and secondary *Ocotea* forest in Kirinyaga include *Macaranga kilimandscharica* (*mukaragati, mukuhakuha*), *Drypetes gerrardii* (*munyenye*), *Tabernaemontana stapfiana* (*mwerere*), *Aningeria adolfi-friederici* (*muna*), *Maytenus keniensis* (*murigi*), *Heywood lucens* (*mutaigoko*), *Neoboutonia macrocalyx* (*mutundu*), *Ekebergia capensis* (*mununga*), *Rytigynia friesiorum* (*wakarigo*), *Grumilea exserta* (*mukomakoma*), *Cassipourea malosana* (*muthathi*), *Ochna keniensis* (*mungarima*), *Rapanea rhododendroides* (*mugaita*), *Albizzia gummifera* (*mukurwe*), *Syzygium guineense* (*muiri, mukui, muriru*), *Polyscias kikuyensis* (*mutati*), *Ocotea kenyensis* (*muthura*), *Apodytes dimidiata* (*mugonyoni*), *Strombosia scheffleri* (*mutheringu*), *Xymalos monospora* (*murendeti*), *Myrica salicifolia, Brucea antidysenterica, Chassalia kenyensis,* and *Chrysophyllum gorungosanum* (Hutchins 1907; Dale and Greenway 1961; Ojiambo 1978; Beentje 1990a, 1990b). The *Albizia-Neoboutonia-Polyscias* forest is probably a variant of the *Ocotea* forest (Beentje 1990b). It is less diverse and found in lower and thus drier areas. Each of the forest types contains a large number of shrubs, herbs, epiphytes, grasses, and other plants. Many deep river valleys, for example, are dominated by tree ferns (*Cyathea sp.*). In addition to indigenous species, several hundred hectares of plantations composed of exotics such as pine, cypress, and eucalyptus have been established.

Moist forest once extended further down the slopes long cultivated by the people of Kirinyaga. A few patches of woodland, sacred groves, and scattered indigenous trees on farms provide some indication of the species that blanketed the tea and coffee zones in earlier times. One needs to be cautious, however, in extrapolating the past composition of the area's primeval forest from today's landscape. The present countryside is not one shaped directly from a pristine wilderness. Rather, it is derived from earlier cultural landscapes long modified by human activities: foraging, farming, herding, afforestation campaigns, other state-sponsored land use interventions, and so on. The main indigenous species encountered today — such as *Cordia abyssinica* (*muringa*) or *Markhamia hildebrandtii* (*muu*) — reveal more about the local propensity to maintain multiple-purpose·species than it does about forest remnants. It is apparent that a turnover in species occurs along the environmental gradient in the tea and coffee zones. A few upland forest trees, including *Albizzia gummifera* or *Prunus africanum* (*muiri, mweria*), range deep into the marginal coffee lands. Others, such as *Tabernaemontana stapfiana* (*mwerere*), are encountered only in the damp and cool tea country. Widespread indigenous species in the tea and coffee zones include *Markhamia hildebrandtii* and *M. platycalyx* (*muu*), *Bridelia micrantha* (*mukoigo*), *Croton megalocarpus* (*mukinduri*), *Croton macrostachyus* (*mutundu*), and the deciduous *Cordia abyssinica* and *Erythrina abyssinica* (*muhuti* or *mubuti*). *Ficus natalensis* (*mugumo*), a tall-growing fig tree often considered sacred by the Gikuyu, is commonplace, particularly in wetter areas. *Pennisetum clandestinum* (Gikuyu Grass, *nyeki ya kigombe*) and *Cyondon dactylon* (Star Grass, *igoka*) are the main grasses.

Agricultural land use has been touched on already in the discussion of agro-ecological zones. Two points bear repeating: the distribution of crops varies according to local climatic, soil, and other conditions; and farming systems in Kirinyaga have experienced considerable change during this century. In particular, many major cultigens have been introduced, such as tea, coffee, cotton, potatoes, rice, new varieties of maize and bean, sunflower, grams, citrus fruits, papaya, mango, macadamia, wattle (*Acacia mearnsii*), eucalyptus, cypress, *Grevillea robusta*, and *Lantana camara*. There has been a corresponding reduction in the production of other crops, including millets, sorghum, *njahi* and other traditional beans, and yam.

In recent years, researchers using remote sensing techniques have carried out a land use inventory for Kirinyaga (see Sinange 1990). Table 2.4, which summarizes the findings of a 1987 survey, depicts land use with broad strokes. The category 'maize', for example, includes intercropped plots as well as pure stands. Nevertheless, the table provides a useful overview of the distribution of crops and land use activities. Half of the recorded land use involved standing food crops (29 per cent), cash crops (18 per cent), and ploughed land (2 per cent). Four-fifths of the district was used for grazing grounds (32 per cent), hedges (3 per cent), woodlots (3 per cent), fallow plots (2 per cent), and forest (1 per cent). Less than one-tenth was absorbed by structures, roads, and other purposes. It is illuminating to compare Kirinyaga with Meru, a larger district (9922 km²) on the north-eastern side of Mount Kenya. Meru has a greater proportion of drylands and a lower population density (83 people per km² in 1979) (see Jaetzold and Schmidt 1983; Sinange 1990). A land use inventory in 1985 revealed that one-fourth of the district consisted of standing food crops (14 per cent), cash crops (5 per cent), and ploughed land (5 per cent). More than two-thirds of it was composed of grazing grounds (58 per cent), forest (8 per cent), fallow plots (3 per cent), and related land uses (2 per cent). Overall, Kirinyaga was more intensively used for agricultural purposes.

Sub-humid woodland and grassland can be found in the cotton agro-ecological zones. The moist fringes include species also found higher up the slopes, such as *Bridelia micrantha*, *Erythrina abyssinica*, and *Markhamia hildebrandtii*. Other trees occurring in the wetter parts of southern Kirinyaga include *Millettia dura* (*muhatia*, *mubatia*), *Azanza garckeana* (*mutoo*), and *Piliostigma thonningii* (*mukuura*), *Kigelia africana* (*muratina*), and *Ficus capensis* (*mukuyu*) (another fig often designated as sacred). The savannah consists of an *Acacia-Combretum* woodland composed of *Acacia tortilis* (*mugaa*), *Combretum molle* (*murama*), *Combretum zeyheri* (*muraba*), *Combretum* sp. (*mutithi*), *Terminalia brownii* (*mururuku*), and *Lonchocarpus eriocalyx* (*muthigiriri*). Among the prevalent introduced trees are eucalyptus, *Grevillea robusta*, *Cassia spectabilis*, and several fruit species. *Euphorbia tirucalli* (*kariaria*) is commonly grown as a living fence. *Lantana camara* is used as a hedge in some places, but it is most notorious for its widespread invasion of bushland and fallowing fields. The lowlands also provide a habitat for a number of grasses.

The foregoing account provides only a broad sketch of the variety and richness of Kirinyaga's flora. There are many localized communities within each of the broadly defined zones. Wetlands are scattered throughout the district, for example, containing reeds, sedges, and other plants. Thus, a wide range of vegetation has been available to the people of Kirinyaga. As will be seen in subsequent chapters, they have responded by developing a considerable and highly utilitarian botanical knowledge. It will also be shown that human activities have greatly modified the environment, and the pace of land use change is accelerating.

Table 2.4:   The use of agricultural land in Kirinyaga district, 1987

Land use/cover	Cover %	Area (ha)
Maize	24.5	27 706
Grazing land	16.6	18 685
Bushland/bush for grazing	15.1	17 082
Coffee	8.7	9788
Rice	4.5	5074
Bananas	3.9	4414
Tea	3,6	4019
Hedge	3.3	3760
Woodlots	3.3	3731
Paths/roads	2.7	3037
Fallow	2.1	2393
Bareground/ploughed	1.7	1863
Napier grass	1.2	1400
Structures	1.1	1264
Forest	1.0	1163
Rivers	1.0	1140
Cotton	0.9	960
Pigeon pea	0.3	282
Sunflower	0.2	226
Tobacco	0.1	90
Sugar cane	0.1	79
Other uses	4.2	4742
Total	100.0	112 899

Source: Adapted from Sinange 1990: 171.

Fauna

In the past, southern Mount Kenya boasted a great variety of wildlife, including mammals, birds, reptiles, and insects (Moreau 1944: 70–2). Missionary May Crawford (1913: 118), who visited the area in 1910, called the lowland plains 'a veritable zoological garden'. There were many numbers of buffalo, rhinoceros, lion, antelope, and other large mammals, plus smaller game. Hippopotamus and crocodile were widespread along lowland rivers and wetlands such as Nguka Swamp. The moist forest and bamboo thicket on Mount Kenya provided a rich habitat for elephants, buffalo, monkeys, leopards, giant forest hogs, eland, porcupines, owls, pigeons, and other species. Some of them, especially elephants, regularly raided farmland along the forest edge. By the early 1900s, however, much of the larger game had been expelled from the densely populated heartland of Ndia and Gichugu. Hyenas, porcupines, and other small mammals were still common in the agricultural areas.

Many aspects of land use related to wildlife will be discussed in detail in later chapters. For present purposes, it suffices to say that the number and variety of wildlife has greatly declined during this century. Several processes have been at work. The expansion of settlements and cultivation in southern Kirinyaga, along with hunting by whites and neighbouring Kamba, led to a substantial decrease in game by the early 1950s. Colonial-initiated 'anti-vermin' campaigns and 'pest control' by game wardens reduced the number of animals in the agricultural areas. The designation of the Mount Kenya forest as a government reserve provided some protection for game. Still, poaching for commercial trophies, the Mau Mau War in the 1950s, and the recent expansion of plantation forests have each disturbed wildlife populations within the reserve.

The peopling of Kirinyaga

Kirinyaga has offered its inhabitants a favourable climate, fertile soils, and diverse flora and fauna. Most of its present residents — the Ndia Gikuyu and Gichugu Gikuyu — descend from Thagicu speakers who settled in the region a thousand or more years ago. They were part of a wider movement of Bantu-speaking peoples into eastern and southern Africa (Phillipson 1985). Numerous oral traditions, some of them contradictory, exist about the ancestral migrations (Muriuki 1974; Mwaniki 1974). Archaeological and linguistic evidence indicate that iron-working Thagicu speakers who kept livestock and crafted Kwale-style pottery were in the region by the twelfth century (Siiriainen 1971; Spear 1981; Mutahi 1983). Population movements continued for centuries as people fled adverse conditions or sought new pasture and farmland (Ambler 1988). Indeed, migration into Kirinyaga never really stopped. Significant numbers of people from surrounding regions settled in the district after the advent of British rule in 1904 (Moris 1973; Mutahi 1983). Between 1930 and 1932, for example, drought and locust drove 1300 Kamba into southern Kirinyaga, though colonial authorities eventually evicted most of them. As will be discussed in later chapters, many Gikuyus displaced by colonial land alienation in Kiambu and Nyeri migrated into the district as well. Immigration has continued, including in recent years a trickle of job-seekers from north of Mount Kenya.

The ancestral Thagicu immigrants eventually absorbed or displaced earlier occupants, including the foraging Gumba or Athi (Orde-Browne 1925; Muriuki 1974). The gradual settlement of the forested slopes was instrumental in forging local socio-cultural identities. Ndia and Gichugu, for example, obtained their names from brothers who were pioneers in the territory (Lambert 1949: 18). As the Thagicu speakers spread out across southern Mount Kenya, their language differentiated into Ki-Ndia, Ki-Gichugu, Ki-Mathira, Ki-Embu, Ki-Mbeere, and related dialects (Spear 1981; Mutahi 1983). In time they came to regard themselves as distinct groups that lived in particular areas. The inhabitants of southern Mount Kenya were 'peoples' rather than 'tribes', however, as their economic, social, and political relations transcended local identities and boundaries (Lonsdale 1992a).

By the late nineteenth century the Ndia and Gichugu were similar to other acephalous agriculturalists of central Kenya (Routledge and Routledge 1910; Dundas 1915; Orde-Browne 1925; Maxwell *et al.* 1929a; Kenyatta 1938; Lambert 1956; Middleton and Kershaw 1965; Saberwal 1970; Kershaw 1972; Muriuki 1974; Mwaniki 1974; Munro 1975; Leakey 1977a, 1977b, 1977c; Spear 1981; Fadiman 1982; Mutahi 1983; Glazier 1985; Ambler 1988; Riley and Brokensha 1988a; Davison 1989; Berman and Lonsdale 1992). They lived in small, independent communities, linked through regular trade and occasional alliances to neighbouring groups and caravans from the coast. Social life revolved around local kinship (clan, lineage, extended family), territorial (homestead, neighbourhood, ridge), and generational (age- and generation-sets) relationships. People resided in scattered homesteads instead of villages. Primordial tenure rights were held by descent groups, but families possessed usufruct rights to descent-group land they occupied. The people of Kirinyaga and their neighbours were skilled farmers who gradually cleared the region's forest to establish relatively prosperous and often thickly populated communities (Gedge 1892; Crawshay 1902; Dickson 1903; Arkell-Hardwick 1903).

From the late nineteenth through the early twentieth century was a difficult period throughout central Kenya. Droughts, epidemics, and epizootics struck different parts of the interior, increasing social tensions (Ambler 1988). Kirinyaga was spared some of the worst disasters, such as the outbreak of rinderpest that wiped out herds in Maasai country and Nyeri between 1889 and 1891 (Muriuki 1974: 88–90). Nevertheless, smallpox and increasingly violent cattle raids caused some decrease in population (see Gedge 1892: 526–8; Arkell-Hardwick 1903: 354; Mwaniki 1974: 272). The biggest blow, however, came from the newly established colonial government. Great Britain declared Kenya a protectorate in 1895, and its military forces set about imposing state rule over the people of the interior. They invaded Kirinyaga and neighbouring Mathira in 1904, killing 1500 people (Mungeam 1966). Another military expedition had to be sent to Ndia and Gichugu in 1905 before the Kirinyaga Gikuyu were controlled. Neighbouring Embu was invaded in 1906, and Meru on the north-eastern slopes came under British control in 1908.

The conquest of Kirinyaga brought Europeans and Asians into the district, where they possessed political power far beyond their numbers. The British administration supplanted the rule of local elders with a political hierarchy based on race. Whites held key administrative and technical posts, while Africans served in positions of strictly local authority such as chief or headman. Some Europeans entered the district as missionaries, where they promoted religious conversion and adoption of Western culture. A few Asians already operated as traders in the Mount Kenya region before the advent of colonial rule (Boyes 1912: 169–70; Mungeam 1966: 62). When Winston Churchill (1908: 35) visited Embu in 1907, the five-month-old station already had two Asian shops. Within a short time Asians operated businesses throughout the district. Still, the numbers of Europeans and Asians remained quite small. As late as 1931, there were only 15 Europeans and 162 Asians in Kirinyaga. By 1962, Kirinyaga and Embu had a combined total of 171 Europeans and 764 Asians, compared to 292 276 Africans. The non-African population has diminished since independence, but it still retains considerable economic influence.

The population of Kirinyaga has steadily increased throughout the twentieth century. Table 2.5 reveals that the population has more than quadrupled since the late 1920s. Accompanying this rise in numbers has been a growing reliance on commercial agriculture and non-farm sources of income.

Agricultural intensification has been evident in increased land clearing and adoption of various soil conservation measures. There is also much landlessness and land-poverty. Yet it would be very misleading to attribute such changes to demographic pressure alone. Labour migration, for example, started with the imposition of monetary taxes following the colonial conquest (Clayton and Savage 1974; Stichter 1982). British administrators attempted to introduce measures such as tree planting for environmental protection as early as 1912 (Dundas 1955). The Swynnerton Plan of the 1950s pushed agricultural intensification by privatizing landholding and expanding production of export commodities such as tea and coffee (Sorrenson 1967; Leo 1984). Since independence the central government has continued to promote agrarian intensification through increased

Table 2.5: Population growth in Kirinyaga, 1927–1979

Year	Ndia	Gichugu	Mwea[1]	Total
1927	55 490	28 341	—	83 831
1939	56 175	31 174	—	87 349
1948[2]	66 680	42 727	—	109 407
1962	97 953	59 993	—	157 946
1969	96 062	62 664	58 262	216 988
1979	123 936	86 441	81 054	291 431
1989[3]	NA	NA	NA	422 000

[1]Mwea appears as an administrative division for the first time in the 1969 census. Previously, its population was included in the figures for Ndia and Gichugu.
[2]The first colony-wide census. Previous figures were based on hut tax estimates.
[3]Projected population
Sources: Kenya National Archives; Embu District Annual Report; East Africa Statistical Department; Kenya Population Census; Ayiemba 1990.

cash-cropping and soil conservation (Moris 1970; Ostberg 1987; Haugerud 1989).

A chronology

The boxed material presents a chronology of significant dates and events related to the social history of Kirinyaga's forestry management. The first covers changes in administrative boundaries during the colonial era. Ndia, Gichugu, and Mwea were incorporated in a framework of provinces and districts that still guides public administration in Kenya. There were a number of reorganizations and changes in names of administrative units during the colonial era. An awareness of these shifts is indispensable for understanding local affairs prior to 1963, when Kirinyaga district was formally established and Kenya became independent. The second depicts key historical events in Kirinyaga, particularly regarding local forest resources.

Year	Event
1895	Great Britain declares Kenya a protectorate.
1904	Kirinyaga is invaded and incorporated into Fort Hall district in Kenia Province.
1907	Gichugu becomes part of Embu district.
1912	Ndia is transferred to Nyeri district.
1920	Nyeri district is split, with Ndia becoming part of South Nyeri district. Kenia province is now called Kikuyu Province.
1922	Gichugu joins with Ndia to become Kerugoya sub-district in South Nyeri district.
1933	Ndia and Gichugu are transferred to Embu district. Kikuyu Province is now called Central Province.
1963	As a result of the Regional Boundary Commission of 1962, Ndia, Gichugu, and northern Mwea form Kirinyaga district. They remain in Central Province, while Embu is absorbed into Eastern Province.

Figure 2.1: *Administrative shifts in colonial Kirinyaga*

Year	Event
1904	Following the conquest, chiefs and headmen are appointed by the colonial regime.
1905	An uprising by the Kirinyaga Gikuyu is suppressed by colonial forces. Monetary taxes are imposed shortly afterwards, and labour migration gets under way.
1906	Timber concession applications for Mount Kenya are forwarded to the Colonial Office.
1910	The Church Missionary Society opens a station at Kabare in Gichugu. A station is established in Mutira in 1912. The demarcation of the Mount Kenya reserve boundary begins in Ndia.
1917	The Nyeri Advisory Council is established.
1925	The Embu and South Nyeri Local Native Councils are established.
1928	The controversy spawned by missionary opposition to female circumcision becomes widespread over the next two years.
1932	The Kenya Land Commission is convened. Its final report is issued two years later, including mention of Nyagithuci forest as part of the settlement of Gikuyu claims.
1933	The desecration of sacred groves in Kirinyaga is brought before the Embu Local Native Council.
1936	Deforestation at Njukiine is initially discussed by the Embu council. Local re-occupation of Nyagithuci is under way.
1940	The Dried Vegetable Project to supply food to British troops begins at Kerugoya and Karatina. The factories will run through 1946, burning large amounts of fuelwood.
1950	Mau Mau, an anti-colonial secret society, is outlawed. Its growth as a political force reflects decades of political activities and increased socio-economic differentiation among the Gikuyu.
1951	The Embu council approves plans for a private sawmill at Sagana which will purchase sawn wood from licensed pit-sawyers in the Mount Kenya reserve.
1952	The Embu council formally establishes 'By-Law Forests', and grants the Forest Department advisory management. Mau Mau guerrillas enter Mount Kenya and the Nyandarua forests. The government declares a State of Emergency in October in an attempt to halt the anti-colonial movement.
1953	Fighting escalates, closing access to Mount Kenya and Njukiine forests.
1956	The capture and execution of Didan Kimathi, military leader of Mau Mau. The fighting winds down. Resumption of Forest Department activities in southern Mount Kenya and Njukiine.
1960	The Forest Department assumes full managerial control of the Embu council's trust forests. The end of the State of Emergency. The Lancaster House Conference announces Kenya's upcoming independence.
1963	Kenya becomes independent, with Jomo Kenyatta as its first president.

Year	Event
1967	Kirinyaga Timber Co-operative Society is organized by the government to co-ordinate production among pit-sawyers.
1978	Daniel arap Moi succeeds Kenyatta as president.
1982	Petroleum shortages throughout the country reflect balance-of-payment problems. The Kenya Tea Development Authority is already converting tea-processing factories to fuelwood use, placing a substantial demand on forest resources.
1984	Public outcry about deforestation in Mount Kenya results in a timber-cutting ban. A presidential directive halts further conversion of forests into tree plantations.
1985	Announcement of the Nyayo Tea Belt Zones to establish buffers around selected forest reserves.
1988	Presidential ban on cutting forest trees.

Figure 2.2:   *Some key dates and events in Kirinyaga's recent history*

Conclusion

Kirinyaga is a small but highly productive district. Located on the southern slopes of Mount Kenya, much of it is blessed with rich volcanic soils and abundant, well-distributed, and reliable rainfall. Significant environmental gradients exist in the district, however, because of differences in elevation, land morphology, rainfall, and other variables. Thus, there are broad differences in indigenous flora and local agro-economic potential. Nevertheless, the area possesses some of the most valuable forest and agricultural land in Kenya. For a millennium or longer the area has supported the descendants of Bantu-speaking immigrants who eventually emerged as the Ndia and Gichugu Gikuyu. Their use and management of the forests, either as independent communities and, since 1905, as part of a nation state, forms the focal point of this study.

3. Indigenous forest management and agroforestry in Ndia and Gichugu

THE NDIA AND GICHUGU GIKUYU were forest dwellers who gradually cleared the land for gardens and settlements. This chapter presents a historical reconstruction of their indigenous forest, tree management, and agricultural practices. It describes ways in which people tried to reconcile competing pressures for retaining and removing trees. In particular, the chapter shows how religious beliefs, tenure relations based on a communal property rights regime, and farm forestry techniques each contributed to the conservation of trees before the onset of colonial rule in 1904. It is argued that indigenous forest management and agroforestry strategies mitigated the impact of deforestation by incorporating valued multi-purpose trees into local production systems. The chapter points out that indigenous conservation practices need to be viewed in the context of local socio-economic and ecological differences. It also considers the impact of the coastal caravan trade on land use during the late 1800s.

The importance of forests and trees

The people of Ndia and Gichugu, like other Gikuyu, customarily regarded Mount Kenya as the resting place of Ngai (also called Murungu) — the supreme deity. When people prayed they faced the sacred peaks. On occasions groups of men went into its forest 'to pour out fat as a sacred offering to God that all things might . . . prosper, and diseases disappear' (Kenya Land Commission 1934: 96).

The sacred mountain was important to the people of Kirinyaga in another way: it was a frontier for the expansion of their agricultural and pastoral economy. The region's forest resources — including trees, plants, and animals — were a vital part of indigenous life. They furnished fundamental items of material culture such as timber, fuel, fencing, foodstuffs, fodder, medicine, utensils, weapons, fibres, and thatch (Middleton and Kershaw 1965; Leakey 1977c). Trees also served a range of other purposes. They provided environmental amenities — shade and windbreak — and were used as boundary markers. Selected forests, groves, and trees were sites of communal worship and local ceremonies, including initiation rites. Traditional dance grounds were sometimes situated in forest clearings. Thick woodland acted as a buffer against outside groups, particularly the Maasai. Not only were frontier homesteads protected by dense foliage (Leakey 1977a), but Gikuyu warriors were adept at carrying out ambushes while hidden in trees (Meinertzhagen 1957).

The multiple uses of trees reflected both the area's diverse flora and the impressive botanical knowledge accumulated by the Gikuyu. In the 1930s, Louis S.B. Leakey (1977a) recorded from Kiambu Gikuyu elders the names of over 400 different trees and plants used during pre-colonial times. Leakey (1977c: 1286) noted that his list was 'not in any way exhaustive'. Tree use in pre-colonial Kirinyaga was not as thoroughly documented, but early colonial accounts suggested that the situation was similar (Crawshay 1902; Orde-Browne 1925).

This utilitarian knowledge of trees and forest resources derived from close interaction with, and dependence on, a range of local eco-zones. People utilized to varying extents the gradient of eco-zones running down the southern slopes of Mount Kenya. The pre-colonial Kirinyaga Kikuyu had only lightly penetrated the upper reaches of the mountain by the early 1900s. Yet, a few people regularly collected medicinal plants from the moors on the alpine slopes (Stigand 1913: 260). A range of products were obtained in the bamboo, moist forest, and sub-humid woodland, including honey, timber, plants for medical or magical uses, ivory, and animal skins. An elderly informant from Nduine sublocation, in Inoi, Ndia, readily illustrated this point during an interview in 1983 by bringing out his bow, quiver, and arrows. He had made the bow from a hardwood that grew in the warm Mwea plains, the quiver was bamboo collected in the Mount Kenya forest, and the arrows were prepared from sorghum stocks and local trees. Regional trade relations allowed people access to forest products from distant areas (Routledge and Routledge 1910; Ambler 1988). Firewood, wooden planks and posts, bamboo poles, honey, and other forest products were available on a regular basis at the local barter markets such as Kagio and Kagumo.

Learning about trees was embedded in the enculturation process, with males and females becoming knowledgeable about different aspects based on the social division of labour (see Leakey 1977a; Riley and Brokensha 1988a). For example, boys grew familiar with the properties of many local trees while helping herd livestock or clear fields, while girls acquired considerable knowledge of flora as they assisted in collecting forest products or preparing food. Informants in contemporary Kirinyaga emphasized that elders were significant repositories of information about vegetation, which they passed on to the young.

There were other people with specialized knowledge of forests resources and their uses. Honey collectors roamed southern Mount Kenya and other woodland in search of wild hives (see Chapter 6). Beekeepers hung their hives throughout the forest, as well as in trees scattered in farmland. The practice of beekeeping required a sophisticated knowledge of trees and plants, especially during hive construction when one must use special scents or smoke for attracting and repelling bees (see Mwaniki 1970, 1974; Leakey 1977a; Riley and Brokensha 1988a). Although the Gikuyu seldom consumed bush meat (Crawshay 1902), some of them engaged in hunting to obtain animal skins or ivory for trade (Maxwell et al. 1929b; Mwaniki 1974; Cavicchi 1977; Leakey 1977a). Healers and sorcerers used the medicinal and magical properties of trees and plants, and they often knew where in the remote forest or wooded savannah to collect such items. Woodworkers and blacksmiths also possessed detailed knowledge about the use of trees for various purposes (Leakey 1977a).

Forests and trees had considerable supernatural or mystical importance. The Gikuyu customarily viewed wooded land and trees as inhabited by spirits and other supernatural forces (Hobley 1967; Itote 1967; Leakey 1977c). These spirits were regarded as capable of intervening in human affairs, sometimes causing misfortune. In addition, the Gikuyu believed that human remains decayed and perished beneath the roots of the mythical *mukongoe* tree (Waciuma 1969: 86). The roots of the *mukongoe* supposedly provided a path for the spirits of the dead to travel to their ultimate resting place in the underworld (Leakey 1977c: 1105). Wooded land was also regarded by people in Kirinyaga as a habitat for dangerous animals and a hiding place for strange or threatening people, including criminals. Tax evaders and others wanted by the law in the colonial era often hid in the forest. The use of forests by Mau Mau guerrillas is well known and described in Chapter 7. Thus, forest resources were valued, respected, and even feared in many ways by the Gikuyu.

Forest clearing

The usefulness of trees competed with the need for farmland. Agriculture in the late 1800s was based on the elementary or polygynous family (*nyumba*) which occupied a homestead (*mucii*). The household was the sole unit of production and consumption, though neighbouring homesteads were usually linked through kinship or forms of mutual assistance such as labour exchange or gift giving. There was a clearly defined division of labour according to sex and age. The technology of farming itself was relatively simple: digging sticks, cultivating knives, and much human labour. The techniques used by the people of Ndia and Gichugu were similar to those employed elsewhere by smallholders: intercropping; multiple gardens in a range of micro-environments; selection of seed varieties according to local conditions; swamp and stream bank cultivation, including use of furrows for irrigation; burning crop residues to fertilize fields; bush fallowing; keeping livestock near the homestead and at distant pasture; and foraging for forest products.

The long process of settlement in central Kenya by Bantu-speaking peoples was accompanied by extensive clearing of primeval forest (Routledge and Routledge 1910; Muriuki 1974). Over the course of many centuries iron axes, cultivating knives, and fire gradually converted woodland into fields and pastures. Stigand (1913: 238), who visited Kirinyaga in 1907, described the arduous process of forest clearing:

> The large trees of the forest are slowly and laboriously cut down with their small soft axes at the height of about the waist from the ground. Yams (*kikwa*) are planted against these stumps up which the plants climb. After a few years' time rot and termites attack these roots and they disappear. Another way more frequently used to dispose of the bigger trees is to pile all the undergrowth and smaller trees cut down round their bases. When this had dried and is fired it kills the big tree, which either falls or dies. If it only dies they wait till its is dry and then light a fire at the base and the trunk slowly smoulders through.

Europeans who ventured into thickly inhabited Gikuyu country, including Kirinyaga, during the late 1800s and early 1900s commented on the lack of tree cover. Ernest Gedge (1892: 526), who travelled through southern Mount Kenya in 1891, noted that 'extensive clearances' caused the forest to be 'some distance' from settlements and fields. The Routledges (1910: 7) observed that Nyeri appeared to be 'one huge garden'. Chauncey Stigand (1913: 235) described Gikuyuland as a 'rolling, almost treeless, cultivated country'. Not only was land cleared for homesteads and gardens, but fires were used to improve grazing grounds (Maher 1938a).

Deforestation had significant cultural dimensions. Oral traditions in Kirinyaga closely connected land clearing with the emergence of a distinct socio-cultural identity. H.E. Lambert (1949) recorded that Ndia and Gichugu were the names of brothers who first cleared land in the district. Another Ndia elder from Nduine stated that, '*Ndemi* ['the cutters'] was the first known generation in Kirinyaga'. He added, 'They were the first Gikuyus to clear the bush, and they gave birth to *Mathathi*, the second generation' (Ndemi and Mathathi are interchanged in other accounts, see Muriuki 1974). Folk histories about the primordial colonization of southern Mount Kenya emphasized the role of forest clearance in establishing or confirming land tenure rights (Routledge and Routledge 1910; Stigand 1913; Dundas 1915; Maher 1938a). An elder from Ndia told H.S.K. Muriuki (1974: 297):

We know that the first lot of people to this place were hunters. Then came the 'axe man' who came with his cattle and cut down shed building material, then put up cattle sheds. When later they came to claim the land, the 'axe man' had a firmer claim than the 'trap man'.

The Ndia and Gichugu Gikuyus' sense of themselves as a people was closely related to their forest environment and their transformation of it. John Lonsdale (1992b: 334) has written:

[The Gikuyu] were brought together by the demands and opportunities of forest clearance. Only then did they become *Agikuyu*, less a boast of ancestral descent than a claim to farming skill. They were people who knew how to civilize the land where the *mukuyu* fig trees grow, to which they brought their harvest offerings.

The related processes of forest clearing and cultural development were gradual, occurring over many centuries (Lambert 1949, 1956; Muriuki 1974; Spear 1981).

Some folk histories link forest clearing with the decline of the foraging Gumba (also called Athi), the previous occupants of the land (Muriuki 1974). Major Granville Orde-Browne (1925: 21), for example, wrote:

It is said these people were originally very numerous, but they gradually dwindled away with the cutting of the forest — although on friendly terms with the invaders — until only a few old men were left. These old men turned into the 'Plantain Birds', which inhabit the forest to this day in large numbers, and they are to be heard talking their original language together in the forest at night.

Embu and Ndia Gikuyu elders interviewed by Orde-Browne generally attributed primordial forest ownership and land use regulations to the Gumba or Athi foragers.

In the late 1800s Okiek (also called Dorobo) hunters roamed the sparsely populated forests, engaged in the ivory trade (Saberwal 1967; Mwaniki 1974). Their presence on the southern slopes was considerably slighter than on the northern and western sides of Mount Kenya (Stigand 1913: 261; also see Gregory 1896; Mackinder 1900; Boyes 1912; Blackburn 1982). Orde-Browne (1925: 22) recorded that the Embu and the Kirinyaga Gikuyu considered the Okiek to be different from the primordial Athi or Gumba: 'The two people are separated, and occupy quite different positions in the minds of the existing native.' In 1929, Kirinyaga and Nyeri spokesmen told the Commission on Native Land Tenure in Kikuyu Province that the Athi and Okiek were different peoples. The spokesmen claimed that the Athi were actually ancestral Gikuyu hunters. Thus, the spokesmen argued that the Okiek were not present when initial settlement took place — a view accepted by the commissioners (Maxwell et al. 1929a: 6–7). A very different situation occurred in Kiambu, where Gikuyu forest clearing and settlements were relatively recent. Kiambu Gikuyu spokesmen acknowledged compensating the Okiek for 'spoiling hunting and honey supply' (Maxwell 1929b: 48). Participation in the payment of goats to the Okiek became a controversial means of defining land ownership among Kiambu *mbari* members in the twentieth century (Kershaw 1972).

Outsiders have sometimes suggested that Gikuyu culture predisposed or caused them to remove tree cover. In the colonial era some officials referred to the Gikuyu as the 'Forest Destroyers' (Baker 1931). A more recent example is a World Bank report (1980: 23) on 'Sociological Aspects of Forestry Project

Design', which states, 'Attitudes towards forests sometimes take on cultural shades . . . In Kenya, the Masai practice range management, while the Kikuyu cut down trees to grow maize.' As will be seen below, there is substantial evidence to suggest that economic and demographic forces, rather than ideology or 'cultural shades', propelled deforestation in pre-colonial central Kenya. Moreover, the Ndia and Gichugu Gikuyu attempted to reconcile competing pressures to retain and to remove tree cover. Restraints on cutting trees were included in customary tenure rights and land use practices, and these were reinforced by cultural beliefs regarding the nature of trees. It needs to be emphasized that their goal was not to halt deforestation, but to mitigate its impact. The application and effectiveness of such practices varied over time.

Land tenure and tree management

The indigenous landholding system exercised much influence over the management of trees. Customary land tenure in Kirinyaga can be classified as a communal property rights regime (see Feeney *et al.* 1990). Primordial land rights were vested in the patrilineal *muhiriga* or clan (Maxwell *et al.* 1929a, 1929b). The clans traced their origins to the daughters of the mythical couple Gikuyu and Muumbi. The number and names of the clans varied throughout Gikuyu country (Muriuki 1974). The following clans were common in Kirinyaga: Ugachiku, Umbui, Unjiru, Aceera, Waitherandu (also called Angeci), Akathigia, Angui (or Aithiegeni), Ithekahuno (or Angari), Ukiuru (or Aithaga), and Icakamuyu (for other versions, see Muriuki 1974; Davison 1989). Because their members were widely dispersed, however, clans were not an effective corporate entity. Instead, the *mbari* (lineage) served as the local residential unit of the clan, the medium through which it carried out its affairs. Thus, the name of a lineage and the clan to which it belonged were always fused together, as in *Ugachiku ya Mbari ya Nyaga*, 'Ugachiku clan, lineage of *Nyaga*'. The extent to which lineages recognized one another as members of the same primordial clan was defined by shared participation in certain functions: initiation rituals; family and kin group sacrifices; contributing blood money; eating animals sacrificed in marriage transactions; and consuming meat at clan ceremonies (Maxwell *et al.* 1929b: 7). 'Reunions' of clan representatives from different lineages throughout Gikuyu country were known to occur, but such meetings were rare (Muriuki 1974: 114). The lineages tended to be highly localized.

All Ndia and Gichugu males were born into a clan and lineage, but active membership required 'application'. An Ugachiko elder described the process for men in his Ndia *mbari*:

> To become a clan member you first had to bring a male goat. This was to say you've brought a head. Then you make four big gourds of *muratina* beer [fermented from the sausage-shaped fruit of the *Kigelia africanum*], and take it to the clan elders.

Informants in present-day Kirinyaga say that applicants were almost always accepted by descent groups, the exception being people with anti-social reputations such as thieves. Outsiders could become *mbari* members by undergoing a 'rebirth' or 'blood-brotherhood' ceremony. A prominent elder was selected as *muramati* (trustee) of the lineage. His duties included overseeing access to and use of the *githaka* by temporary land occupants. The heads of the different families assisted the *muramati*.

Each lineage had a *githaka* or estate. It consisted of homestead sites, cultivated plots, and fallowing fields, plus forest and bush, claimed by the *mbari*. There was a wide range in the size and aggregate holdings of the lineages (Middleton and Kershaw 1965: 26–7). The largest ones included hundreds of members and covered thousands of hectares, but many of them were much smaller. The Maxwell Commission (1929a: 9) claimed that the 'average' githaka in Gikuyuland covered 80 to 120 hectares. A *nyumba* (family) held usufruct rights to the portion of *githaka* it occupied. Families resided on scattered homesteads, cultivating small fields scattered throughout the countryside. Men inherited property from their father, but those from land-scarce families could ask for farm plots from relatives or the *muramati*. Women gained access to land through marriage. An unmarried women had rights to land in her mother's name. Land could be obtained as well through socially recognized forms of borrowing, through fictive kinship (re-birthing), and by redeemable purchase. The landholding system was inclusive, reflecting the demand for labour among households and descent groups (see Kershaw 1972).

Rights to trees were enmeshed in a web of social obligations that included neighbours as well as kinfolk. Tenure rights were defined within the context of local territorial groups: *itura* (village), composed of several homesteads; *mwaki* (neighbourhood), a collection of *itura*; and *rugongo* (ridge), consisting of several *mwaki*. These entities were not always composed of kinfolk because in many places members of different descent groups were intermingled (Hobley 1971: 138). Instead, proximity of residence, mutual assistance, and joint participation in decision-making about local affairs fostered a sense of community. For example, the term *mwaki* (fire) referred to homesteads which shared hot embers for re-lighting fires. Neighbours helped one another through labour exchanges for harvesting and other tasks. Common participation in ceremonies and in the elders' council (*kiama*), reinforced local group identities. Both the *mwaki* and the *rugongo* had a *kiama*, which male elders could join as along as they paid the required entrance fee of goats. Thus, a condition of 'social predictability' existed within the Ndia and Gichugu communities (cf. Erasmus 1977: 47–48). People had long lived and worked together, and they developed 'means of controlling each other's outcomes'. Individuals who cheated on communal obligations were branded as anti-social and cut-off from mutual assistance.

As mentioned previously, rights of first clearance had been an important means of establishing claim to land in the southern Mount Kenya area. But trees did not have to be cut down to be involved in the assertion of land ownership. On the contrary, the Ndia and Gichugu Gikuyu protected and planted trees as means of establishing land ownership. Folk histories of early Kirinyaga included accounts of trees being used as markers for dividing land between and within clans. Mwaniki (1974: 297), for example, was told that Ndemi generation 'demarcated' boundaries using trees such as *Kigelia africana* and *Markhamia hildebrandtii*. The Maxwell Committee recorded the following trees being used by the Nyeri and Kirinyaga Gikuyu as boundary markers: *Cordia abyssinica* (*muringa*), *Commiphora zimmermanni* (*mukungugu*), and *Syndadenium compactum* (*mwatha*). *Crinum kirkii* (*gitoka*) was also used for indicating *mbari* borders (Maxwell *et al.* 1929b: 2). In present-day Ndia several informants recalled that descent groups sometimes used particular species to divide the landholdings of individual homesteads. If an already standing tree was not conveniently located, people used transplants or cuttings to set the boundary. An elder from Nduine sublocation stated:

Table 3.1:   Common indigenous agroforestry trees in Ndia and Gichugu

This table is meant to be illustrative rather than comprehensive. It lists in alphabeti-cal order indigenous agroforestry trees traditionally utilized in Ndia and Gichugu divisions, Kirinyaga district. Botanical and vernacular terms for the species are given, followed by major traditional uses and, in parentheses, properties of the tree which fostered its incorporation into local production systems.

Bridelia micanthra, mukoigo. Poles, timber, and firewood (propagation by cuttings, pollarding, drought resistant).

Commiphora zimmermanni, mukungugu. Vine props, poles, utensils, quick-set hedges (cuttings, intercropping, pruning).

Cordia abyssinica, muringa. Beehives, stools, mortars, well covers, and building timber (cuttings, volunteers, pruning, intercropping).

Croton macrostachyus, mutundu. Poles, medicinal uses, and boundary markers (coppicing).

Croton megalocarpus, mukinduri. Poles, boundary marker, cattle shade (profusely seeding, fast growing).

Erythrina abyssinica, mubuti or *muhuti.* Living fence, medicinal uses, weather in-dicator (cuttings, pruning, some intercropping).

Ficus natalensis, mugumo. Ceremonial and medicinal uses (cuttings).

Kigelia africana, muratina. Fruit used as a fermenting agent (intercropping, pruning).

Markhamia hildebrandtii and *Markhamia platycalyx, muu.* Poles, building timber, and firewood (cloning, volunteers, pollarding, intercropping).

Pygeum africanum, mweria. Mortars, pestles, poles, building timber, and cattle enclosures (coppicing, pruning).

Ricinus communis, mubariki. Castor seed and oil (profuse seeds, fast growing)

Source: Castro 1983; Leakey 1977c; Riley and Brokensha 1988b.

Each *mbari* planted its own type of tree [to mark boundaries]. For example, they would use *mukoigo* [*Bridelia micanthra*] and *muu* [*Markhamia hi-ldebrandtii*], and others would use *muringa* [*Cordia abyssinica*], *muumbo* [*Ficus wakefieldii*] and *mugumo* [*Ficus natalensis*]. My *mbari* used *muu*, *mukoigo*, and *muringa*.

All of the above species were commonly grown in Kirinyaga from cuttings or transplants of volunteer seedlings (see Table 3.1).

Controls on tree cutting

By the late 1800s, communal controls had been placed on the clearing of forest by descent and neighbourhood groups. Permission was supposed to be obtained from local elders and rightholders before harvesting trees or farming along the forest frontier on the slopes of Mount Kenya. In a memorandum prepared for the Kenya Land Commission in 1932, H.E. Lambert, the district commissioner of Embu, reported about traditional access to the forest:

Natives from the lower areas who wished to cultivate in the higher land had to get the permission of the individual owners of pieces of land already demar-cated and recognized as the individual's ngamba [plots]; they could not merely choose any convenient sites higher up; the upper boundaries of definitely owned ngambas were the upper limits of cultivation.

Lambert added that cutting trees above the line of cultivation was prohibited by the local community. Small patches of hilltop and riverine woodland such as Njukiine forest were also set aside by kin and neighbourhood groups as 'timber reserves' or woodlots (see Chapter 10). Although such areas were protected from indiscriminate clearing, they were usually treated as land banks, to be opened to cultivation as needed.

Descent groups exercised rights of encumbrance over certain trees located on farmland. Two highly valued multi-purpose species, *Cordia abyssinica* and *Pygeum africanum* (*mweria*), were almost always considered clan property. Lineage elders also exercised control over any large, locally valued timber tree on its *githaka*. Even the household that possessed usufruct rights to the particular parcel had to seek the approval of *mbari* elders before felling such trees. Informants agreed that a payment of a goat to the elders was expected. Only newlyweds who needed building timber were not subject to this requirement.

Extended families and households were recognized as having exclusive rights to trees, especially ones within enclosed compounds and cultivated fields. Exclusivity was especially acknowledged if the trees had been pollarded, coppiced, or deliberately propagated. Rights of encumbrance and commonality obliged homesteads to share certain forest products with their kinfolk and neighbours. In many cases kinfolk or friends asked permission to cut timber as a formality or an act of etiquette; people were not required 'to beg' or to pay. Customary tenure rights also allowed neighbours to collect deadwood, shrubs, herbs, most wild fruits, and other forest products as long as the trees, crops, and other property were not damaged or disturbed.

A rightholder (*mwene githaka*) could limit felling on his or her land. Such restrictions were placed on timber and other valued trees. A curse (*kirumi*) was sometimes placed on such trees to protect them from encroachment. This was common with *Kigelia africana* (*muratina*), whose sausage-shaped fruits were used as a fermenting agent for brewing. Sickness or death awaited those who violated such supernatural sanctions. In the 1980s many people in Kirinyaga still believed that evil would befall anyone who took fruit from another's *muratina*. Curses could also be placed on an entire stand of trees (Leakey 1977a). The Aithaga clan, whose members in Ndia were renowned for their potent curses, 'were believed to have the power of protecting forests' (Hobley 1967: 183; Orde-Browne 1925). Nyeri officials observed in 1914 that curses protected 'practically every patch of forest' in the district. Placing a curse on woodland was sometimes considered anti-social, however, and kin folk and neighbours were known to pressure a rightholder into removing it (Dundas 1915).

Farm-level strategies to conserve trees

Individual households used several strategies to retain tree cover on their particular holdings. Families sometimes set aside small plots of heavily wooded land to supply building material, fuel, and other items (Routledge and Routledge 1910; Dundas 1915; Kenyatta 1938; Hobley 1967; Leakey 1977a). Present-day practices suggest that these small stands of trees were situated in a variety of settings, including along steep ridges and at the head of narrow valleys and ravines. Such copses were protected during clearing, with individual trees cut as need arose.

Probably more common was the protection of individual or small groups of trees during clearing. When preparing land or a fallow plot for farming, certain trees would be spared the axe. Before setting fire to the plot, brush and cuttings would be removed from around the trees to shield them from flames. The ground was often turned over both to work the soil and to provide added protection from fire. This practice was motivated by spiritual and utilitarian concerns.

Selective clearing was influenced by traditional religious beliefs. The Gikuyu believed that trees possessed spirits capable of intervening in human affairs (Leakey 1977c). A tree spirit was not upset when its abode was cut, as long as it had another tree nearby to go to. When clearing land, people were supposed to leave 'a large and conspicuous tree' at intervals to absorb the spirits from the ones cut down (Hobley 1967: 31–2; Leakey 1977c: 1,117–8). Such a tree was called a *murema kiriti* ('one which resists the cutting of the forest'), and it was not supposed to be cut or allowed to fall without a ceremony transferring the spirits to another tree. The angry spirit would kill a person who reportedly failed to perform the ceremony (Leakey 1977c). Young people who used the wood from such a tree for fuel would 'become ill or die', though senior male elders and very old women could burn it without danger (Hobley 1967: 32). Certain groves were set aside as sites for communal sacrifice (see Chapter 9). These sacred groves were also protected by supernatural sanctions.

Trees were often left standing for a more mundane reason: to maintain a convenient supply of forest products for family consumption. One of the most visible reasons why Gikuyus spared large trees was to hang beehives on them (Routledge and Routledge 1910). Crawshay (1902: 33), an early European visitor to Kirinyaga, wrote, 'Many a fine tree owes its existence to the bees.' *Ficus natalensis* and *Cordia abyssinica* were favourite 'bee trees', but any large tree with sprawling limbs could be used to hang hives. Honey was especially valued for brewing purposes. Besides being a popular drink, honey beer was required for a number of ceremonies (see Leakey 1977a).

Certain tree species were preferred because they directly supplied multiple or special products. Table 3.1 lists common indigenous agroforestry trees in Kirinyaga, including their major uses and key botanical properties. The list is not exhaustive because other species were used to varying extents. There was no single pattern of indigenous agroforestry. Rather, there were numerous variations on a similar theme of trying to incorporate trees into household production systems. This diversity reflected both the physical and social environments. The district is characterized by considerable local differences in topography, rainfall, soils, and natural vegetation. Families faced different situations regarding the availability of land and labour, the extent of their ethno-botanical knowledge, and the crop mixes possible within their particular eco-zone. What is important to emphasize is that households were utilitarian in their management of and use of trees.

The present-day incidence of the species in Table 3.1 should not be used as guides to their past distribution. Forestry programmes, agrarian intensification, and other changes in land use since 1904 have influenced contemporary patterns. *Commiphora zimmermanni*, for example, was said to be 'the commonest' farm-land tree in Gikuyuland at the turn of the century (Stigand 1913: 239). Easily propagated from cuttings, it was valued highly as a quick-set hedge and a vine prop. The tree also supplied leaves for goat fodder, poles, and wood for utensils. Although still widely grown, this tree has been surpassed in local popularity and spatial distribution by exotics, including fast-growing and multi-purpose *Grevillea robusta* (*mukema* or *mubariti*). Several informants stated that *Croton megalocarpus* (*mukinduri*), a native species, is grown more widely today than in the past.

The indigenous agroforestry species often possessed botanical properties — seeding profusely, easy sown or transplanted, propagation from cuttings — which facilitated their reproduction and retention. Species producing seeds in large quantities included *Croton megalocarpus*, *Cordia abyssinica*, *Markhamia hildebrandtii*, *Markhamia platycalyx*, and *Albizia gummifera*. Volunteer seedlings from several species, including *Kigelia africana*, were often protected. The extent to which direct sowing was used in the pre-colonial era is unclear. A careful reading of available historical accounts and observation of current agroforestry practices suggested that the pre-colonial Kirinyaga Gikuyu probably relied more on taking cuttings to grow new trees. Cuttings from *Markhamia hildebrandtii*, *Cordia abyssinica*, and *Ficus natalensis*, for example, were used to mark boundaries. *Erythrina abyssinica*, *Euphorbia tirucalli*, and *Commiphora zimmermanni* were propagated from cuttings for living fences. The Ndia and Gichugu Gikuyu also took cuttings of *Ficus natalensis* and other fig species to establish new sacred trees.

Pruning, pollarding, and coppicing were used to sustain certain species on farmland, including *Markhamia hildebrandtii*, *Markhamia platycalyx*, *Croton macrostachyus* (*mutundu*), *Croton megalocarpus*, *Pygeum africanum*, and *Cordia abyssinica*. Pollarding involves removing most or all of a tree's branches, while coppicing is a method of cutting certain species to foster regrowth from the stump. These periodic tree-management practices minimized competition for water and light with neighbouring food crops, and they increased the tree's productivity (see Poulson 1983). Seasonal and multi-year rhythms were often involved. *Markhamia hildebrandtii* (*muu*), for example, was pollarded during the dry season, before the onset of the planting or harvest seasons. During this time labour demands were relatively low. The prunings furnished firewood to be stored for use during peak work periods. In addition, poles and other small timbers were obtained. Food crops, including maize and beans, were planted next to the pollarded *muu*. Tree regrowth quickly occurred, so that within a couple of years another pollarding took place. Meanwhile the tree's girth and height continued to increase over the years. Thus, a number of harvests of branches and shoots were possible on a regular basis over many years before the whole tree was felled. The popularity of the exotic *Grevillea robusta* in present-day Kirinyaga owes much to its capacity for being pollarded.

Multi-purpose trees that could be intercropped with staple foods were especially valued. As mentioned previously, various food crops were grown next to *Commiphora zimmermanni* and *Markhamia hildebrandtii*. Maize, beans, and other foods were sometimes interplanted with *Cordia abyssinica* and *Erythrina abyssinica*, both deciduous species. Grain and pulses were sown under *Kigelia africana* as well. *Croton megalocarpus* and *Albizzia gummifera* commonly furnished shade for cattle.

Thus, indigenous agroforestry practices constituted a form of practical conservation that was highly selective in terms of species. While *Cordia abyssinica*, *Bridelia micrantha*, and similar multi-purpose trees might be protected, other species decreased in number. Some historical evidence and oral traditions suggested that species such as *Heywood lucens* (*mutaigoko*), *Drypetes gerrardii* (*munyenye*), *Ekebergia capensis* (*mununga*), *Blighia unijugata* (*muikuni*), and

Milletia oblata (*mwanga*) became increasingly scarce as settlements and fields expanded in the late nineteenth and twentieth centuries (see Hutchins 1907; Maher 1938a).

Economic inequalities of the pre-colonial era were sometimes manifested or reflected in the use and physical distribution of trees. The Routledges (1910: 43) recorded that people who were too poor to obtain mutton fat rubbed castor oil from the seed of *Ricinus communis* (*mubariki*) on their garments. An informant from Baricho, Mutira, Ndia, stated that having *muringa* near a homestead was an indicator of a prosperous family, 'People liked *muringa* [*Cordia abyssinica*]. Where you had one, the family was well to do, having many cows and so on.' Another informant suggested that *Kigelia africana* was connected with prosperous livestock keepers, since the tree grew often on the sites of old cattle enclosures.

Tree propagation was carried out on a limited scale in the pre-colonial era. It was carried out to meet needs such as marking boundaries, making fences, setting hedges, and supporting vines. Planting trees in large numbers for the purpose of reafforesting farmland was not part of indigenous land use strategies. In the indigenous Gikuyu world view, only 'God planted trees' on a large scale (Dundas 1955: 67). Gikuyu leaders from Kirinyaga and neighbouring areas told the 1929 Maxwell Committee, 'Trees have only been planted since Europeans came' (Maxwell *et al.* 1929: 8). Nevertheless, the pre-colonial Gikuyu had developed several strategies and techniques for incorporating trees into local production systems.

The issue of shifting cultivation

Early colonial administrative and technical officers depicted the Gikuyu as practising a highly destructive form of shifting cultivation (Eliot 1905; Hutchins 1907, 1909; Cranworth 1912). Geologist H.B. Muff claimed that Gikuyu shifting cultivators converted fertile soils into 'bare rock' (Hutchins 1907: 30, 1909: 67). Sidney H. Hinde, provincial sub-commissioner and a strong proponent of opening the Mount Kenya region to white settlement, agreed that their shifting cultivation caused severe land degradation, including heavy soil erosion (Hutchins 1907: 30). According to Hinde, Gikuyu forest clearing also decreased rainfall and disrupted stream flow. He asserted that the Gikuyu were reducing the Nyandarua Forest at a rate of half a mile a year (Hutchins 1909: 66–7). Forester Sir David. Hutchins, who visited southern Mount Kenya in the initial days of colonial rule, accepted Muff's and Hinde's assessments as accurate. The characterization of the Gikuyu as destructive shifting cultivators was used to justify the colonial appropriation of the Mount Kenya and Nyandarua forests (see Chapter 4).

Subsequent colonial writers accepted the notion that the Gikuyu practised a form of shifting agriculture that wantonly destroyed forests and soil quality. Forester S.H. Wimbush (1930: 195–6), for example, summarized the conventional wisdom regarding Gikuyu agriculture:

A hundred years ago the forests on the east and south of the mountain [Mount Kenya] must have covered a vast area, extending right down to the edge of savannah country bordering the valley of the river Tana. But the native cultivator of the Kikuyu tribe, at the time a stranger to methods of improving or harbouring the fertility of the soil, desiring fresh virgin land for his crops every few years, encroached little by little on the apparently inexhaustible forest.

According to Wimbush (1930: 196), the Gikuyu 'devastated' the forest until the colonial administration 'impressed' on them the need to conserve resources. Richard Baker (1931: 22), assistant conservator of forests, emphasized that the Gikuyu did not destroy forests 'in any spirit of mischief'. Instead: 'They were merely ignorant of the consequences of their recklessness.' In a more modern interpretation, conservation specialist Colin Maher (1938a, 1938b) claimed that Kirinyaga Gikuyu shifting cultivation had been appropriate in the past because of low population density, but now it had become quite harmful due to reduced fallows because of land scarcity.

Colonial claims about Gikuyu farming practices have been accepted by some recent writers. Thomas P. Ofcansky (1984: 137), in an otherwise informative history of forest administration in Kenya, states: 'Agricultural peoples such as the Kikuyu practiced a particularly destructive form of shifting cultivation by clearing and burning large patches of forest to grow crops and, when the soil was exhausted, moving on to the repeat the process elsewhere.' Ofcansky cited a Kenya Arbor Society publication from 1937 as reference for his comments. Similarly, an otherwise impressive report by Peter Dewees on forestry in Murang'a issued recently by the Food and Agriculture Organization cites without question the claims of Hinde and Hutchins regarding the supposed destructiveness of Gikuyu shifting agriculture.

William Allan (1965: 178–89) challenged many of the assumptions about Gikuyu shifting cultivation. He pointed out the lack of detailed knowledge about indigenous Gikuyu farming practices, including the length of fallowing. It was evident to Allan, however, that many colonial writers had underestimated the ability of the highlands to support permanent agriculture. Large parts of Gikuyu country such as Kirinyaga possessed deep, rich volcanic soils, allowing intensive cultivation. Allan believed that 'traditional' farming practices were capable of supporting over 100 people per km^2 without land degradation. Moreover, because of the soil's strength, Gikuyu farmland seemed capable of 'rapid recovery even after prolonged and punishing misuse' (Allan 1965: 180).

Many of the widespread assumptions about Gikuyu land use were seriously questioned by district-level agricultural officers in the colonial era. For example, Maher (1938a: 35–6) claimed that Gichugu shifting cultivators fallowed their fields after only two years in production. In contrast, a 1939 survey by the Embu assistant agricultural officer showed that plots cultivated for two or three years produced higher yields than freshly farmed land, and gardens cultivated for four years showed 'no signs of deterioration'. This pattern of productivity occurred throughout the Kenyan highlands (Logie and Dyson 1962: 18). It derived from the large quantity of organic matter in the soil of newly cleared upland forest. As decomposition took place, crop yields improved. The farming techniques used by the Gikuyu — such as limited tilling, incomplete clearing, and intercropping — allowed garden plots in some areas to remain under almost continuous cultivation. Dense bracken and weed growth, rather than soil exhaustion *per se*, frequently prompted households to withdraw land from farm production.

Fallowing fields remained a valuable source of forest products such as firewood, medicinal plants, thatch, and fodder. The length of the fallow period probably varied according to local circumstances, though such plots were always brought back into cultivation long before they could revert into secondary forest growth. The presence of large purple flowers on *Vernonia auriculifera* (*muthakwa*), a quick-growing shrub common in fallow regrowth, was sometimes used as an indicator to reopen a plot. Several present-day elders stated that the only shifting cultivation they knew about was the *taungya* (*shamba* or 'squatter') system of reforestation used by the Forest Department in the Mount Kenya reserve. In general, fallowing allowed coppiced or small trees and bush to regenerate, but there was no long-term rotation involving farmland and trees.

Deforestation in the late pre-colonial era

The regional and long-distance caravan trade expanded throughout central Kenya in the late 1800s (Saberwal 1967; Beachey 1967, 1976; Marris and Somerset 1971; Moris 1973; Mwaniki 1974; Ambler 1988). Caravans from the coast, often with several hundred porters, offered a substantial, if erratic and sometimes troublesome, market for foodstuffs, plus ivory and slaves (see Crawshay 1902; Muriuki 1974; Mwaniki 1974). By the 1860s people in Kiambu and other areas deliberately extended their cultivated area to meet the rising commercial demand (Kershaw 1972; also see Miracle 1974; Ambler 1988). Perhaps one-third of the farmland in southern Gikuyuland became directed towards growing surpluses for the caravan trade (Kershaw cited in Molnos 1972: 216).

The situation was similar in Kirinyaga, which Captain B. Dickson (1903: 39) called in 1903 'a great centre for the native caravans' (also see Saberwal 1967; Powell-Cotton 1973; Mwaniki 1974; Ambler 1988). Ernest Gedge (1892: 526) observed in 1891 that, 'The plantations appeared like market-gardens, so well were they kept.' In fact, they often were market-gardens, providing an 'unlimited food supply' to Arab and Swahili caravans (Arkell-Hardwick 1903: 51–60). Coastal merchants not only maintained long-term contacts with local communities to supply food, ivory, and other commodities, they also established regular camps or settlements. 'In those days there were Swahili traders on many of the ridges', recalled an African witness before the Kenya Land Commission in 1932. As many as seven camps were operated by Swahilis and Arabs in Kirinyaga and Embu (Saberwal 1967: 36). The most important settlements was located at Kagio, near the crossroads between the north-eastern and north-western caravan routes around the mountain. A 1907 European visitor pointed out that its 'village of square, rectangular huts' greatly contrasted with the 'round, Bantu type' in the surrounding countryside (Stigand 1913: 253–4). As late as 1911, there were 62 Swahili trading plots at Kagio. Colonial authorities eventually expelled them, accusing the Swahili of encouraging women to run away from their husbands. Farm surpluses from Kirinyaga were also exchanged in local and regional trade circuits, particularly with the Kamba (Moris 1973; Ambler 1988).

Expanding market and population pressures overwhelmed tree maintenance strategies in some areas during the late 1800s. Acute tree scarcity emerged in places heavily trafficked by caravans, such as near Ngongo Bagas on the southern edge of Gikuyuland and Maruka in Murang'a (von Hohnel 1968; Lugard 1893; Dickson 1903). From Nyeri the Routledges (1910: 6–7) observed, 'In the heart of Kikuyu, except for a sacred grove here and there, scarcely a tree remains. As far as the eye can reach, in all directions, spreads one huge garden.' Of course such gardens still included heavily pollarded and coppiced trees. The lack of tree cover in densely settled sections of southern Mount Kenya caused the 1891 Dundas expedition to have difficulties procuring firewood (Gedge 1892). In general, though, acute tree scarcity was not widespread in Ndia and Gichugu, but a highly localized phenomenon. Many places still possessed a smattering of tree cover. While quality timber trees might become locally scarce, fuel and other products could be obtained from fallowing fields and 'bush' (Arkell-Hardwick 1903: 59; Crawshay 1902).

The decrease in tree cover was not necessarily synonymous with increased land degradation. Instead, it often simply meant a shift in cropping patterns, with grains, pulses, tubers, and other foodstuffs, or grassland for livestock, replacing trees. Techniques such as intercropping, nutrient recycling by burning or burying crop residues and other plants, and low-till farming using digging sticks and cultivating knives, made it possible to expand farmland without undermining soil management.

Still, tree scarcity often caused hardship, especially for women, who were responsible for collecting wood. The Routledges (1910: 122) recorded the considerable time and effort spent by women in densely populated, tree-scarce parts of Nyeri to collect firewood for their domestic needs. Women often left at 5:00 a.m. for a four-hour walk to the forest, where they collected loads weighing up to 30 kg, then returned home in the evening. A robust trade in foodstuffs and forest products developed in Nyeri between the grain-abundant but wood-scarce region and the wood-abundant but often food-short villages on the Nyandarua forest frontier. Several elders in contemporary Kirinyaga recalled a trade between villages near the Mount Kenya forest and the more densely settled areas. A man from Kanyei sublocation, Mutira, Ndia, stated,

> Forest region people used to come here to trade firewood. We exchanged maize and beans for wood . . . They [the firewood sellers] came to the home areas. It was done by women who brought head loads.

Studies of the caravan trade often conclude that men, especially wealthy and powerful brokers, were its major local beneficiaries (Cavicchi 1977; Ambler 1988). In contrast, the foregoing analysis suggests that women in tree-scarce areas bore many of its costs through increased difficulty in procuring firewood. Ironically, in the first years of colonial rule Paramount Chief Githai wa Giti of Ndia took advantage of the scarcity of firewood near Kagio market by setting up 'a wood-pile, and [exacting] compensation for it, thus making a good living out of passersby' (Madeira 1909: 62).

Conclusion

This chapter has emphasized the importance of understanding indigenous tree management practices in a historical perspective. The peopling of southern Mount Kenya has long involved the clearance of forest and woodland. Yet, forests and trees also constituted invaluable socio-economic and cultural resources. Through experimentation and experience the people of pre-colonial Kirinyaga developed a range of communal and farm-level strategies to incorporate trees into their agrarian and socio-cultural systems. These strategies included the communal protection of forests, sacred groves, and locally valued timber species, the setting aside by households of small copses as woodlots, selective clearing, fallowing, and pollarding. The goal of such practices was not to re-afforest farmland and pasture, but to maintain economically and culturally valued multi-purpose trees near homesteads and fields. As in perhaps most traditional resource management systems (see Berkes 1987), this practical conservation was not based on 'scientific reasoning' or some indigenous environmentalism regarding trees. Rather, a complex combination of factors — cultural beliefs and values, local social relations, economic concerns, and population pressures — governed the use and management of trees. Commercial and demographic expansion in the late 1800s led to accelerated land clearing and localized tree scarcity. However, the decrease in tree cover was not necessarily synonymous with increased land degradation.

Large-scale tree planting for environmental protection or commercial purposes was an innovation of the colonial era (see Castro 1983, 1993, forthcoming). Nevertheless, indigenous tree management practices provided the foundation for past and recent successes with farm-level forestry interventions in Kirinyaga. Households continue to rely on time-tested and resilient indigenous techniques and strategies to meet the challenges of rising population pressures and the growing demand for economic development.

4. Conquest and concessions: the rise of British control, 1885 to 1915

THIS CHAPTER IS the first of five examining state-local conflicts over the use and management of the southern Mount Kenya forest. It describes and analyses the European penetration, conquest, and imposition of colonial control over the forest between the 1880s and 1915. The purpose is to elucidate the dramatic shift from a customary and decentralized common property management regime to one based on centralized and custodial government management. Over the course of a few years control of Mount Kenya passed from indigenous communities to colonial bureaucrats and technicians. The chapter describes and explains the complexity of motives and options involved in the colonial take-over of the forest. As will be seen, British officials, prospective entrepreneurs, and state foresters in London and Kenya often differed among themselves as to the best way to promote colonial political and economic interests. As in the other parts of the tropics, Western business interests sought exclusive access to the forest for large-scale commercial ventures. They were opposed by proponents of scientific forestry, who ultimately triumphed in imposing a state forest management regime. Their victory led to the eviction of the Kirinyaga Gikuyu and their neighbours from the forested slopes of the sacred mountain.

Colonial penetration and conquest

Anglican missionary Johann Ludwig Krapf (1860: 294) was the first European to see Mount Kenya. He observed its snow-capped peaks from Kitui, over 150 km away, in 1849. Mbeere warriors thwarted Krapf's (1860: 311–15) attempt to enter the region in 1851. More than three decades passed before another European, Joseph Thomson (1885), ventured near the mountain. The pace of European exploration of central Kenya soon accelerated, as the scramble to claim colonial territories was under way. Imperial ambition, commercial interest, scientific exploration, and other motives prompted Europeans to penetrate the interior of Africa (Hallet 1974). Austrian Count Teleki led a caravan that reached the upper slopes on the mountain's western face in 1887 (von Hohnel 1894). German explorer Carl Peters (1891) travelled along the southern edge of the Mount Kenya region in 1889. British Captain F.D. Dundas tried to scale the mountain from the south in 1891, but the steep terrain and dense forest proved too difficult (Gedge 1892). J.W. Gregory (1896), a British naturalist, investigated the western slopes in 1893. Explorations continued through the turn of the century (see Crawshay 1902; Dickson 1903). By 1899, even the tallest peak on the mountain had been scaled by Europeans (Mackinder 1900). Still, the region remained independent.

Many of the early explorers were impressed by Gikuyuland, including Kirinyaga. They depicted the region as land of pleasant climate where primeval forests gave way to exceptionally fertile and productive gardens tended by an industrious people (Thomson 1885: 306–8; Peters 1891: 210–16; Gedge 1892: 526–9; Lugard 1893: 323–33; von Hohnel 1894: 286–377; Gregory 1896: 157–2; Crawshay 1902; Arkell-Hardwick 1903: 59–61; Dickson 1903). An ivory trader travelling through Ndia and Gichugu, for example, wrote that the land was 'extraordinarily rich and fertile . . . and produces . . . a practically unlimited food supply' (Arkell-Hardwick 1903: 59). Winston Churchill (1908: 33), who visited Kirinyaga and Embu in 1907, wrote:

> The landscape is superb. In beauty, in fertility, in verdure, in the coolness of the air, in the abundance of running water, in its rich red soil, in the variety of its vegetation, the scenery about [Mount] Kenya far surpasses anything I have ever seen in India or South Africa, and challenges comparison with the fairest countries of Europe.

Many of the explorers especially appreciated the agricultural wealth of Gikuyu because their caravans depended on local food surpluses for provisions.

Great Britain declared Kenya a protectorate in 1895. By 1899, the railroad reached Nairobi, which became the seat of colonial administration. The government gradually extended its control towards north-eastern Gikuyuland. Fort Hall was founded in 1900 near the south-western edge of Ndia. Hostile relations with the northern Gikuyu temporarily halted state expansion (Mungeam 1966; Rogers 1979). A military expedition conquered Nyeri in 1902, where another outpost was established. Colonial forces invaded Gichugu, Ndia, and neighbouring Mathira between 25 February and 17 March 1904. Richard Meinertzhagen (1957: 152), who led troops through Kirinyaga, recorded in his diary: 'During the first phase of the expedition against the Irryeni [Ndia and Mathira] we killed about 796 niggers, and during the second phase against the Embo [Gichugu] we killed about 250.' He added that the Gichugu had not been 'sufficiently hammered' and expressed a desire to 'go back at once and have another go at them'. More than 1500 Africans were killed during the invasion, plus thousands of cattle confiscated, compared to a handful of losses for the colonial forces. The attack probably resulted in the highest death toll from a single British military operation in the Kenya highlands between 1895 and 1911 (Lonsdale 1992a: 28–9). Fearing a reprimand from the Foreign Office in London, authorities in Kenya reported only 400 African deaths (Mungeam 1966: 84). Government control now reached as far as the Rupingazi River, the boundary between Gichugu and Embu.

The European evaluation of Kenya underwent considerable change in the early 1900s. The building of the railroad and the attractiveness of the highlands to white settlers altered the potential value and use of land, natural resources, and the labour of the native peoples. The imperial goal became to make Kenya a self-supporting colony based on exports by European enterprises (Huxley 1956; Wolff 1974; Tignor 1976; Stichter 1982; Leo 1984; Berman 1990; Berman and Lonsdale 1992). This new attitude was heralded by Sir Charles Eliot, protectorate commissioner from 1901 to 1904, who wanted to make Kenya a 'white man's country'. He believed that the Africans were too backward to generate the exports needed to relieve the British exchequer of the burden of supporting the administration and railroad (Mungeam 1966).

Forests now became commercial assets, another resource to contribute to the development of the budding colonial economy. The government increasingly perceived the Africans as a threat to the forests and their utilization by Europeans. Eliot (1905: 74) led the way by depicting the Gikuyu as destructive shifting cultivators, clearing forests and abandoning the land once it became exhausted. He argued that the colonial administration 'must not allow nomadic tribes to monopolise huge areas of which they can make no real use' (Eliot 1905: 104). Instead, the government was obliged to assist whites to develop resources.

Eliot regarded the Mount Kenya region as ideal for European settlement. He envisioned thousands of white families living between the mountain and the

Tanzanian border (Meinertzhagen 1957: 31). Yet, Eliot (1905: 196) feared 'a catastrophe' would occur if colonists moved into the area before the Africans were subjugated. Kirinyaga and Embu were declared 'outlying districts' in May 1903, which barred unauthorized entry by whites. Even after the conquest of Kirinyaga, the area stayed closed. A 1905 uprising in Ndia and Gichugu, squelched by another military expedition, revealed the government's tenuous control over southern Mount Kenya (Mungeam 1966).

The Colonial Office and timber concessions

Despite its status as a closed district, southern Mount Kenya attracted interest among white entrepreneurs. In 1905 Moreton Frewen and others began investigating the mountain's resources. Their explorations included the forest along the Ruamuthambi and Kamweti rivers in Ndia (Hutchins 1907: 7). These investigations culminated in joint applications by two syndicates for large-scale timber concessions. Frewen headed one of the groups; the other syndicate was organized by Lord Warwick and Lord Brooke. They presented their proposal to Sir James Hayes Sadler, the new provincial commissioner, in March 1906. The syndicates planned to divide Mount Kenya between themselves, with the Thiba River as the southern boundary. Warwick's group intended to take the eastern face of mountain, while Frewen's syndicate would work the western side. Each lease was estimated to cover 40 000 ha. The syndicates jointly proposed building a railroad to transport the timber to national and export markets.

These requests for extensive tracts of forest were by no means unprecedented in Kenya. Ewart Grogan and associates had already acquired over 51 000 ha of forests at Eldama Ravine. As late as 1912, approximately one-fifth of the land appropriated by Europeans in the protectorate was held by only five individuals or syndicates (Berman 1990: 56). Many colonial officials assumed that large estates were an important means for promoting rapid economic development.

Sadler forwarded the applications to the East African Department in the Colonial Office in London. It had recently assumed responsibility for Kenyan affairs in the British government. The Colonial Office usually had a supervisory rather than executive role (Maxon 1993). Headed by the secretary of state of the colonies, the department reviewed local policy, appointments, and budgets. Only the colonial secretary could grant large concessions. According to Winston Churchill, an under-secretary at the time, the Colonial Office defined its task as reconciling Crown, European settler, African, and Asian interests (*The East African Standard*, 16 Nov. 1907: 9). Three colonial secretaries served in the period under consideration: Lord Elgin (1905–1908), Lord Crewe (1908–1910), and Lewis Harcourt (1910–1915). Their administrations, especially Elgin's, strongly shaped land use on Mount Kenya.

Sadler supplied a four-page appraisal of the applications. It emphasized the paucity of information about the region and the proposed lease terms. The concession on the eastern slopes appeared jeopardized because the Embu and neighbouring peoples were beyond colonial control. Yet, Sadler viewed the concessions favourably, provided the applicants guaranteed sufficient capital for their scheme. If they met this condition, he advised approving them on terms similar to those granted for timber concessions elsewhere in Kenya: long-term land leases at very low prices.

Minutes by two Kenyan officials — Sidney Hinde of the provincial administration and Andrew Linton of the agriculture and forestry departments —

accompanied Sadler's report. Hinde thought such concessions were the 'cheapest and best way' to manage the forest. The timber industry also offered the possibility of attracting white settlers to the fertile lower slopes. Yet, Hinde raised several issues about the applications: whether the sketch plan accurately depicted the forest; if the concession included the tapping of wild rubber (*landolphia* vines); how logs would be transported to market; and the need for a reafforestation plan. He emphasized that Embu would have to be conquered and a government station opened nearby before white colonization could begin. Although Hinde refused to endorse the concession outright, he made it clear that such schemes were welcomed.

Linton, concurrent director of agriculture and forestry in the protectorate, admitted lacking basic information about the Mount Kenya region. Still, he claimed the concessions fitted into the aims of public forest management in Kenya: environmental protection and income generation. Mature timber could be removed 'with advantage to the forest and the revenue of the country'. Because large amounts of capital were needed for the concessions, Linton argued against reducing their size. He strongly recommended approving the application, but emphasized that further exploration of the forest was required for a complete assessment.

The support of the timber concessions by Sadler and Linton reflected the prevailing weakness of state forestry in Kenya. A small Forest Department had been formed in 1902 to manage wood supplies for the railroad. Regulations were passed that same year enabling the administration to set up forest reserves. Although some few reserves were established, the department lacked the staff and resources to protect them. It also experienced a high turnover in leadership, with four people in charge of forestry between 1905 and 1907 (Ofcansky 1984: 139).

Colonial Office minutes revealed that there was considerable disagreement about the timber applications. Churchill wanted a speedy decision (Mungeam 1966: 162). He believed that concessions to private enterprise were needed to foster rapid development (Hyam 1968: 436). In contrast, Elgin and many of the East African Department staff wanted more information about the forest and the proposed timber concessions before reaching a decision. The colonial secretary distrusted speculative concessionaires, often preferring government control over natural resources as a more appropriate policy (Hyam 1968: 435–8). He delayed any decision until reports were received from Sadler and David Hutchins, a South African forester.

Meanwhile, a major obstacle to colonial development of southern Mount Kenya was removed when government forces invaded Embu in June 1906. The Embu suffered over 400 dead (Lonsdale 1992a: 28–9). The attack was carried out without prior approval from London. In fact, protectorate officials waited nearly two months before informing the Colonial Office about the action (Mungeam 1966: 163–64). Hinde justified the invasion as a punitive measure prompted by Embu raids. However, his report mentioned the need to conquer the Africans before opening the fertile region to white settlers.

Sadler ventured to southern Mount Kenya in August 1906. In spite of reduced visibility because of heavy mists and smoke, he observed that the forest covered a larger area than indicated by the applications. His reports provided few details about the forest and its inhabitants. However, he did suggest that the concessions be limited to the southern slopes until Meru could be subjugated. Sadler's dispatches were regarded as inconclusive by the East African Department, which now eagerly awaited Hutchins' report.

Hutchins' reports on Mount Kenya

Hutchins (1907) visited northern Ndia, Gichugu and Embu in December 1906, but 'native trouble' prevented travel east of the Rupingazi. The short time-span of his study only allowed for a preliminary assessment of the montane forest. Yet, the report had monumental consequences for the future forest management. At a basic level it described how forest composition varied according to geographic position and elevation. The *Ocotea* forest on the south-eastern slopes, dominated by giant East African camphor (*Ocotea usambarensis*) trees, had the 'best' timber. However, the Juniperus–Olea forest on the western slopes seemed to be more accessible for harvesting. Other potentially valuable plants were identified: *landolphia* vines that yielded rubber; and moss and lichen, which could be used as packing materials for shipping fruit. Hutchins (1907: 14) estimated that the southern half of Mount Kenya covered 200 000 ha and was worth £11 500 000. Thus, the forest was larger and more valuable than previously assumed. The report also noted the immense watershed and climatic value of the forest (Hutchins 1907: 29–33).

Because of the considerable economic and environmental value of the forest, Hutchins (1907: 31–3) advised placing Mount Kenya under government management instead of private ownership. This recommendation reflected his extensive experience in public forest administration. Hutchins had studied at the *Ecole des Eaux et Forets* in Nancy, France, a leading school on the philosophy and methods of scientific forestry (Ofcansky 1984: 139). He had a long career in the Indian and South African forest services. Long steeped in the practice of state forestry, Hutchins argued that the specialized technical expertise of the Forest Department was needed to ensure proper natural resource management.

He was not against commercial development of the forest. On the contrary, Hutchins (1907: 34) strongly supported opening the region to commercial lumbering and farming by dividing the area into four administrative blocks of roughly 40 000 ha each. The Forest Department would invite public bids for harvesting timber in each block subject to its supervision. The forest north of Ndia and Gichugu was to be placed in Block B, running from Nyeri station to the summit, then southwards again along the Rupingazi River. Although it had fewer camphor trees, the block was rich in podocarpus, a commercially valuable softwood. Block A contained most of the *Ocotea* forest, extending north-easterly from the Rupingazi into Meru. The state-supervised timber concessions would use a railroad or the Tana River to carry the logs to the coast for export. Suggested timber lease terms, including stumpage rates, were presented in detail (Hutchins 1907: 33–7). The conditions proposed by Hutchins were far less generous than those originally sought by the syndicates.

The report proposed establishing a buffer zone of white farms along the forest rim (Hutchins 1907: 24). Gikuyu land use practices were depicted as too destructive to allow them to stay next to the forest. Their 'shifting cultivation' supposedly destroyed large tracts of woodland, caused soil erosion, reduced rainfall, and disturbed stream flow (Hutchins 1907: 13, 30). Leaving the Africans adjacent to the forest also posed a security risk. In a subsequent report Hutchins (1909: 69) stated that in South Africa rebellious tribes sought refuge in the forest. To dislodge them 'entailed an expenditure of millions and the loss of many lives'. His warning proved prophetic half a century later, when the forest provided cover for Mau Mau guerrillas.

The Colonial Office received Hutchins' report in March 1907. H.J. Read, a senior officer, concluded that the study was 'sound and reasonable'. Two weeks later Lord Elgin agreed to place Mount Kenya under state control. The Forest Department would be responsible for its management. The Colonial Office decided to invite public bids for the four large timber concessions, though not until a forest survey was completed. The two existing applications were to remain in the running for the concessions, but they were not to receive preferential treatment. London officials rejected claims by Frewen and Warwick that they had 'discovered' the forest and thus deserved special consideration. Before its decisions could be announced, the Colonial Office was approached with a new offer by the timber concession applicants.

Railways and delays

Reginald Antrobus, an assistant under-secretary in the Colonial Office, received a new proposal in May 1907. The plan was submitted by a syndicate consisting of Frewen, Lord Warwick, and Lord Brooke, plus Lord Winchester, Lord Dudley, C. Newton Ogle, Fred W. Baker, and other financial backers. It was entitled 'Soft Wood Forests on Mt. Kenya' and presented a more detailed and ambitious scheme regarding the economic development of the region's forest and agricultural resources. The syndicate offered to construct and operate a railroad to the podocarpus and cedar forests of Mount Kenya. The track was expected to extend over 200 km from Nairobi to the forest. They planned to establish sawmills and woodworking industries, using skilled labourers imported from Canada. Large numbers of 'cheap' Gikuyu workers were to be employed felling trees and manufacturing windows and doors. The syndicate wanted to gear its production towards overseas markets in the British Empire. The firm expected to export 150 000 tons of lumber and logs annually.

The applicants claimed to be ready to invest £500 000 on the railway, mills, and machinery. In return they asked for exclusive timber rights on Mount Kenya, free of fees. The government could supervise forest use, however, and the syndicate offered to plant three trees for each one cut. An alternative plan called for allocating 12 140 ha of free timber for 65 km of railroad constructed, plus 2.59 km² for each additional 1.6 km of track laid. The syndicate estimated that the latter plan would yield 48 560 ha of forest and 41 440 ha of 'unoccupied prairie' near Mount Kenya. The prairie would be divided into farms for white colonists. The proposal argued that such a 'white oasis' would be of strategic value in case of trouble with the Africans.

The syndicate requested a meeting with Lord Elgin about their proposal. Frewen and the others were also interested in obtaining a copy of Hutchins' report, which had yet to be released to the public. Colonial Office minutes showed that the staff considered on several occasions how to handle the request. They confirmed the decision to turn Mount Kenya over to the Forest Department, yet the officials were reluctant to provide information regarding their intentions.

The Colonial Office wanted to resolve the problem of transporting timber from the forest before granting any concessions. No one was certain whether the Tana was capable of floating logs to the coast. Many officials believed that a railroad needed to be built if commercial timber development were to take place. The key issue was whether private or public funds were to be used. As mentioned, the syndicate proposed building a feeder line as part of their concession. Although not against private financing of railroads, Elgin and some of the staff were sceptical about the offer. They were weary of speculative ventures

(Hyam 1968: 437). Antrobus and others also wanted the government to benefit from the considerable rail revenue likely to be generated by forestry and agricultural development. Yet, as Churchill pointed out, the British Treasury seemed reluctant to commit public funds for further rail expansion.

Shortly before Elgin's meeting, Read queried the forester about his findings and the syndicate's latest proposal. Hutchins emphasized that the estimate of the forest's commercial value was conservative. He suggested that the cost of a railroad, even at £500 000, was 'a mere flea-bite compared with the value of forest'. Hutchins was optimistic about public financing once leases were signed with syndicates of approved financial standing. However, he proposed a more direct means for acquiring railroad funds: ask the four prospective leaseholders to deposit £50 000 with Crown Agents as a guarantee to work the forest. This money could be invested in the railroad. Hutchins also recommended that the rail route go via southern Mount Kenya to tap into the 'rich Embu country'. His views were endorsed by Antrobus, Read, and other officials.

Hutchins' report was released in mid-1907, and the timber applicants were informed that Mount Kenya would be placed under Forest Department control. Both Frewen and Warwick quickly disputed Hutchins' findings and recommendations. They were especially upset about the estimated size and value of the forest, plus the proposed lease terms. Frewen thought that Hutchins overestimated the total areas of forest by a factor of four. He complained that the report exaggerated the commercial prospects of unknown species in the world timber market, such as East African camphor. The economic analysis was said to have underestimated haulage costs. Frewen concluded that 'no timber will ever be cut on Kenia on the conditions he outlines . . . he would make the business impossible.' Officials forwarded their criticisms to the forester, who defended his methods and recommendations. Hutchins convincingly argued his case to the Colonial Office. Comments in several East African Department minutes revealed that the forester was highly regarded by the London officials.

Elgin deferred a decision on the new proposal, claiming that lease and transport issues needed clarification. Some reorganization of the Kenya Forest Department was expected to facilitate the resolution of these issues. In July 1907, the Colonial Office informed the syndicate that it could not provide any definite statement at the present time about the application.

The colonial population of Kenya was informed of Hutchins' report in August 1907. A Nairobi weekly published a memorandum from Elgin to Commissioner Sadler stating 'the urgent need' to protect Mount Kenya from 'irregular exploitation' (*The East African Standard*, 24 Aug. 1907: 11). Elgin announced Hutchins' appointment as conservator of forests, a post now directly responsible to the colonial secretary. For the first time in the protectorate's history, Elgin wrote, its Forest Department had a leader to deal with 'various projects without the danger of either hindering legal enterprise or of surrendering public property to the individual speculators for an inadequate consideration'. He avoided any specific mention of the pending applications, while offering the possibility of future commercial forestry development.

Churchill addressed the issue of Mount Kenya during his visit to the protectorate in late 1907. In a revealing speech at Nairobi the colonial under-secretary stated:

There is a great project which is coming rapidly into the area of practical politics, whatever that phrase means. I refer to the extension of a line in the direction of Mount Kenia, which will put East Africa in touch with those great forests — which, whether they have before them a great export future or not, are at any rate the source from which East Africa should draw its own timber . . . (*The East African Standard*, 16 Nov. 1907: 9).

His own scepticism about timber exports was quite evident. When Churchill returned, the *London Times* expressed doubts about the economics of building a railway to move timber from the mountain. It also argued that clearing would cause forest degradation. Quite clearly, the proposal had critics in Britain who worried about its costs and ecological impact.

State forestry in doubt

Lord Crewe became secretary of state for the colonies in early 1908. By that time the conquest of Meru placed the British in control of the entire mountain (Fadiman 1979). These new circumstances failed to generate any immediate change in the Colonial Office's cautious approach towards Mount Kenya timber concessions. As late as 1909, for example, Frewen and Warwick were told that their application could not be judged until a survey could determine if the Tana River was capable of floating logs to the coast. The survey revealed that river transport was not feasible (Hutchins 1909: 21). Even that bit of knowledge failed to bring about a decision on the concessions. Protectorate officials were slow in providing London with prospective terms for timber leases and the railroad, adding to the delay.

Meanwhile, the Forest Department had yet to assume control of Mount Kenya, and the future of the agency appeared uncertain. European colonists attacked the department for restricting forest exploitation. State reserves were portrayed as an attempt to 'choke off' resources that 'cry for development' (Cranworth 1912: 156). The government was accused of 'hoarding' forests because it feared 'private individuals or companies, or worse still, a speculator [might] make a profit' (Cranworth 1912: 155–6, 1919: 207–8). T.A. Wood, a member of Kenya's Legislative Council, wanted the department merged with the Police Service because the foresters spent so much of their budget on forest protection.

The department also had many critics among powerful civil servants in the colonial administration who objected to it on economic grounds (Ofcansky 1984: 139–40). The foresters constantly faced severe financial and labour constraints. In 1908, for example, forestry received only 60 per cent of its requested budget. Hutchins complained to the colonial secretary that vital activities could not be carried out, including forest protection and developing timber working plans. Sir Percy Girouard, who succeeded Sadler in 1909, asked the Colonial Office to abolish the post of conservator of forests. He argued that the department was 'a waste of money', but London officials denied the request (Mungeam 1966: 211). Charles Bowring, who succeeded Girouard, accused Hutchins of 'retrograde forest policy' (quoted in Ofcansky 1984: 140).

The existence of the forest reserves was threatened by ambiguities in forest legislation. The 1902 regulation permitted the establishment of forest reserves, but it failed to specify procedures for excising land from such areas. Controversy erupted in 1908 when protectorate officials granted parcels of land in the forest reserves to private companies without consulting the department. Hutchins once again appealed directly to the Colonial Office. He complained that the department was not taken seriously by protectorate officials. It made little sense to halt encroachment by Africans, Hutchins argued, only to allow white speculators to

seize control of government forests. Without security of tenure for the department, there could be no forest conservancy. The issue was not resolved until the
passage of a new forest ordinance in 1911.

Similar themes were repeated in a report by Hutchins on Kenya's forest resources in October 1909. The highland forests were depicted as under severe
threat from both Gikuyu farmers and white entrepreneurs. The questionable accounts of Hinde and H.B. Muff about Gikuyu shifting cultivation were cited to
document the destructiveness of indigenous land use (Hutchins 1909: 66–7). The
report also attacked 'speculators and fortune-hunters' seeking forest concessions
(Hutchins 1909: 63). It noted that private interests already controlled over 100 000
ha of woodland. Hutchins called for the demarcation of state reserves and the
promulgation of a comprehensive forest ordinance. He also revived the plan for a
protective buffer zone of white farms around Mount Kenya and the Nyandarua
range. The report also insisted that the forestry staff had to be increased before
Mount Kenya could be opened for timber development (Hutchins 1909: 71).

The final years of local control

While the fate of Mount Kenya was debated in London and Nairobi, the people
of Kirinyaga and their neighbours still occupied the forest. Since 1905 they had
been ordered by the provincial administration to stop clearing new fields in the
highland forest. Colonial officials perceived ambiguities in the situation,
however, because the forests in Gikuyu country had yet to be gazetted. Local
forest use continued to be governed by customary communal controls, including
regulations regarding land clearing.

Gikuyu forest use became a subject of controversy within Kenya's white community. It was said that 'Pax Britannica' — the supposed end of tribal warfare by
colonialism — accelerated deforestation. According to Lord Cranworth (1912:
157, 1919: 209), the Maasai had been 'the real forest conservator' because their
raiding had forced the Gikuyu to maintain a belt of forest as a buffer zone. Once
the Maasai threat was eliminated, it was argued, the Gikuyu initiated their
'wholesale spoliation' of the forest (Cranworth 1912: 47). Hinde estimated that
the Nyandarua forest alone was retreating at a rate of half a mile per year
(Hutchins 1909: 66–7). The Routledges (1910: 6–8), who observed forest clearing
near Nyeri, protested the lack of preventive action by officials. McGregor Ross,
director of public works for many years and a staunch defender of African rights,
testified at the Kenya Land Commission that massive deforestation occurred in
the decade after 1900. The reports issued by Hutchins (1907, 1909) supported the
claims of wide-scale forest destruction. In the colonial era the Gikuyu were
known as the 'Forest Destroyers' (Baker 1931).

The foregoing accounts contrast with descriptions of southern Mount Kenya
by Hayes Sadler in 1906 and by Chauncey H. Stigand a year later. Sadler observed in a report to the Colonial Office that a belt of thick bushland extended
over a mile between the forest and cultivated plots in Ndia and Gichugu. The
area appeared to be abandoned farmland. Similarly, Stigand (1913: 258) reported about the forest in Kirinyaga:

> Much of the country round here is covered by scrub and bush which pushes up
> to the forest edge. It appears that this land used to be either good grazing
> ground or under cultivation. The people having lost many of their cattle, the
> undergrowth has quickly again claimed the land.

Unfortunately Sadler and Stigand failed to mention the reasons for this agricultural retrenchment along the forest edge. These were the costly punitive expeditions, including the loss of many human lives and the confiscation of thousands of head of livestock. The collapse of the caravan trade may have contributed as well, though new markets for food surpluses quickly arose. Whatever the cause, Stigand (1913: 259) was amazed by the lack of clearing in the southern forest.

The accounts by Stigand and others can be reconciled to some extent. Major Granville Orde-Browne (1925: 19–20), an official in Embu from 1909 to 1916, observed that deforestation in southern Mount Kenya was 'retarded' compared to the Nyandarua range. Land clearing may have increased in some places after Stigand's visit because of new market opportunities. According to a protectorate report, for example, Kirinyaga exported large quantities of grain to Nairobi in 1908. Its households also continued to trade their substantial food surpluses in regional markets. There is no reference in the Kenya Land Commission of the early 1930s to a break down in communal controls along the forest frontier. Misconceptions about Gikuyu agriculture led many writers to exaggerate or overestimate its environmental impact. Smallholder farming systems worldwide, particularly shifting cultivators, have been commonly portrayed as destructive (see Dove 1983 and Warner 1992 for insightful analyses of this phenomenon). More importantly, the depiction of the Gikuyu as Forest Destroyers justified the colonial appropriation of their land and resources.

The demarcation of the reserve

The outcry about forest clearing caused the administration to order the demarcation of the Mount Kenya reserve boundaries. District records showed that work began in Ndia and Gichugu by early 1910. Despite numerous claims about deforestation, officials lacked maps showing the actual extent of the montane forest. Furthermore, there was no firm operational definition of what constituted 'forest'. Aware of this, the central government instructed provincial and forestry officials not to wait for precise yet time-consuming surveys before marking the borders. At the Kenya Land Commission some officials who supervised boundary cutting recalled that only land 'honestly described as forest' was included within the reserve. Yet, the chief conservator of forests told the commission that the borderlines were often 'give-and-take' ones. That is, in some places farmland and pasture were included within the reserve line, while patches of forest were occasionally excluded. To facilitate demarcation, officials preferred to draw long, straight boundaries. These 'lines of conveniences' added an element of arbitrariness to the selection of forest (*The East African Standard* 1925: 173). The provincial administration was delegated responsibility for settling any border disputes.

The boundary consisted of a three-metre-wide strip or road separating forest claimed by the government and land belonging to the Africans. Officials used several means to recruit workers for the task. Compulsory and unpaid labour was often used. In other cases men who worked on the forest boundary received credit towards their hut tax. Representatives from Kirinyaga and Embu later told the Kenya Land Commission that officials used deception in demarcating the reserve. According to one account, people were informed that a road was to be built from Nyeri to Meru so that the Gikuyu could buy sheep and travel without difficulty. In another version the strip was said to be a buffer for preventing the spread of fires. Both accounts agreed that people had no idea that the clearing was meant to be a barrier to separate them from their forest, farms, and homesteads. The Progressive Kikuyu Party of South Nyeri, a politically moderate group, wrote to the commission: 'we were not told, nor did we know, that the boundary lines were to be like walls of a cattle byre'.

Labourers planted fast-growing eucalyptus trees along the clearing to mark the boundary. The Africans were told they would be fined or imprisoned if they harmed the trees. Officials then ordered people living within the reserve to leave. Government-appointed chiefs, headmen, and their tribal retainers were responsible for clearing out any remaining homesteads and herds. In Kirinyaga Chiefs Gutu wa Kibetu and Njega wa Gioko, both of them local leaders of the pre-colonial era, carried out the destruction of the forest homesteads. Evicted families were warned never to return. Because they were regarded as forest encroachers, no compensation was provided. In some places they were allowed to harvest standing crops prior to eviction. No records were kept of the number of people displaced by the boundary demarcation. The boundaries of the reserve were officially gazetted in 1913, thus formally terminating aboriginal rights to the forest.

Only sporadic resistance occurred in response to forest appropriation in southern Mount Kenya. It took the form of families trying to re-occupy their holdings, occasionally with the tacit approval of local headmen. In 1910, households in one northern Embu location households not only cleared new plots in the forest, they also refused to pay their taxes. Tribal police destroyed the fields and suppressed the tax uprising. That same year a Gichugu headman in Kabare was fined for allowing people to cultivate in the reserve. To prevent further unauthorized use of the forest, headmen whose territory was adjacent to the reserve were paid a small amount to monitor the boundary and keep it clear. They were eventually replaced by guards who possessed powers of arrest. The guards were posted along the reserve boundary to supervise its everyday use. Several of the early forest guards in Kirinyaga were Sudanese.

When the forest evictions took place, no formal protests occurred among the people of southern Mount Kenya. Years later, at the Kenya Land Commission, some administrative and forestry officers interpreted this as African acceptance of the legitimacy of the government's actions. Veteran provincial administrator C.R.W. Lane, for example, stated, 'I do not consider [the Gikuyu] having any claim to the forest at all. When we put forest guards there, there was no protest at all'. John Pease, district commissioner of South Nyeri, argued, however, that the Gikuyu lacked the political organization and educational skills to present their views when the forest was demarcated. Even Lane admitted that in the early days of colonial rule, before Africans received schooling, they would have taken such orders 'without question'. Despite the absence of organized protests, the appropriation of the forest emerged as a major source of tension between the people of southern Mount Kenya and the colonial administration.

Colonial officials were satisfied in the years immediately after the demarcation of the reserve that forest 'encroachment' had been halted. The impact of state forest restrictions was softened by the Nyeri forester, who allowed people in fuel-scarce areas to gather deadwood for free as long as they left their axes behind. Women and men who volunteered their labour for such tasks as clearing boundaries or paths were given firewood in exchange. White settlers, though, were the primary beneficiaries of free issues of wood from the forest reserve during this period.

Concessions redux

The demarcation of the forest boundary coincided with the opening of the western side of the mountain to white settlement. Once the Maasai were expelled, the colonial government surveyed the region north of Nyeri for allotment into farms (Sorrenson 1968: 101). The lease conditions included an annual rent of £9 per year, plus requirements regarding eventual land improvements (Anderson *et al.* 1962: 51). There was no attempt to create a buffer zone of white farms along the southern rim of the forest. Orde-Browne testified at the Kenya Land Commission that officials believed Mathira, Kirinyaga, and Embu to be too thickly populated to allow white immigration. To have opened the region to Europeans would have been a great 'injustice' to the Africans. The southern slopes of Mount Kenya reportedly contained as much cultivation as the rest of the central highlands (Cranworth 1912: 160). However, the importance of the forest to the Gikuyu was not seen in a similar manner by officials.

The Colonial Office and the Forest Department loosened their grip on Mount Kenya in 1910. They sanctioned the collection of wild rubber in the forest (see Chapter 6). A small timber lease was granted on the western slopes: 800 ha to Lord Cranworth, with an option for another 800 ha. Officials wanted his sawmill to service the white farms in the allotment zone. He pursued more ambitious plans, requesting a 40 000 ha concession in the *Ocotea* forest. Neither the Forest Department nor the Colonial Office took action. Cranworth (1912: 162) believed that officials were overly protective of the camphor forest, noting, 'These trees have been to the authorities even as an only child to its mother.' The application was soon switched to the Juniperus–Olea forest on the western slopes. Once again, the Colonial Office refused to discuss the matter until Warwick and Frewen's proposal was settled. An irritated Cranworth (1912: 160) commented about Mount Kenya:

> The dealings of the Government with this magnificent property up to the present have been somewhat peculiar, or at all events, shrouded in mystery. In 1905–06, the whole forest appears to have been alienated or leased to a syndicate . . . What their position is no one appears to know, but certainly in all this time no steps have been taken by them to develop their concession, if concession there be. It is by no means improbable that no definite proposals have ever been put before them to accept or decline.

It appeared to Cranworth (1919: 207–8) that the Forest Department was resisting any efforts 'to establish private enterprise on Mount Kenya'.

In the meantime an increasingly frustrated Frewen and partners bombarded the Colonial Office with various proposals and queries. The main points of contention continued to be the railroad and the timber lease terms. As another timber applicant noted, there seemed to be 'a vicious circle': no concession would be allowed without a railroad, and no railroad would be approved without the concession agreed. The Frewen syndicate also revived its request for preferential treatment on the basis of having 'discovered' the forest. This claim only drew testy responses from East Africa Department staff familiar with the long years of correspondence. One official regarded it as 'a direct challenge' to the colonial secretary's power to grant concessions. The Colonial Office reiterated in 1911 and 1913 its assertion that no such discovery or preferential rights existed.

The issue of preferential treatment became important because other syndicates expressed interest in obtaining concessions. Although public tenders had yet to be offered, several queries and proposals were sent to the Colonial Office between 1911 and 1915. Governor Girouard encouraged Cranworth to maintain his application for a large-scale concession. The McDonell brothers discussed the possibility of carrying out timber operations. W.F. Leeson, G. Lloyd, and T.H. Hiker submitted separate proposals as well, each involving a series of negotiations.

In 1912 the Colonial Office finally drafted a three-page statement specifying terms for the Mount Kenya railroad and timber concession. It proposed a single concession covering 40 000 ha on the southern slopes between Nyeri and Embu. The exact site was to be chosen by the conservator of forests and the concessionaire. Besides paying a fixed rent, the leaseholder would be charged a royalty for timber removed. The concessionaire was to be responsible for building a feeder line to the Thika tramline, the northern railhead by that time. Rail rates for public traffic were to be similar to those charged by the Uganda Railroad. Colonial Secretary Harcourt accepted the draft as policy in December 1912. Some members of the East African Department, however, felt uneasy opening Mount Kenya to timber exploitation. In late 1912, H.J. Read wrote to Sir George V. Fiddes (who replaced Antrobus as head of the department):

> Personally, I think that it would not be a bad thing if the whole affair were closed down for two or three years. None of the present applicants are really sound and substantial people and I doubt whether public invitation to tender would produce a better lot.

Read also believed that the government ought to build the railway, rather than relying on the private sector.

As events turned out, Read and other officials worried unnecessarily about their prospective concessionaires. The Colonial Office's terms met with disapproval from Frewen, Cranworth, and Leeson. Counter-proposals were presented by the different parties. In 1914, Cranworth offered to raise £500 000, for example, to build a railroad to north-western Mount Kenya. In return, he asked for modifications of the timber lease terms. The Colonial Office refused to modify the conditions. Ultimately, none of the concession proposals was approved.

The onset of the First World War effectively marked the end of consideration for large-scale Mount Kenya timber concessions. Many of the prospective entrepreneurs, such as Lord Cranworth, joined the military. The Colonial Office also became absorbed in the war effort, and its influence over Kenyan affairs waned until the early 1920s (Maxon 1993). As will be discussed in Chapter 6, the Forest Department decided to offer timber leases on a much smaller scale. A government railroad through northern Gikuyu country and the western side of the mountain was built only in the mid-1920s. The feeder line to Embu or the southern forest along Kirinyaga was never constructed.

Conclusion

The British government appropriated the southern Mount Kenya forest in the early years of colonial rule. Officials insisted on seizing control of Mount Kenya from the people of Kirinyaga and their neighbours in order to protect the forest from encroachment. In addition, many officials and entrepreneurs wanted to open the area to commercial timber and agricultural exploitation by white settlers. There was, however, much debate within the Colonial Office and the branches of the protectorate government regarding the management and use of the forest. Although the British government desired the economic development of the region's resources, Lord Elgin and others in the Colonial Office and the Kenya Forest Department wanted to avoid turning the forest over to speculators. After years of negotiation, imperial officials and prospective entrepreneurs failed to reach agreement on terms for railroad construction and timber leases. By 1915, the Colonial Office dropped plans to offer large-scale concessions in the southern forest. Thus, the unfolding events represented a victory to forestry officials interested in controlling African and European access to the reserves. Frustrated concession applicant Lord Cranworth (1919: 209) claimed that forestry expert Sir David Hutchins 'spared no pains to save the trees he loved'. The people of Kirinyaga found little solace, however, since their claims to the forest were rejected by the government. Colonial officials evicted the Africans from the newly demarcated state reserve.

5. Contested forest claims: 1925 to 1940

MOUNT KENYA CONTAINED several traditional ritual sites where sacrifices to God were performed to ensure local prosperity. When the forest reserve was established, the men whose duty it was to carry out the rites continued to go 'by stealth over the old boundary offering the sacrifice as of old' (Kenya Land Commission 1934: 96). The defiance of state regulations both ensured cultural continuity and provided a form of resistance to colonial control. In the years after forest demarcation the Gikuyu used such 'weapons of the weak' (cf. Scott 1985) as unauthorized removal of firewood to defy colonial rule. During World War 1, with the forestry staff depleted by military requirements, provincial reports indicated that wood theft reached substantial proportions. The return of forest officers at the end of the war diminished the scope and magnitude of informal challenges to state authority along southern Mount Kenya. Some forests bordering Gikuyuland and the White Highlands, however, remained difficult to control after the First World War. For years illegal cultivation and herding by Africans continued along western Mount Kenya and the Nyandarua range (van Zwanenberg 1975: 249–51). Forests also served as a hide-out for fugitives and tax evaders.

Beginning in the 1920s, local grievances about colonial appropriation of the forest were also expressed through officially sanctioned means. This chapter examines the voicing of such grievances through two prominent channels: the local native council, established in the mid-1920s as part of the colonial policy of indirect rule; and, especially, the Kenya Land Commission, a body convened in 1932 to adjudicate African land claims against the state and white settlers. The chapter also describes the colonial government's attempted settlement of the Gikuyu land grievances in southern Mount Kenya. It involved the return to African control of an 800 ha forest parcel called Nyagithuci. The negotiations and conflicts among the Africans and the British administrators regarding resettlement at Nyagithuci are highly revealing of the contradictory motives and actions that characterized the colonial experience. An examination of the debates about Nyagithuci also elucidates many of the assumptions about Gikuyu life and politics that guided colonial policy.

The Local Native Councils

By the early 1920s the British government pursued a policy of indirect rule in Kenya, allowing Africans control over certain local administrative affairs (see Kitching 1980; Maxon 1993). The Native Authority Ordinance of 1924 allowed for the creation of local councils in each of the African reserves. These bodies were supposed to be loosely based on indigenous elders' council, though the new institutions were explicitly derived from official decree rather than from 'any latent indigenous powers recognized by treaty or agreement' (Native Affairs Department 1947: 20). British administrators in Nyeri had actually set up an advisory council composed of African members as early as 1917. The new entities, which were formed in 1925, had greater authority than the advisory council.

The council was composed of appointees and publicly elected members who served three-year terms. Chiefs often served as councillors, and the Christian missions usually had at least one representative. The district commissioner presided over the meetings and possessed veto power. Councillors passed resolutions governing a range of local affairs, including agriculture and land tenure, woodland (excluding Crown Forest), trade, health, education, and roads. They served as trustees for public land such as markets and roads. The council levied a rate (about one Shilling per adult in the 1920s), hired its own technical staff, and carried out its own administrative activities and programmes. In fact, as Majorie Ruth Dilley (1966: 29) observed in 1937, the councils often embarrassed the colonial government by their willingness to finance and operate public services. The Embu council, for example, long resisted Forest Department efforts to take over local woodland by successfully operating its own forestry programme (see Chapter 10).

The Local Native Council was also created as a channel through which local political views could be expressed to the colonial government. The Gikuyu protest movement led by Harry Thuku and others in the early 1920s made policy-makers in Nairobi and London keenly aware of the rising tide of African political grievances (see Rosberg and Nottingham 1970; Clayton and Savage 1974; Clough 1990; Berman and Lonsdale 1992; Maxon 1993). British policy-makers wanted the councils to serve as 'a safety valve for a constitutional approach in controversial matters' (Native Affairs Department 1935: 45). They were utilized as such. Chief Njega wa Gioko stated in 1932 that every time a council meeting occurred, 'from every quarter there came complaints about the land' (Kenya Land Commission 1934: 86).

The minutes of the Embu and South Nyeri councils provided ample examples of African protests about the appropriation of Mount Kenya. At the opening of the Embu council in July 1925, Senior Chief Runyenjes followed a speech by Kenya Governor Edward Denham by denouncing the exclusion of beekeepers from the forest. Runyenjes again attacked the appropriation of the Mount Kenya forest at the second meeting. A year later Chief Muruatetu asked 'by what right Government had reserved the forest'? Councillors complained at other meetings about Forest Department controls on removing timber, collecting firewood, hanging beehives, and taking cattle to salt-licks. They also claimed that Asian traders and white missionaries were not prosecuted when they cut trees in the reserve without permission. British officials denied any discrimination in enforcement of forest regulations. Restoration of the forest was said by the district commissioner to be the most pressing land issue in Embu by the early 1930s.

South Nyeri councillors also attacked colonial forest appropriation. Paramount Chief Wambugu pointed out at a 1932 meeting that people evicted from the forest never relinquished their claims to the land. He also stated that the Gikuyu 'did not know [the forest] was to be given to Europeans'. Once again, the colonial appropriation of Mount Kenya was portrayed as an illegitimate action.

The Mount Kenya forest became a source of conflict between the South Nyeri council and the colonial government in 1928. The councillors requested 12 ha in the reserve for an experimental farm. The proposed farm was to carry out agricultural research and serve as a tree nursery for the benefit of the local people. In spite of its purpose, the councillors and their constituents were wary of surrendering local land for government purposes, even if they retained nominal control. The council received only a short-term lease and was compelled to pay a small rent. These conditions enraged the councillors, who had assumed the land would be available free of charge on a long-term basis (Huxley 1931: 182). After two years the Forest Department reclaimed the plot. Even politically moderate Gikuyus complained to the Kenya Land Commission that the council lost the money it invested in the farm. Coinciding with the forest farm issue was a protest by the Tetu Gikuyu over the lost of Nyeri Hill, a sacred site long appropriated as Crown Forest (Tignor 1976: 28).

The protests about Mount Kenya were connected to wider African dissatisfaction about colonial rule. By the late 1920s the issue of European land alienation pervaded Kenyan politics (see Rosberg and Nottingham 1970; Tignor 1976; Clough 1990; Berman and Lonsdale 1992). Missionary attempts to ban the Gikuyu practice of female circumcision also caused an uproar (Kenyatta 1938; Murray 1974; Davison 1989). Racial consciousness and cultural nationalism were developing rapidly, particularly in Kiambu. Many white settlers and officials feared that a Gikuyu insurrection was imminent (Huxley 1931: 176). British administrators sought a means to diffuse an increasingly explosive situation.

Governor Sir Edward Grigg appointed a special committee in 1929 to examine Gikuyu land issues, though it focused almost exclusively on the definition of tenure rights (Maxwell *et al.* 1929a). The committee consisted of G.V. Maxwell, the chief native commissioner, L.S.B. Leakey, the well-known archaeologist who spoke Gikuyu fluently, and S.H. Fazan, an administrator. It spent three weeks meeting with elders and chiefs in different parts of the province (see Leakey 1937: 262–71, for an inside account). Kirinyaga representatives, such as Chief Njega, were interviewed at Karatina with the rest of the South Nyeri Gikuyu on 25 September 1929. Although the session dealt with land customs, the elders mentioned that their main honey collection grounds in the forest had been closed to them (Maxwell *et al.* 1929b: 2). The final report in November 1929 provided important insights into the traditions and changing nature of tenure rights, but it ignored the crucial Gikuyu land grievances against the administration and white settlers. A special commission would be needed to address such issues.

The Kenya Land Commission

In this atmosphere of crisis, the colonial secretary convened the Kenya Land Commission in April 1932. The commission was asked to adjudicate African land claims against the government and white settlers. The commission's findings were to serve as the basis for drawing up permanent racial and tribal boundaries. The Africans were to receive security of tenure within their assigned reserves. British officials hoped the commission would remove the uncertainty and fear created by the 1915 Crown Land Ordinance, which had nullified aboriginal land rights. The commission was headed by Sir Moris Carter, former chief justice in East Africa who had served as chairman of the 1925 Southern Rhodesia Land Commission. The other two members were white settlers, while Fazan served as secretary.

The task of the commission was enormous: 736 witnesses testified and over 900 documents were presented (Clough 1990: 161). It eventually collected 17 volumes of original evidence in typescript pages about land claims, including eight volumes specially dealing with Gikuyu grievances. Most of the material dealt with land lost to European settlers, particularly in southern Gikuyu country. Only a small amount of the testimony and submissions related directly to Mount Kenya. Still, for those involved, it was a matter of upmost importance.

The commission collected written and oral African evidence about the forest at hearings in Nyeri during November 1932 and January 1933. Over 90 South

Nyeri lineages, including ones in Kirinyaga, submitted claims to lands occupied by the Forest Department. Some of them dealt with Mount Kenya, while others concerned the Nyandarua range or Nyeri hill. A petition by the South Nyeri council mentioned the evictions and criticized state policies that limited access to the forest. It stated that 1343 district residents had lost land through colonial land appropriation, including 104 people in Ndia and Gichugu. The council's figure had been derived from the South Nyeri Progressive Kikuyu Party, a politically moderate group that supported Protestant missionaries in their attempt to ban female circumcision. The party submitted its own memorandum contesting the forest alienation, asserting that 'we were not told, nor did we know, that the boundary lines were to be like walls of a cattle byre' (Kenya Land Commission 1934: 96). It argued that the Gikuyu did not know that their forest would be taken away 'forever'. The Embu branch of the Kikuyu Central Association presented a similar view. All of the written submissions pressed the commission to return their original forest land, including salt licks and ceremonial sites, plus adequate space for current farming and wood requirements.

Testimony about southern Mount Kenya was presented by prominent elders and chiefs. Juhena Ngungi from Ndia described showing district officials 'the remains of huts and deserted places' in the forest (Kenya Land Commission 1934: 257). 'This land originally belonged to us and we used to get our best cultivation there and best wood,' he attested. Ngungi recalled that the evictions took place around 1911 or 1912. Chief Njega of Ndia and Chief Gutu of Gichugu 'were told to burn down all these huts on this land and they did it. There were over 100 and less than 1000 huts.' Chief Njega himself testified to the commission. A stalwart of local land rights, yet also a public servant in the colonial state, Njega confirmed Ngungi's account:

After this boundary was marked out we could not get into the forest and we had our important trees there and we cannot go inside there again and get sufficient wood. As I was the Chief, Government came and told me that I should go into the forest and turn out all the people who were living there and burn down there huts, which I did. The huts were uncountable, very, very many. Even now you can see the remains of the huts. They were the huts of people who lived there before Government came to this country (Kenya Land Commission 1934: 258).

The final sentence quoted above, about people living in the forest before the coming of 'Government', was of critical importance to the commission. Because the British believed that the onset of colonial rule actually led to the acceleration of deforestation, the commission considered Gikuyu forest occupation as legitimate only if it existed prior to 1895. Similar testimony about indigenous forest rights and colonial evictions was received from Chief Muruatetu of Embu, Headman Kareithe of Karatina, and others along the southern rim of Mount Kenya.

The district commissioners of South Nyeri and Embu also testified at the hearings. As the head administrative officer at the district level, they were in a key position to gather and to evaluate the various land grievances. Before the commission convened, they consulted with the Local Native Council about the upcoming hearings. The administrators also held special public meetings to discuss the land claims, including visits to the forest to see where the evictions had supposedly occurred. The commission sought their advice as to the legitimacy of the claims.

Both district commissioners — John Pease in South Nyeri and H.E. Lambert in Embu — largely supported local claims to the forest. Each man's experience in the area he administered may have influenced this outcome. At the time the colonial government frequently transferred provincial and district officials after serving only one or two years in a place (Trzebinski 1985). Thus, officials often lacked sufficient time to acquire a grasp of local affairs. Both Pease and Lambert had been posted to their respective sites since 1929, and Pease originally visited Kirinyaga as early as 1918. Lambert had a strong interest in African culture, reflected in the books he wrote about the Gikuyu and related peoples (Lambert 1949, 1956). Pease's presentation to the commission also revealed a person who took an interest in local perspectives. To call them advocates for their African populations would be an exaggeration; however, they were clearly knowledgeable about, and sympathetic towards, local land grievances.

Pease testified that a large number of Ndia and Gichugu farms had been located within the forest reserve boundary. They had long-standing tenure rights extending as far as the bamboo zone, though lineage boundaries were marked only in thickly populated areas. He estimated that in 1910 probably 600 to 800 people were evicted in Kirinyaga, particularly in the forest north of present-day Inoi, Mutira, and Mwerua. Perhaps two-thirds of the forest farms existed before 1895, with some having been occupied for a long period. This covered an area of roughly 15 km². Pease concluded that the Forest Department's demarcation of the reserve had been motivated by a concern to save the forest from destruction, rather than with 'administrative questions and the needs and interests of the local Kikuyu' (Kenya Land Commission 1934: 518).

Lambert's testimony supported the Embu claims. He emphasized that their grievances were put forward by 'responsible persons' not 'agitators'. The root of the land issue was said to be the government's lack of knowledge about native culture. When forest demarcation occurred, officials were ignorant about local tenure rights and thus ignored them. 'The line demarcated was a convenient line and not a line which administered native claims' (Kenya Land Commission 1934: 551). He refuted the notion that indigenous forest use had been unregulated. Tenure rights had been defined within the reserve boundary 'to a varying depth of about two miles'. The original owners and their boundaries could still be identified 20 years after the evictions. Farming had been limited to small clearings or glades. Large trees within the cultivated zone were communal property and could not be cut without the approval of local elders. The forests outside the clan lands were also protected as a communal resource. Lambert sided with Embu claims that they were not told the purpose of forest demarcation. He concluded that the Embu had 'definitely suffered a hardship in the loss of land and salt-lick'.

Neither Lambert nor Pease recommended that the forest be returned directly to the local people. Lambert suggested that part of the forest be designated as African Reserve Forest, where limited cultivation could occur and the Local Native Council would earn revenue from the removed forest produce fees. Pease proposed a sort of profit-sharing *taungya* system, with the Gikuyu leasing land from the Forest Department to plant food crops and trees. When the trees matured, the proceeds from their harvest would be divided between the Africans and the department.

Other colonial officials disputed the African claims. Major Granville Orde-Browne, who supervised the demarcation of the Embu boundary, testified that the local people had been fully informed about the government's intentions. He added that the border carefully distinguished between forest and farmland.

Orde-Browne suggested that the Gikuyu always claimed a larger area than they could have possibly occupied. C.R.W. Lane, a provincial administrator at the time of demarcation, stated: 'The natives have no claim whatsoever to the forests. They did not occupy them or cultivate them' (Kenya Land Commission 1934: 404). Edward Battiscombe, former conservator of forests, said the reserve boundary followed the line of actual forest and cultivation. In contrast, A.G. Baker, the surveyor general of Kenya, and H.M. Gardner, the conservator of forest, recalled that reserve boundaries were often lines of convenience, involving a trade-off between farmland or forest. Charles Dundas thought that the Gikuyu might be 'justified' in claiming remote territory which they used. Thus, the commission confronted a problem of conflicting memories and interpretations.

The announcement of the Kenya Land Commission had generated 'great expectation and hope' (Rosberg and Nottingham 1970: 155). Some Africans expected their claims to the forest to be settled immediately. Several incidents of people threatening the forest guard were reported by the assistant conservator of forests to the Embu district commissioner in September 1932. In one case an African waving a *panga* (machete) told the guard that the boundary no longer existed and the eucalyptus boundary markers would be chopped down. Months later the local people were still said to 'very unruly', disputing the guard's authority to prevent them from grazing livestock or removing forest produce. The assistant conservator asked the district commissioner for 'moral support', as well as any available tribal policemen.

There was much anxiety as people awaited the commission's final report. Some Africans had been very sceptical about the proceedings. Chief Njega told the commissioners that the cards seemed to be already stacked against African claims. The astute chief's comments were made without the knowledge of Carter's secret 'terms of reference'. Indeed, unknown to the British parliament or other concerned parties, the colonial secretary had told the commission chairman to assume that the racial character of landholding in the highlands would not be changed (Clough 1990: 160). Several colonial officials doubted the commission's ability to resolve the land grievances. The Native Affairs Department's annual report for 1933 stated, '. . . it is obvious to any one who knows the native mind that many people will be unsatisfied'.

The final report of the Kenya Land Commission was published in May 1934. The distribution of its copies set the tone for things to come (Clough 1990: 163). No translations were available in any African languages. No reports were sent to local native councils, even though European district councils received complimentary copies. The district commissioner summarized the findings a few months later to the Embu council. And no meeting took place between Colonial Secretary Philip Cunliffe-Lister and any African representative when he travelled to Kenya to discuss the report.

In evaluating African land claims, the commission used the criteria of 'effective use' and 'true loss sustained'. Prior to 1895, the commission felt that clear evidence had to be present showing that the Africans had occupied an area in sufficient numbers. Sparsely populated or frontier areas were not recognized as having been in effective use. Thus, the commission concluded that the Gikuyu failed to demonstrate their rights to most of the forest surrounding their agricultural lands in the pre-colonial era. It acknowledged that 'a few venturesome individuals' may have penetrated deep into the forest, but their activities were not sufficient to establish tribal ownership. Forested areas that had sufficient settlement, however, could be considered as being in effective use.

The commission dedicated a single paragraph to the Ndia and Gichugu forest claims. It decided that the people of Kirinyaga had suffered some legitimate loss of land during forest demarcation. The report placed the boundary of effective Ndia and Gichugu Gikuyu occupation to be one mile north of the existing forest line. This interpretation was acknowledged to be a conservative estimate. The rest of the forest claimed by the people of Kirinyaga was ruled to be ownerless. In contrast, the commission rejected all of the Embu claims, despite Lambert's strong support for them. The report did suggest that arrangements could be made to open some forest salt-licks to local use. Still, the judgement disappointed the Embu.

The denial of the Embu forest claims nearly undermined the government's attempt to introduce coffee growing in the district. Until the early 1930s, coffee cultivation was officially limited to white farmers. This restriction was nominally imposed to prevent the spread of crop pests, but it also served to prevent economic competition from Africans. In 1933, the administration decided to allow cultivation of the crop in Embu, Meru, and Kisii districts on an experimental basis (Barnes 1976). Although the Embu council petitioned the government as early as 1926 for the right to plant coffee, no one applied for a growing permit when offered by British officials in early 1934. Records in the Embu District Archives indicated that many people from the proposed site feared the loss of their land to the colonialists if they planted coffee on it. Embu representatives mentioned the administration's earlier use of deception to seize control of Mount Kenya. At a meeting attended by the provincial commissioner in September 1934, several local speakers argued that the government's recent refusal to compensate the Embu for the loss of the forest demonstrated its hostile character. Further negotiations were needed before Embu farmers in Njuu location agreed to the experimental planting.

Nyagithuci forest: whose land?

The final settlement of the Gikuyu claims was based on the assumption that all land grievances be considered in terms of the 'tribe' as a whole. Although individuals and lineages had presented specific claims, the commission felt that the Gikuyu themselves actually viewed land losses as a tribal affair. The commission members, like many Europeans, believed that the tribe was the fundamental socio-political unit in African society. This was a serious misconception. The Gikuyu certainly formed a cultural entity in terms of a group of people who shared cultural and linguistic attributes. But in the pre-colonial era the Gikuyu never formed a 'tribe' in a socio-economic or political sense as conceived by Westerners. Ironically, colonialism forged a sense of wider political identity among the Gikuyu peoples, but it also set into motion other cultural changes that undermined group unity. There were growing divisions on the basis of religion (Christians and adherents of traditional religion) and economic status (the prosperous, particularly those with lucrative non-farm income, and the land-poor or landless without steady employment). The substantial gap between European ideals and African reality became evident when the colonial government attempted to carry out the commission's recommended settlement.

The commission recommended 8500 ha of land excised from the various government forests adjacent to the Gikuyu reserve as partial compensation for the tribe's losses. According to the commission's final report, the chief conservator deliberately selected scrub-covered instead of heavily wooded land. An 800 ha block of land in South Kenya called 'Narkothi Hill' was included in the settlement. It was situated adjacent to Ndia and Gichugu. The colonial secretary told district officials not to allocate the land without instructions from the central government. By this time Kirinyaga had been transferred from South Nyeri to Embu, and Lambert had been replaced by Kenneth Lindsay. The new district commissioner reported in August that no action had been taken other than informing the Local Native Council of the decision. Indeed, correspondence in the Embu District Archives showed that Lindsay and forestry officials had problems locating the parcel, which was known by a variety of names: Neakochi, Narkothi, Nyakithuci, and the one usually used today: Nyagithuci.

The Ndia and Gichugu Gikuyu assumed that Nyagithuci had been awarded to settle their land claims. By early 1935 people complained at a public meeting in Kerugoya about the delay in handing back the land. They were also disappointed by its lack of trees. The provincial commissioner, who attended the meeting to talk about cotton production, stated that the land could not be distributed until the Forest Department finished demarcating it. He added that the commission never promised to return wooded land to them. The local reaction to his statements was not recorded. Less than a week later, though, Lindsay felt compelled to write to the provincial commissioner: 'I feel that politically the confirming of . . . land empty of timber could have a most undesirable effect on the attitude of the natives and the good faith of Government in the land matter' (Embu District Archives). He mentioned the need for timber to construct rat-proof stores. At the time Ndia was known as one of the worst plague centres in Kenya. Outbreaks of the disease occurred sporadically during the 1920s and 1930s.

The survey of Nyagithuci tract was completed in early February. The forest surveyor informed the people of the locality that the area was to remain closed until further notice. About a week later the Embu district officer visited the land to assess its agricultural potential. He estimated that one-fifth of it contained trees, and the land appeared suitable for agriculture.

Acting Provincial Commissioner M.R. Vidal submitted a proposal for resettlement of forest parcels in October 1935, suggesting that the Local Native Council organize the actual redistribution of parcels. Clans would be instructed to give preference to their landless members. Other conditions stipulated by Vidal included prohibition of land sales and tenure security for the resettled. He urged the commissioner for local government to carry out immediate transfer of the land. On 2 December 1935, the colonial secretariat in Nairobi approved the plan. Two months later Lindsay reported that the Nyagithuci tract had been 'surveyed and handed over for occupation'.

Nyagithuci resettlement seemed to be resolved. A change in key administrative personnel — a source of policy discontinuity throughout colonial times — undermined its apparent conclusion. Correspondence in the Embu District Archives revealed that a significant shift occurred in 1936, when S.H. La Fontaine took over as provincial commissioner. He proposed giving the Kiambu Gikuyu priority in obtaining added lands such as Nyagithuci. They had experienced most of the colonial land alienation, yet only half the areas to be returned were adjacent to Kiambu. He warned that 'there would be no end to trouble and agitation' if Kiambu needs were not addressed.

The new provincial commissioner returned to these themes a few days later in a dramatic letter to the colonial secretary. La Fontaine explained that his proposal came in response to the intense anger felt by the Kiambu Gikuyu about the commission. Unrest was not limited to a few agitators but widespread. Senior

Kiambu Chief Koinange reported intervening to prevent 'serious trouble recalling the earlier days'. The letter added: 'This was undoubtedly an exaggeration but it is significant of what the best Kikuyu in Kiambu are thinking.' According to La Fontaine, part of the problem was that so much of the land returned to the Gikuyu was in Embu and Nyeri. Instead of benefitting the entire tribe as the commission intended, this land was likely to become the property of local residents. Kiambu leaders already had been informed by Gikuyus elsewhere that immigrants would be welcomed only if they entered as land borrowers or were 'reborn' into a local lineage. La Fontaine attributed such conditions, which the Kiambu elders and chiefs regarded as demeaning, to the breakdown in clan solidarity. His interpretation underestimated the extent to which descent group loyalties were always localized. What had changed, however, was the growing competition for land, which meant that strangers were no longer as welcome as in the past (see Moris 1973; also see Chapter 10). La Fontaine asked that forest areas such as Nyagithuci be used exclusively for Kiambu resettlement. Once again, he warned that the situation 'might easily burst into flame and have irrevocable results' without positive action.

Lindsay informed La Fontaine that Nyagithuci had been returned to the Ndia locations adjacent to it. He added that it was the most thickly populated part of the district. Elders had been told that only landless people could be resettled there. Perhaps as a ploy to make the area seem unattractive, Lindsay described the land as bracken-covered and 'untimbered'. He suggested that Nyagithuci did not hold much potential for the Kiambu Gikuyu. Instead, Lindsay suggested that they migrate as individuals to southern Kirinyaga or Embu. In fact, many of them had been moving into the region on their own (Moris 1973).

La Fontaine rebuked Lindsay for allowing the Ndia to reoccupy Nyagithuci, stating that the land was likely to be reserved for Kiambu Gikuyu resettlement. La Fontaine's comments provoked a quick response from Lindsay, who summarized the orders issued by Vidal and approved by the colonial secretary allowing resettlement. The Embu district commissioner sounded his own warnings about local discontent if Nyagithuci was set aside for outsiders. To resolve the issue, La Fontaine placed the topic on the agenda of the provincial meeting of local native councils and district administrators in late August.

In the meantime an agricultural survey shed new light on the suitability of Nyagithuci for resettlement. It consisted mainly of dense bush, though some places were thickly forested. The soils appeared very fertile. Weed growth, rather than soil exhaustion, was the main reason why farmers in its vicinity fallowed their fields. The land was suitable for a range of food and cash crops, including *Acacia mearnsii* (wattle). The survey also noted that goats could graze without affecting plant succession. The agricultural official concluded that Nyagithuci could easily support Kiambu Gikuyu resettlement.

The Nyagithuci issue seemed to be resolved at the provincial meeting of the Local Native Councils and district administrators in late August 1936. Although the Embu councillors were 'not happy', they agreed to offer no resistance to Kiambu Gikuyu resettlement on three-quarters of Nyagithuci. The wooded parts of the tract were to remain under local control. British officials felt that the agreement was appropriate, given the dire need for land in Kiambu. Both white farmers and Maasai herders were evicting Gikuyu squatters, swelling the ranks of the landless. However, subsequent events revealed that the Ndia accepted the plan because they thought the Kiambu Gikuyu would become temporary land occupants (*ahoi*), with the original rightholders still retaining ownership of the area.

Resettlement at Nyagithuci: whose blame?

For two years Nyagithuci attracted very little official attention. Controversy arose once again, however, following a November 1938 visit to the site by Governor Sir Robert Brooke-Popham. Once again, key personnel changes in the administration contributed to new conflicts. Brooke-Popham, who assumed office in 1937, encountered local cultivators and saw evidence of deforestation. He was not aware during the visit that an order had been given setting aside the land for Kiambu resettlement. When he returned to Nairobi, the governor conferred with La Fontaine, now the acting chief native commissioner, about the situation. Brooke-Popham learned that 'definite orders' had been given closing Nyagithuci to local families. The governor now wanted the Kirinyaga Gikuyu removed from the site.

Brooke-Popham's comments generated a wave of charges and counter-charges among officials concerning the responsibility for allowing 'encroachment' at Nyagithuci. Much of the blame was initially directed towards the incumbent administrative officers: C. Tomkinson, the provincial commissioner, and Ivor R. Gillespie, the district commissioner. Both were assumed to have neglected directives set forth by their predecessors. Gillespie did not help his case by admitting that he possessed a bad memory and had lost his notes on the subject. Yet, despite claims by La Fontaine and Lindsay, who was transferred in March 1937 to Uasin Gishu district, no order restricting local access to Nyagithuci was found in district, provincial, or central government records.

While this investigation was going on, Tomkinson was asked by C.E. Mortimer, the commissioner of lands and settlement, to prepare for the removal of the Kirinyaga Gikuyu from Nyagithuci. Eviction was to take place once their crops were harvested. Both Tomkinson and Gillespie opposed the proposed evictions, predicting 'the gravest discontent' if the Ndia were driven off. An order was issued prohibiting the clearing of new ground. Nairobi officials ordered Gillespie to survey Nyagithuci's occupants, finding out when they arrived and if they possessed land elsewhere.

Meanwhile, Tomkinson met with local chiefs to obtain their version of the events. The chiefs denied that any orders had been issued prohibiting resettlement. Chief Mugera of Inoi stated that land disputes were absent in Nyagithuci because 'everyone admitted the right of the old rightful owners. *Mbaris* [lineages] did it on their own'. Chief Justin of Mutira bluntly pointed out that local people 'did not want strangers. Landless Kiambu came to find an area. We said ours is small and our people are sueing one another below [the] old [forest] line as land hunger' (Embu District Archives). The Ndia chiefs stated that the Kiambu people were welcome, but only as temporary land occupants.

Gillespie and J.P. Benson, the assistant agricultural officer, interviewed many of Nyagithuci's occupants in early January 1939. Their reports provided significant insights into the process of resettlement. They found that 344 people cultivated slightly more than 320 ha. Almost half (163, 47 per cent) of them belonged to the Unjiru clan, but 10 other clans were represented as well. More than 80 per cent (277) of the people claimed land through ancestral rights. Gillespie wrote:

> The information was given to me in a quiet and confident manner, without undue emphasis or verbiage. The questions put were: 'Why have you come to live here?' or 'What claims do you say you have here?' or 'Are you a Muhoi [temporary occupant] here?' The replies were usually, 'This was my father's land' or 'This was my grandfather's land.' 'I was born here. I can show you

where the huts were' or 'When I was driven out of this area by Government, I went back to beg land lower down; now I have come back to my own land.'I inspected a number of the alleged sites of old huts. I am no archaeologist. I cannot swear that they were the sites of old huts, though there was usually something to suggest that the statement was true. . . . It is about 28 years since the people were driven out; they build a particularly poor type of hut even to this day, so that it is hardly to be expected that after years under bush, and three or more seasons of cultivation, there would be much sign of the buildings. The whole appearance of the land in the vicinity, however, suggests cultivation in the past. . . . A number of persons claimed that their Ithaka [descent group holding] ran in strips from below the old line into the new area. . . . The claim was not an extravagant one; indeed no excessive claims were made to us (Embu District Archives).

Another 16 per cent (55) borrowed their plots from the original rightholders. Only 3 per cent (12) of the occupants had 'indefinite' or 'no claims' to their plots. Gillespie noted, 'These areas are probably owned but the cultivators have not asked leave to use the land.'

The colonial officers reported difficulty in determining when people returned to Nyagithuci. They eventually estimated the year of entry by asking occupants how many harvests had been obtained. Over one-third (123, or 36 per cent) had returned just before the second wet season of 1936. Slightly more than one-quarter (91, or 26 per cent) of them entered in 1937, and the bulk (130, or 38 per cent) returned in 1938. Some of them delayed moving back until land they had purchased elsewhere had been 'redeemed' — the purchase price of goats or money returned by the original rightholder. Only 29 per cent (100) of the people reported having farmland outside Nyagithuci, yet fewer than that number of adults (91, or 26 per cent) actually resided on the tract. Gillespie observed that men mainly occupied temporary huts for guarding crops, while women usually lived in homesteads located outside Nyagithuci.

The agricultural survey confirmed that Nyagithuci was fertile and capable of producing high yields. The main crops were *njahi* (lablab bean), sweet potato, calocasia, maize, beans, tobacco, wattle, millet, and yam. There was no evidence of soil erosion, even on steep slopes. Nor had soil quality deteriorated. In fact, yields appeared better in the fields that had been cultivated the longest. Only 18 ha had been deforested, which Gillespie called modest given local timber and firewood shortages.

After reviewing the Kenya Land Commission evidence and his own findings, Gillespie recommended leaving the parcel under Ndia and Gichugu control: 'They are now happy and confident in having recovered part of what they claimed. If this is taken from them, the damage to Government's prestige will be quite irreparable. Money can buy land but it cannot buy confidence, and it is the confidence of the native that we need' (Embu District Archives) Based on Gillespie's account and the discussion with the chiefs, Tomkinson advised the central government to allow the local people to retain Nyagithuci. The colonial secretariat eventually approved the recommendation, specifying that 120 ha of uncultivated land be set aside to accommodate any Kiambu Gikuyu who might be resettled in the future.

Kiambu resettlement: Nyagithuci and elsewhere

The central government announced another plan to resolve Kiambu Gikuyu land grievances in August 1939. It excised an additional 1600 ha of forest reserve near Kiambu for resettlement. In exchange, 1200 ha of forest reserve originally set aside as compensation by the commission were returned to the colonial administration. Officials in Embu were informed that the unoccupied portion of Nyagithuci might be returned to the Forest Department as part of the agreement. There was also a possibility that Nyagithuci might be allocated to the Local Native Council for resettling people displaced by the proposed construction of an African agricultural school in Embu township. In the end, the government decided to keep Nyagithuci open to Kiambu Gikuyu resettlement. Only four large Kiambu families took up the offer, receiving a total of 40 ha in 1940. The Embu council eventually assumed trusteeship of the remaining portion of the tract.

The lack of Kiambu Gikuyu support for resettlement at Nyagithuci was a missing ingredient in the central government's land compensation plans. It needs to be emphasized that the people of Kiambu were greatly disappointed by the commission's refusal to return their lands. Marshall Clough (1990: 163) points out that the commission's report disillusioned 'those who had believed in the value of constitutional, reformist action'. The offer of Nyagithuci for resettlement, even if well intended, ignored the specific land grievances of both the Kiambu and Ndia peoples. It was based on the false premise that the Gikuyu had tribal tenure that allowed members of the group access to any uncultivated land (see Leakey 1937: 263).

Other factors influenced the unwillingness of the Kiambu Gikuyu to resettle in Nyagithuci: the distance from relatives, potential crop damage from forest wildlife such as elephants, and 'the cold reception' they might receive from local people. Perhaps more important was the availability of land in the lower, warmer zone of Kirinyaga and Embu called Weru, located between the densely populated ridges and dry plains (see Moris 1973; also see Chapter 10). The region increasingly attracted immigrants from Kiambu and Nyeri, willing to relocate far from relatives, risk attack from game, and even accept ritual 'rebirth' into a local descent group or status as a temporary occupant. The crucial differences were that in the Weru two crops of maize per year could be grown, and the area's flatness and sparse population were ideal for a new farm innovation — the plough, which allows cultivation of larger areas. In contrast, only one crop of maize could be grown annually in the cool, damp, ridges of Nyagithuci. Because of colonial restrictions on African production of tea and coffee, maize was a major cash crop for the Gikuyu. Thus, the Kiambu outsiders and the local Gikuyus arranged· necessary transactions without much colonial interference. Instead of accepting Nyagithuci and having to battle the local Gikuyus, Kiambu immigrants carried out their own resettlement movement into the Weru while denouncing the land commission's settlement as unjust and insufficient.

Conclusion

The administration tried to channel the expression of African grievances within a constitutional framework: the local native council and the Kenya Land Commission. This political strategy proved effective to some extent, particularly regarding the local native council. In Kirinyaga the council served as a vehicle in the 1920s and 1930s for questioning or denouncing state forestry and the appropriation of Mount Kenya. As will be seen in subsequent chapters, the council continued to fulfil this role throughout the colonial era. Later chapters will also show how the council became a mechanism through which people resisted Forest

Department proposals to take over local woodland. Thus, the council not only benefited the colonial state by serving as a 'safety valve' for local frustration, it contributed to limited African empowerment by furnishing an institutional means for maintaining control over local resources.

The Kenya Land Commission proved more problematic. It was never intended by the British administration to address in full the land grievances of the Gikuyu and other indigenous peoples. Although the commission collected information in a comprehensive manner, its proposed settlement was very limited in scope and magnitude. Moreover, the commission's assumptions about tribal tenure were flawed and led to many problems when officials tried to implement them. The saga of the Nyagithuci resettlement stands as a monument to cultural misunderstanding and myopic colonial politics. The resettlement controversy also demonstrated the considerable disagreement that often existed at the district, provincial, central government, and imperial levels about what constituted colonial interests. The ultimate failure of the Kenya Land Commission became evident in the early 1950s, with the Mau Mau War, much of which was fought in the forest.

6. Colonial forest management: 1911 to 1952

BRITISH CONTROL OVER Mount Kenya led to major changes in forest management and exploitation. Imperial policy-makers imposed the doctrines and organizational forms of scientific forestry developed in other colonial situations (see
Troup 1940; Guha 1990; Martin 1991; Peluso 1992). This chapter describes the
policies and practices established by the Forest Department, as well as their
specific effects on local access and use of the reserve, from 1911 to 1952 — on the
eve of the Mau Mau emergency. As will be seen, southern Mount Kenya never
supported the large-scale timber industry envisaged by early proponents of forestry development. However, a small but significant local timber sector was
fostered in the guise of African pit-sawyers. They emerged as a major economic
and political force in the forest by the early 1950s. The pit-sawyers and their
grievances over forest use would emerge as a focal point for the anti-colonial
Mau Mau movement.

Colonial forest administration

The Forest Department justified its appropriation of Mount Kenya on the assumption that scientific forestry provided a superior basis for natural resource
management. The Gikuyu and other indigenous peoples were portrayed as destroyers of forests. European land speculators and timber entrepreneurs were
also seen as a threat to forests. In contrast, David E. Hutchins, wrote in a 1908
department report: 'The modern science of forestry has for its objective to
improve, not to destroy the forest'. Just as cultivated fruits were superior to wild
fruits, Hutchins argued, a 'cultivated forest' would prove more valuable than
'wild' ones. He cited the example of German state forests, whose value per acre
had reportedly tripled since the 1830s.

Protectorate officials passed regulations governing forest use as early as 1897,
but a forestry bureaucracy was not formed until 1902. Kenya adopted a similar
model to the centralized and custodial-oriented forest administrations established
in India, South Africa, and other parts of the British Empire (see Troup 1940;
Guha 1990). The 1911 ordinance that provided the legal framework for the department was based on the Indian Forest Act and the Cape Forest Ordinance (*The
East African Standard* 1925: 163). The head of the department was known as the
conservator of forests, and the first one appointed, C.F. Elliot, had served in the
Indian Forest Service. Hutchins, whose tenure from 1907 to 1911 proved so influential, had been in both the Indian and South African forest services.

The department took as its main task the expansion and management of
'Crown Forests' — the government forest estate. Forests were nominally set
aside for environmental protection and to ensure resource exploitation on a
sustained yield basis (Logie and Dyson 1962). By 1915, state forests covered over
3500 km^2, much of it situated in the Mount Kenya region (Ofcansky 1984: 140).
State forest lands were divided into several conservancy units managed by a
hierarchy of officers: divisional foresters, assistant conservators, foresters, and
forest rangers. Most colonial forestry officers were Europeans, though by the
early 1930s a few Asians and Africans had been appointed to junior positions. In
contrast, the guards, resident workers, and day labourers were entirely African.

Kirinyaga's share of the Mount Kenya reserve was called South Kenya and
usually included in Nyeri forest division. Its administrative outpost consisted of

Castle station, built in the heart of what a 1908 official report called 'the best' camphor forest. Castle remained the only station in Kirinyaga's part of the reserve until the late 1950s, when Kamweti opened. There were, however, several nearby forest stations: Chehe along the Ndia—Nyeri border, Ragati in Nyeri, and Irangi in Embu. Castle often served as a substation for these other posts. A shortage of professional staff and financial difficulties proved to be chronic conditions for the department (Ofcansky 1984), and rendered it difficult to keep Castle in operation. The lack of a full-time forester in South Kenya to some extent reduced the overall supervision of the reserve.

Forest regulations

The 1902 and 1911 ordinances severely restricted local use of state forest lands. They prohibited building dwellings, cutting trees, setting fires, farming, or herding in forest reserves without official authorization. A system of fees and penalties was instituted for the use or removal of forest resources. People were required to purchase a licence to harvest timber, gather deadwood, hang beehives, collect thatching grass, graze cattle, or dig ochre in the Crown Forest. In the early 1930s, for example, a permit to gather firewood usually cost two Shillings a month for a headload a day. John Pease, the South Nyeri district commissioner, called this fee 'reasonable' at the Kenya Land Commission. However, several African witnesses disagreed. At the time monthly wages for farm workers in the White Highlands averaged only seven to eight Shillings (Clayton and Savage 1974: 173). Thus, a monthly fuel ticket represented a significant expense for families. The collection of revenue from forest users was important for the department, which operated on a semi-commercial basis. It always faced a challenge of balancing conservation and budgetary needs.

The range of local forest use permitted under colonial regulations was considerably narrower than in the pre-colonial era. The department restricted access to salt-licks and mineral springs. It prohibited goats from grazing in the reserve. Medicinal and magical uses of forest products were curtailed. Foresters, for example, rejected requests by the Embu Local Native Council in 1940 to gather *Rapanea rhododendroides* (*ngaita*) seeds and *Ocotea kenyensis* (*muthura*) bark for use in the treatment of respiratory problems and other ailments. Officials promised to arrange for their collection and sale at Ragati station if either item ever proved medicinally valuable. The significance of such plants, however, was not taken seriously.

Violators of forest regulations faced jail or fines. Serious offences were handled in the courts. Under the 1911 ordinance, however, the Forest Department could adjudicate suspected minor offences. It set up a system of 'compounding', which allowed a forester or the district commissioner to assess fines, usually up to three times the value of the alleged violation. Forest guards could not compound offences. Such fines were usually less severe than the maximum allowed, and people often preferred to settle charges quickly rather than risk court and stiffer penalties. More than two-fifths of the accused forest violators in Nyeri forest division had their offences compounded in 1938. By 1950, over 90 per cent of suspected forest offences in the colony were handled by compounding.

With few exceptions, the southern Mount Kenya reserve was generally free of major crime or violence prior to the onset of Mau Mau. As mentioned in Chapter 5, some forest guards were threatened during the Kenya Land Commission in the early 1930s. There were also occasional crime waves, such as in the early 1940s, when several camphor trees were damaged by honey hunters (see below). Available records, however, suggest that forest ordinance violations were probably never widespread nor serious in Kirinyaga. Table 6.1 shows the range in offences and fines compounded between August 1937 and March 1940 in Embu and Kirinyaga by district officials. Penalties were meted out according to each particular case, but illicit grazing and honey hunting tended to receive heavier fines. Theft of firewood was the most common offence. The cost of disobeying regulations could be higher than following them. A monthly fuel ticket cost two Shillings, while the compounded fine for removing a single headload of firewood averaged three Shillings.

Table 6.1: Compounded forest offences, Embu and Kirinyaga, August 1937 to March 1940

Date	Offence	Penalty (KSh)
Aug. 1937	Fuel cutting	5
	Stock grazing	10
Jan. 1938	Honey hunting	10
	Cutting poles	4
	Fuel cutting	4 to 6
Mar. 1938	Fuel cutting	2
July 1938	Fuel cutting	1 to 3/50
Sept. 1938	Goat grazing	3 to 6
	Fuel cutting	1
Oct. 1938	Fuel cutting	2
Nov. 1938	Fuel cutting	2 to 4
Jan. 1939	Fuel cutting	5
Apr. 1939	Fuel cutting	2 to 6
Feb. 1940	Fuel cutting	3
Mar. 1940	Goat grazing	8
	Sheep grazing	3/50

Source: Embu District Archives. Gaps between months indicate either no offences were recorded or the page was missing.

Violations of forest regulations can be interpreted as an 'everyday form of resistance' to government control (see Scott 1985). As such, they constituted in Kirinyaga a persistent, yet very diffuse and small-scale form of political activity. Of course some undetected or unreported removal of forest products took place, though officials appeared satisfied with the level of vigilance maintained by the guards. The department provided some opportunities for cash-strapped households to obtain access to forest products. People worked as day labourers, performing such tasks as clearing boundaries or trails, in exchange for rights to collect firewood or hang beehives. To encourage the removal of deadwood from plantation sites such as Thiba, the department sometimes lowered the price of fuel tickets to one Shilling.

Beekeepers and honey hunters

Honey collectors were the most difficult forest users to supervise. The sweet, viscid fluid produced by bees was primarily used for ritual and brewing purposes. Lineage elders poured honey on sacrificial rams, for example, when marking farm boundaries (Maxwell *et al.* 1929b: 2). Honey beer was traditionally consumed as part of kin group, initiation, marriage, and religious rites. It was also a drink for recreational purposes by married men and older women. Louis Leakey (1977a: 254) observed that 'every Kikuyu was keen to obtain wild honey'. Not everyone, however, was willing to climb trees or risk bee stings. Certain men became known for their skill and bravery in harvesting wild hives. The *Ocotea* forest was prime honey-hunting country, since bees often built hives in the hollow branches of camphor trees (Wimbush 1930: 196). Honey collection tended to be seasonal, mainly occurring in the *thano*, or dry season, from late December to early March (Mwaniki 1970: 37). Men often went in small groups, staying in temporary camps or caves.

Besides seeking out wild hives, some individuals specialized in beekeeping. These men had a detailed knowledge of different bee species and their care (see Mwaniki 1970, 1973; Leakey 1977a: 251–4; Riley and Brokensha 1988a: 162–71). They also knew how to use particular plants and leaves to attract bees to hives and to smoke them out. Fire management was important, since the honey collectors were well aware of the dangers of accidental blazes. The trunks of camphor (*muthaiti*) and *Cordia abyssinica* (*muringa*) were favoured for making the barrel-shaped hives. Beekeepers often possessed dozens of hives scattered throughout forests and fields to take advantage of a variety of flowering trees, plants, and crops (Leakey 1977a: 251). Each bee-box carried an owner's mark, and charms and curses were used to protect them from theft. The Mount Kenya forest contained the main beekeeping grounds of the Kirinyaga Gikuyu before the demarcation of the government reserve (Maxwell *et al.* 1929b: 1; Mwaniki 1970, 1974: 291).

Correspondence in the Embu District Archives showed that department often blamed careless honey harvesters for starting forest fires while smoking out bees. It attributed 40 per cent of all Kenyan forest fires in 1935 to them. Foresters were especially concerned because the fires often damaged commercially valuable camphor trees. The courts were criticized by forestry officials for making the problem worse by giving too-lenient sentences for setting fires in the reserve. Some honey collectors also cut trees and branches trying to reach wild hives in high or inaccessible places. An unusually high number of damaged camphor trees was recorded in 1944 near Castle forest station. In one month alone honey hunters in three separate cases were arrested for cutting, burning, or otherwise damaging 20, 16, and nine camphor trees, respectively. A large camphor, even a hollow one, could contain more than five tons of timber. Given camphor's commercial value, each destroyed tree represented a considerable financial loss to the department. Whether the aforementioned 1944 cases were examples of 'saboteurs in the forest' (cf. Guha 1990), or simply inept honey hunters, is unclear from available evidence. Although arson was sometimes used as a form of resistance to state forestry, experienced honey collectors prided themselves on their management of fire. While one must be aware of the context of conflict, there is also a corresponding need to avoid attributing motives where specific information is lacking.

Officials tried various means to restrict honey collection. Foresters sometimes closed all or part of the reserve to them. Extra forest guards were posted in the Nyandarua range to handle the honey collectors, but similar measures were not taken in South Kenya. Eventually, foresters differentiated between beekeepers and hunters of wild hives. The tending of bee-boxes was seen as less prone to cause forest damage than obtaining honey from hollow trees. Permits were issued without charge to beekeepers to hang their hives in the forest. About 250 men, many of them elderly, had permits in the early 1950s.

Certain areas were designated for beekeeping. An account in the Kenya National Archives written by W.G. Dyson, a forester in southern Mount Kenya during the 1950s, provides many insights into the department's policy. The licensed beekeepers acted as informal forest controllers, keeping illegal honey collectors out of the reserve more effectively than the guards. Beekeepers also served as environmental monitors, providing information about the forest acquired through their travels to remote areas. In addition, they often performed tasks such as clearing paths. Dyson concluded that the beekeepers were 'useful people' to have in the forest. Thus, the department reached a long-term and mutually advantageous accommodation with local beekeepers.

Shamba labour

The department had other 'useful people' who provided services in return for access to forest resources: its resident labour force. These workers usually consisted of landless men and their families. They were sometimes the very households whose gardens had been appropriated for the forest reserve. The men signed contracts to work roughly nine months a year for the department, carrying out such tasks as land clearing, tree planting, road maintenance, and nursery upkeep. In return they received a small monthly wage, access to small plots for food crops and keeping a few sheep or cattle, and housing. Until the 1950s very few, if any, public services such as dispensaries, were provided for the workers. The terms of labour and work conditions for the department's resident work force were similar to those for 'squatters' on white estates (see van Zwanenberg 1975). In fact, the department's labourers were often called 'forest squatters'.

Furnishing land to labourers was central to the department's main mode of reafforestation: the *taungya* system of combining tree planting with the rotation of garden plots. First introduced on Burmese teak plantations in the 1860s, *taungya* has been one of the cheapest and most satisfactory means of planting trees on a large scale (Troup 1940: 174). The technique was known in Kenya as 'the forest *shamba*'. The conservator of forests noted in 1934 that it permitted the department to reafforest 'at a cost which will bear comparison with that of any country in the world'. Labourers and their households were responsible for clearing small plots (0.4 to 0.8 ha), in which they interplanted maize and other food crops with tree seedlings. Women and children usually weeded and protected the young trees. People who failed to maintain their trees could be dismissed or fined. After three years, workers were assigned another plot for reafforesting.

There was a small resident workforce in South Kenya during the first decades of colonial rule, reflecting the modest level of reafforestation activities. In 1931 there were only 26 *shamba* labourers and their families at Chehe, and 369 forest workers in all of Nyeri forest division. The expansion of plantation forestry after the Second World War resulted in a corresponding growth in the *shamba* labour force. By the end of the colonial era the number of resident workers at Chehe reached nearly 200 families. The *shamba* labour force similarly increased at Castle and Kamweti in Kirinyaga to almost 200 workers by 1960.

Forest rubber extraction

In the midst of the debate about timber concessions, the colonial government sanctioned the first European commercial enterprise on the southern slopes of Mount Kenya: latex extraction from *landolphia* vines. This climbing shrub, called *muugu* by the Gikuyu, was mainly used as a rope or cord. There were also medicinal uses for its roots. The tapping of *landolphia* latex for export had been taking place in coastal forests for decades (Fitzgerald 1970). Uganda also possessed a sizeable *landolphia*-extraction industry (*The African Standard* 9 Jan. 1904).

The presence of wild rubber vines in the Mount Kenya forest was noted by a colonial officer during the invasion of Kirinyaga in 1904 (Meinertzhagen 1957: 150). Hutchins (1907: 23) also observed *landolphia* 'in the wettest and warmest part of the forest' near the Rupingazi River. He identified the plant as *Landolphia kirkii*, but subsequent study showed it to be mainly *Landolphia ugandensis* (Battiscombe 1926: 99). Both vines yielded latex with export value at the time. Hutchins (1907: 5) concluded that *landolphia* was not in sufficient quantity to support commercial development.

A syndicate organized by McDonald, Dunman, and Company, however, obtained permission in 1910 to tap *landolphia* vines in the southern Mount Kenya forest. They recruited Gikuyu, Embu, and Mbeere labourers as tappers. The workers were attracted by the possibility of earning their tax money so close to home. The usual method for tapping vines was to slice the bark and allow the latex to drip out on banana leaves, then transfer it to a bottle, a slow and often inefficient process. The plants were easily damaged or destroyed by tapping (Ward and Milligan 1912: 116). Even with the best harvesting techniques, vines took years to yield another crop of latex. The processing of the latex often took place in the forest, since the rubber was prone to putrefaction. The syndicate regarded its initial harvest as a success: nearly 2050 kg of latex valued at £670. The Forest Department received a royalty of £120.

The budding southern Mount Kenya *landolphia* latex industry soon suffered a major setback: world market prices for rubber collapsed in 1912 (*The East African Standard* 1925: 147). The syndicate also encountered supply problems. The second-year rubber harvest dropped to 1040 kg. The syndicate considered abandoning the trade unless it could devise a more profitable method of tapping. Mechanical tappers were available, though it was unclear whether such machines offered any economic advantage over the African labour force. Although perhaps more effective in squeezing out latex, vines still required several years before yielding another harvest. The 1912–13 season yielded only 542 kg. The syndicate ceased operating, citing high production costs and low profits.

Landolphia tapping was only a distant memory until the Second World War, when widespread rubber shortages occurred. British officials revived wild rubber collection in 1943. Africans throughout southern Mount Kenya were encouraged to engage in tapping, and a buying centre was established near Chuka on the eastern slopes. Only a few people responded because of the low prices offered for latex, the distance of the tapping zone from settlements, and difficult conditions in the forest. Colonial administrators considered using local conscripts to collect rubber, but the Embu Local Native Council insisted that workers receive adequate compensation. Instead, officials organized a week in February 1944 when people were exhorted to engage in tapping as a 'voluntary war effort'. Despite a large turn-out, only a small quantity of rubber was collected. The district commissioner blamed low production on a lack of effort by the tappers.

He acknowledged, however, that volunteers were unfamiliar with *landolphia* tapping. The assistant agriculture officer initiated another rubber collection campaign that eventually yielded 520 kg of latex. In general tapping proved too unprofitable and unpopular, and it soon halted altogether. Once again, the wild rubber vine industry vanished into obscurity.

Sawmills and fuelwood contractors, 1915 to 1945

By 1915 the department no longer sought a single, long-term industrial concessionaire for the *Ocotea* forest on the southern slopes. Instead, it focused attention on opening the Juniperus-Olea forests in western Mount Kenya to small-scale, short-term timber licences. Sawmills obtained licences on a five-year basis, with renewals possible. The licences specified the harvest site, licence fee, and royalty rates (Cranworth 1919: 209). Two mills were in operation shortly after the allotment of farms to white settlers, and a few others took up the trade by 1915. The mills often consisted of a white owner-operator, a handful of Asian carpenters or sawyers, and African workers who served as sawyers and day labourers. Selective clearing was practised. Instead of reaching world markets, the wood cut by the West Kenya sawmills was sold to white farmers and businesses in the immediate vicinity. The 'bush mills' easily captured their local markets because high freight costs made timber produced elsewhere too expensive (Cranworth 1919: 217, 1939: 45–6). They generally declined during the First World War as some of the owners and many of their customers entered the military.

The Kenyan timber industry experienced little growth in the decades between the world wars (Logie and Dyson 1962: 12). A severe depression engulfed the industry in the early 1920s. A slight recovery occurred in the middle of the decade, only to be undermined by the widespread economic crisis of the late 1920s. Even in the best of times, the colony's commercial timber market had a low saturation point. Quite simply, the capacity of Kenya's sawmills greatly exceeded the commercial demand for sawn wood (Nicholson 1931: 66).

Early proponents of opening Mount Kenya to industrial forestry had emphasized the possibility of selling timber overseas. Wood exports began in 1920, but Kenyan sawmills found it difficult to compete in world timber markets. High production and transport costs, plus poor communications, hindered their efforts. By the late 1930s their penetration of international markets remained minimal (Logie and Dyson 1962: 12). Thus, the Colonial Office's suspicions about the speculative nature of the proposed Mount Kenya concessions in many ways proved accurate.

Although sawmilling increased in the Mount Kenya reserve during the 1920s and 1930s, it failed to attain the lofty success predicted by early proponents of timber development. At least one sawmill harvested timber on the southern and south-western slopes by the 1920s: West Kenya Saw Mills, run by two British partners named Harwood and Holmes. They operated a water-powered mill in Karatina market, a short distance from Ndia. Their mill cut camphor, podocarpus, and other trees from a licensed area covering 2400 ha. The Nyeri foresters established a working plan for their operation. However, their firm failed to survive the depressed economic conditions of the early 1930s. Its timber lease was taken over for several years by the South Kenya Saw Mill. The Yacoob Deen Company eventually opened a sawmill in Karatina, obtaining licences for Castle, Thiba, Chehe, and other areas within or near Kirinyaga. Its sawmill in Karatina continued operating after independence (see Ojiambo 1978: 56–8).

Several Asian businessmen sought permission to establish a sawmill in Kirinyaga and Embu in the 1930s, but British officials refused their requests. A typical case involved Lachmandass Deviditta, a major produce merchant who sought permission in 1938 for a sawmill in Embu. His letter of request pointed out that the nearest 'proper' sawmill to Embu township was roughly 90 km away in Nyeri. Deviditta argued that 'progress' would inevitably increase African demand for sawn wood for houses, shops, and other purposes. Officials were not persuaded, and his application was turned down. Asian businessmen eventually opened small sawmills in Embu, Kutus, and Kerugoya in the 1950s.

Mount Kenya's western and northern slopes became the focal point for the region's limited timber development. By the early 1930s the following firms held large timber licences in Nyeri forest division: Thaie Company, 13 870 ha; Keith Timber Company, 7280 ha; West Kenya (later South Kenya) Saw Mill, 2400 ha; and Nanyuki Saw Mill, 700 ha. The Thaie Company's licence mainly covered African-held lands in Meru, rather than government forest reserve. Timber harvesting in Nyeri forest division peaked at 4760 m³ in 1929, then sharply declined because of the worldwide economic depression. The Mount Kenya sawmills experienced an upturn in business by 1938, when they cut over 5000 m³ of timber.

Fuel contractors also bought large amounts of wood. They removed deadwood and cut trees rejected by sawmills, usually in places slated for reafforestation by the Forest Department. The extension of the railroad to Nanyuki on the north-western side of the mountain in the late 1920s generated a substantial demand for fuelwood. For example, contractors for the railroad purchased 12 600 m³ of stacked wood in Nyeri forest division in 1937. That same year they obtained an additional 3300 m³ of stacked wood for sale to other customers. The latter included local businesses, schools, and government agencies. It appears that most of the fuel contractors in south-western and southern Mount Kenya were Asians.

The expansion of sawmills and fuelwood contracting in the Mount Kenya region was accompanied by reafforestation activities. As early as 1916, the Forest Department established small cypress and cedar plantations on the western slopes and utilized natural regeneration near Nyeri. The planting of both indigenous and exotic species, plus the use of a variety of reforestation techniques, reflected ongoing debates within the department (Logie and Dyson 1962: 17). Hutchins (1907: 4) felt that the indigenous forest was largely incapable of regenerating itself. He strongly advocated growing exotic species on plantations. His 1909 report on Kenyan forests included a long list of Mexican, Central American, Australian, and Indian timber species for possible introduction (Hutchins 1909: 85–102). Edward Battiscombe, who succeeded Hutchins as conservator of forests, favoured natural regeneration and planting of indigenous trees. Battiscombe acknowledged in 1916 that it was generally a slow process, but it ensured 'the reproduction of species which [were] climatically suited to the locality' (Embu District Archives). The department often used natural regeneration during Battiscombe's administration from 1911 to 1925, particularly in the *Ocotea* forest. Camphor was easily reproduced through suckers as well as seeds, and its young trees grew up to 1.8 m per year. Subsequent conservators emphasized growing exotic species in large-scale plantations (Logie and Dyson 1962). They argued that native species were too slow growing or required too much care. For example, elephants often raided camphor seedlings and saplings. A department report noted that camphor could be raised artificially, 'provided that elephants can be kept away indefinitely'. The problem was that only small areas of regenerating camphor could be effectively protected at any given time. Nevertheless, both exotic plantations and natural regeneration continued to be used. In 1937, the department established over 80 ha of exotic plantations in South Kenya, compared to only 12 ha set aside for the camphor regeneration. Two years later it added another 70 ha of exotic plantations, but department workers also prepared over 70 ha for the natural regeneration of camphor in South Kenya.

The onset of the Second World War led to a substantial increase in the demand for timber, fuelwood, and other forest products. Timber harvesting by sawmills in Nyeri forest division increased to nearly 5550 m³ in 1939. Mills throughout Central Province worked at full capacity by 1942. The department issued many temporary licences to new sawmills in order to meet the urgent demand for wood. A department report after the war admitted that cutting greatly exceeded sustained yield levels.

The most significant role allocated to the southern Mount Kenya forest was supplying fuelwood for the government's large vegetable dehydration factories at Kerugoya and Karatina. The Dried Vegetable Project was established in 1940 to supply food for British soldiers in the Middle East (see Moris 1973). These factories processed vegetables grown by hundreds of local Gikuyu through production contracts and direct employment. Akub Khan and Krishanar Stores of Nyeri were awarded the fuel contract for the Kerugoya factory in late 1941. The primary site selected for providing firewood was Ritui forest, situated between the Mukengeria and Rundu rivers in northern Kirinyaga. An informant who worked for the Kerugoya scheme recalled:

> Wood for the Dried Vegetable Project was from Mount Kenya . . . [It was cut from] the Ritui forest, the source of the river Ritui. There used to be a thick forest. Also, wood was taken from the Kangaita forest nearby. Both places used to have many trees.

Foresters selected the areas to be cut, exempting timber trees. These were sold separately to timber licence holders. The fuel contractors hired Gikuyu workers to harvest the trees and used ox carts to transport the wood to Kerugoya.

A large volume of fuelwood was used by the project. In September 1943, for example, 96 per cent of the 2115 m³ of the stacked fuelwood burned by the Kerugoya factory came from Ritui forest. During 1944 the factory consumed about 2800 m³ of stacked fuelwood per month, nearly all of it from Mount Kenya. Before the Kerugoya factory closed in 1946, monthly wood-fuel consumption reached 3700 stacked m³. There was no comparable industrial consumer of fuelwood in the district until the early 1980s, when tea factories switched from furnace oil to wood in processing.

After the war, forestry officials acknowledged that wood extraction from government reserves had occurred in a chaotic manner. An official history of the Forest Department recorded: 'The heavy felling . . . left huge areas of forest cut over and partially cut over with no exact records of the areas or the degree of exploitation' (Logie and Dyson 1962: 16). The Embu district commissioner complained in 1945 that extensive areas of South Kenya had been cleared without any plans to reafforest it. Forestry staff shortages immediately following the war delayed reafforestation. As late as 1949, British administrators in Embu bemoaned the lack of a firm schedule for rehabilitating denuded areas.

The pit-sawyers: 1930s to 1948

The wartime demand for timber led the Forest Department to open the southern Mount Kenya reserve to small groups of Gikuyu pit-sawyers. Pit-sawing is a labour-intensive means of cutting timber, requiring much strength, endurance, and skill (see Ojiambo 1978). Sawyers begin by digging a deep pit and putting poles over it. The log is then placed on the supports. Using a long saw, one man cuts while standing on top of the log, while the other works from inside the pit. They produce baulks, planks, and boards that can be used as is or transported to a mill for further processing.

Hutchins (1909: 77) recommended the introduction of European sawyers from South Africa as cheap labour for sawmills. The first pit-sawyers, however, probably arrived from India. Kenyan sawmills employed about 80 Asian pit-sawyers by 1910. The pit-sawyers were especially used by sawmills to handle trees with thick girths such as camphor or podo, thus facilitating their transport from the harvest site. Gikuyus soon learned the trade, becoming known for their high standards of workmanship (Logie and Dyson 1962: 13). Many of them functioned as independent pit-sawing contractors. An experienced or 'master' sawyer often supervised a number of employees, including apprentices. The size of their operation could be measured by the number of saws they owned and used. A small outfit might have only one saw, while a large concern could possess three or more saws and many workers. Several pit-sawing companies were in Kirinyaga by the mid-1930s. These early sawyers were usually Gikuyu immigrants from Kiambu, Murang'a or Nyeri. Many colonial officials considered the Gikuyu adoption of pit-sawing to be a positive development. It provided employment, increased the quantity and quality of timber, and contributed to the spread of Western-style wooden housing and shops. But some officials also viewed the sawyers as a potential threat to communal woodland and state forest lands. Thus, the colonial administration attempted to exert close control over them.

Independent pit-sawyers initially operated in the African reserves, obtaining trees from rightholders and selling the timber locally. By the late 1930s the Forest Department granted timber-cutting licences to a small number of Gikuyu sawyers in government forest reserves in Kiambu and along the Nyandarua range. The department set forth conditions to minimize competition between sawmills and pit-sawyers for wood supplies and timber markets. The pit-sawyers were largely restricted to already-fallen trees, usually ones situated in places regarded as inaccessible for sawmills. The department sometimes permitted them to harvest trees rejected by sawmills. It specified that pit-sawyers could only sell their timber in the native reserves adjacent to the forest. Thus, sawyers were prohibited from shipping their wood to urban areas or other outside markets. The administration justified the order as a means to increase the timber supply for 'improved' (Western-style) housing for Africans. J.C. Rammell, the acting conservator of forests, acknowledged in 1939 that the policies were to prevent pit-sawyers from undermining the market share or profits of the sawmills. Kiambu Gikuyu sawyers attacked the policies as racist. The issue of pit-sawyer access to wood supplies and timber markets remained a source of conflict throughout the colonial era and resurfaced after independence.

Despite the restrictions, pit-sawing in forest reserves rapidly grew in popularity. Provincial records showed that in 1939 the department sold 640 m^3 of timber to Gikuyu pit-sawyers, 13 per cent of the total for entire forest division. Officials reported that the demand for pit-sawing licences was so strong it would have been possible to sell five times that amount. The foresters increasingly viewed sawyers as a significant source of revenue. They also appreciated the sawyers' work in salvaging timber rejected by the sawmills. In addition, the sawyers were used in places slated for selective clearing.

Southern Mount Kenya was opened on a very limited scale to pit-sawing in 1941. The Forest Department offered licences to cut four fallen camphor trees. Each camphor was capable of yielding several tons of timber. The licence terms were similar to those used elsewhere for pit-sawing, including a ban on shipping the wood outside the district. In spite of high fees and timber royalties, the trees were quickly sold. British officials were disappointed by the poor quality and low output of the sawyers. Nevertheless, the timber was readily purchased by the Embu Local Native Council and others. Pit-sawing licences were soon issued for Chehe, Ritui, and Kapingazi near Irangi.

The availability of the wartime pit-sawing concessions was announced at Embu council meetings. Officials were surprised in the early 1940s by the lack of local applications for pit-sawing concessions. When timber licences were offered at Chehe in 1943, for example, no one from Ndia applied. The district commissioner reported that pit-sawing was largely done by 'a number of strangers, persons living in the district as tenants at-will free of any kind of payment'. Local interest in pit-sawing licences increased by the end of the war. At the request of the Embu council in late 1945, the Forest Department agreed to restrict future timber licences to local people only. It was decided by all parties that immigrant sawyers could stay at existing concessions as long as their work continued to be satisfactory.

A register of licensed master sawyers from April 1946 in the Kenya National Archives provides insights into the scope and magnitude of pit-sawing in southern Mount Kenya. There were 13 master sawyers with 42 registered saws in the forest between Chehe and Irangi. As mentioned previously, the size of their operation could be ascertained by the number of saws they owned. Eight of them possessed three to four saws. In contrast, most licensed pit-sawyers (14 of 27) in Nyeri forest division only had two saws. Johana M. Gakau of Chehe owned seven saws, the highest total in Nyeri division. Pit-sawing largely focused on Chehe along the Ndia-Nyeri border and on Embu from Gichugu to Irangi. Only a single sawyer with three saws worked at Kangaita along the Ndia-Gichugu. The register shows that a few of the master sawyers had Christian names, and one of them was clearly a Muslim (Dishon Ali). Unfortunately, their district of origin was not specified.

British officials in Embu issued a five-year district development plan in 1945 calling for increased pit-sawing in the Mount Kenya reserve. Forestry staff shortages, however, hindered the issuing of new timber licences. As early as 1944, the department denied requests for pit-sawing concession in Kamweti because no forest officer was available to mark trees and supervise cutting. The situation became worse immediately following the war. South Kenya lacked a forester for most of time between 1946 and 1948. The forester from Ragati station occasionally visited the area to mark trees for already-licensed concessions. Much to the chagrin of the indigenous population, though, he would not issue new licences. Because most of the concessions continued to be held by Gikuyu immigrants, local sawyers felt that the department unjustly restricted their opportunity to enter the lucrative timber trade. The district commissioner reported in 1947 that the situation made the Forest Department 'unpopular with local inhabitants'. The licensed pit-sawyers themselves were unhappy about the continued ban on exporting timber from the district. The Embu council supported the export ban as a means of increasing the supply of sawn wood for Ndia and Gichugu.

The department's restrictions on pit-sawing was not the only example of thwarted African entrepreneurship in the forest sector. The experience of War-uhiu Itote from Mathira near Ndia offers an insightful example. After returning from military service in Asia at the end of the Second World War, Itote (1967: 32–8) earned a living around Nanyuki hiring workers to clear land for European farmers. The fallen wood was converted into charcoal, which Itote sold by the bag at Karatina. He tried to expand his business by supplying firewood to the railroad, but Asian contractors 'monopolized' the trade. Itote and a partner were not even allowed to set up a wood lot on their own property. Itote (1967: 34) later recalled his reaction:

> I boiled with rage and could not control my indignation for many days. First the Europeans took our land from us, encircled us and stuffed us into cages they called 'Reserves' . . . Then . . . the Asians came along and stifled us economically.

His feelings about discrimination and exploitation were shared by thousands of other Gikuyu. Itote's attempt to find outlets in Nairobi for their wood-fuel business, was unsuccessful because of numerous travel and export controls. He eventually obtained a job in the city, came into contact with militant anti-colonial Gikuyus, and emerged as a military leader of the Mau Mau forces in the Mount Kenya forest. There were many reasons why Gikuyus became increasingly involved in anti-colonial politics in the post-war years (for recent works, see Throup 1988; Furedi 1989; Atieno-Odhiambo 1991; Kershaw 1991; Presley 1992; Berman and Lonsdale 1992). Very clearly, though, the sorts of racial and economic discrimination encountered by pit-sawyers and frustrated forest entrepreneurs such as Itote contributed to the emergence of the Mau Mau movement.

Timber development: 1949 to 1952

A full-time forester was finally stationed at Irangi in late 1948. Thus, 1949 marked the first time since the end of war that a forest officer was present throughout the year in South Kenya. There was a slight increase in pit-sawing licences, but the demand for concessions substantially exceeded the capacity or willingness of the department to grant them. Some of the new licence holders may have been immigrant Gikuyus. The presence of a new forester at Irangi in 1950 failed to change the no-growth policy regarding pit-sawing concessions. The department claimed that it lacked the resources to supervise more sawyers. Meanwhile, local sawyers were increasingly upset that immigrants possessed timber licences, while their applications for licences were ignored. Embu councillors accused forestry officials of discriminating against local pit-sawyers. The foresters denied the charge of bias. Nevertheless, the district commissioner observed that the department was seen by the local population as 'repressive rather than . . . helpful'.

The ire of the prospective sawyers was undoubtedly raised by the decision in the late 1940s to permit timber exports. Although much of their wood continued to be sold within the district, pit-sawyers were allowed to find buyers from other areas as well. They exported 1500 tons of timber in 1949. The following year sawyers earned nearly £8000 from shipping wood outside the district. Quite clearly, the attractiveness of pit-sawing was enhanced by the widening of the timber market. The spectre of possible expanded commercial timber development in South Kenya during the early 1950s, added to local concerns about access to pit-sawing licences.

The colonial government promoted two schemes in the early 1950s involving the pit-sawyers. First, the Forest Department organized the Embu Pit-sawyer Co-operative Society. The cooperative sought to co-ordinate production and marketing activities among master pit-sawyers. It planned to set up purchasing depots to facilitate timber sales. The pit-sawyer co-operative was also to serve as a channel for introducing technical innovations. Members were to obtain credit through the society for improving their individual operations. In addition, the department wanted the co-operative members to supply baulks of camphor and other commercial timber to a large sawmill planned for Kirinyaga. Forestry officials believed that having the pit-sawyers only cut baulks, with the rest of the wood processed by sawmill machinery, would increase productivity and timber quality.

Bond Timber Limited sought permission for a sawmill at Sagana in south-western Ndia. Its proprietor, British businessman M.A. Bond, intended to convert baulks cut by pit-sawyers into planks and other wood products for national and overseas markets. The Forest Department supported the scheme, arguing that it would increase the efficiency of pit-sawing. British administrators in Embu favoured the idea, having endorsed the establishment of a sawmill in the 1945 district development plan. The district commissioner introduced Bond's proposal to the Embu council in August 1951. Its approval of the scheme was needed for the mill to obtain a plot in Sagana from the Local Land Board. Sagana was regarded a choice site because of its location as a railroad depot and as a crossroad for north-south and east-west routes around the mountain.

The district commissioner described the sawmill scheme to the councillors, emphasizing that it would be accompanied by a substantial increase in pit-sawing. The council members were receptive to the proposal, but they sought several conditions before giving approval. One of their concerns dealt with the pit-sawyer timber marketing. The councillors wanted pit-sawyers to retain the right to sell wood independently of the mill. British officials were sensitive about this issue, fearing that the sawmill could suffer wood shortages if local prices proved to be higher than those offered by the mill. Because much of the wood was supposed to be supplied through independent pit-sawyers rather than mill employees, the issue was quite germane.

Of even greater importance to the council was the allocation of pit-sawing licences. The councillors renewed their efforts to pressure forestry and administrative officials into increasing opportunities for local sawyers. They asked that timber licences be granted only to those individuals who were recommended by the council's forest committee. Before making a final decision on the matter, the councillors wanted to meet with the Forest Department to discuss the scheme and related issues. Administrative and forestry officers agreed to a special session. Although the council lacked jurisdiction in the Crown Forest, colonial officials acknowledged that the adjacent reserve be regarded as being within its sphere of influence.

At the same August meeting councillors discussed ways of exerting control over pit-sawyers, particularly the immigrants. The imposition of a special council tax or licence was considered and rejected. Instead, a resolution was passed compelling sawyers who worked outside their division or district to obtain a letter from their home area attesting to their good character. The nominal reason for the letter was to eliminate 'lawless' individuals from pit-sawing. The letters of clearance were not only to root out tax evaders and fugitives, but also political subversives. As will be discussed later in this chapter, some pit-sawyers were among the earliest and strongest proponents of the anti-colonial Mau Mau movement in the district. Embu administrators quickly informed officials in other parts of Central Province about the new requirement. Of course each master sawyer or employee who failed to obtain clearance created a potential job opening.

In September 1951 the council's forest committee met with the district commissioner and the Irangi forester to devise guide-lines for issuing future pit-sawing licences. The various parties agreed that already-licensed immigrant sawyers could continue to work in the forest. However, only indigenous residents of Embu and Kirinyaga were to receive future timber-cutting concessions. Procedures for reviewing applications were established at the meeting. Because of the backlog of requests for licences, it was decided that candidates ought to be chosen on merit rather than on the original date of their submission. The Irangi forester, the forest committee, and district commissioner were to meet to screen the applications. Based on their joint review, the names of qualified sawyers would be forwarded to the Forest Department for final approval. Forestry officials vowed to follow as closely as possible the recommendation of the reviewers.

Bond soon reached an accord with the pit-sawyers, including the co-operative. Essentially he accepted the terms specified by the council at the August meeting. Informed of the matter in mid-November, the council decided to delay any decision regarding the scheme until a special meeting scheduled for early December. The councillors invited the conservator of forests and other officials, pit-sawyers, Bond, and the registrar of co-operative societies. All but the latter attended the meeting.

The special session was held on 8 December 1951. The councillors quickly approved the scheme, recommending that the Local Land Board provide a plot for the mill. They refused to be a formal party in the agreement between Bond and the pit-sawyers, arguing that it was a private affair. Probably the most important part of the meeting was the dialogue between the councillors and R.R. Waterer, the conservator of forests. Waterer announced that the pit-sawyers' production for the mill was planned at 'a sustained yield' of 300 tons of timber per month. New cutting sites were to be opened, while present ones were to be phased out gradually. The conservator agreed to give preference to sawyers from the district in the Embu forest. He concluded by suggesting that in the future the people of the district might be allowed to run their own sawmill.

A reportedly well-equipped sawmill started processing large volumes of baulks cut by pit-sawyers in 1952. In spite of a promising beginning, the scheme soon appeared as luckless as the early concession applications by Lord Warwick and Moreton Frewen. The pit-sawyer co-operative had many problems trying to co-ordinate production and marketing among its members. The leader of the co-operative was convicted of embezzlement, undermining confidence in the organization. The sawmill also suffered from mismanagement. The owner left before the end of the year. According to one official account, he later committed suicide, apparently because of financial troubles. Management of the sawmill was taken over by other businessmen, but its operations were overtaken by wider political events: the Mau Mau Emergency.

Conclusion

The colonial government took a custodial approach to forest administration. Its Forest Department implemented a system of bureaucratic and scientific management, emphasizing both environmental protection and commercial use of resources. A series of ordinances governed forest use, and the reserve itself was monitored by guards and officers. Reafforestation emphasized plantation forestry using exotic species. South Kenya never supported a large-scale timber industry. However, a small but significant timber sector developed among Gikuyu pit-sawyers, particularly immigrants from other districts.

Conflict was inherent in the relationship between the colonial foresters and the people of southern Mount Kenya. The department's restrictions on forest use, including pit-sawing, made it one of the most unpopular agencies in the colonial regime. Yet, the department and local communities reached accommodation on certain aspects of reserve management. The foresters learned to treat beekeepers as informal watchers of the reserve, for example, and the Embu council was included in the decision-making regarding the Bond sawmill. Such accommodations reduced some of the tension regarding the forest, allowing the colonial government to control the reserve without serious challenge for over 40 years. In the early 1950s, though, the precarious peace was about to be broken.

7. From Mau Mau to independence: southern Mount Kenya, 1952 to 1963

THE DECLARATION BY the governor of a State of Emergency in October 1952 set in motion the most violent period of Kenyan history since the British conquest at the turn of the century. Armed Mau Mau supporters and their sympathizers used Mount Kenya as a base for guerrilla warfare against the colonial regime and its perceived local allies. Only a brutal counter-insurgency campaign contained the anti-colonial movement. Forced to cease its southern Mount Kenya operations in 1953, the Forest Department resumed activities three years later. In 1963 Kenya received its independence.

This chapter examines the Mau Mau movement as it relates to state forestry in southern Mount Kenya. It is not intended as a comprehensive review of the complex anti-colonial movement or the subsequent counter-insurgency campaign in Kirinyaga (see Castro and Ettenger 1994). Rather, the focus is on the nexus between forest-dwelling populations and Mau Mau, as well as the impact of warfare on state forestry. The chapter also examines the acceleration of the plantation forestry development that took place in the last years of colonial rule. The last seven years of colonial forestry management are more than a transition period, for the policies and practices established during that time influenced public forestry for years to come.

Mau Mau

The Mau Mau movement challenged the legitimacy of colonial rule, including the administrative and cultural foundations of British dominance (Rosberg and Nottingham 1970; Edgerton 1991; Maloba 1993). Long-standing land grievances, as well as post-war policies compelling soil conservation on Gikuyu homesteads, contributed to its rise (Barnett and Njama 1966; Wachanga 1975; Kanogo 1987; Throup 1988; Furedi 1989). Increased socio-economic differentiation, inter-generational tensions, land disputes among the Gikuyu, and urbanization also fuelled tensions that manifested themselves in the movement (Kershaw 1972, 1991; Kaggia 1975; Kitching 1980; Berman and Lonsdale 1992). Thus, Mau Mau represented the outcome of very diverse and complex political and social forces.

Four decades after Mau Mau was outlawed in colonial Kenya its nature and significance continue to be debated (see, for example, Buijtenhuijs 1973; Ochieng' and Janmohamed 1977; Atieno-Odhiambo 1991; Kershaw 1991; Berman and Lonsdale 1992; Presley 1992; Maloba 1993). The duration of this controversy reflects the complexity of Mau Mau, Gikuyu society, and post-colonial Kenyan politics. As a political movement in the early 1950s, Mau Mau expressed 'the distinctive cultural content of Gikuyu internal conflicts as much as anti-colonial liberation struggle' (Berman 1991: 200). At the time colonial officials and settlers failed to comprehend the importance of nationalism, land conflicts, and socio-economic differentiation in generating Mau Mau (Edgerton 1991). Government psychiatrist J.C. Carothers (1954: 4–5), for example, claimed that the Gikuyu had a 'forest psychology' inclining them towards secretiveness, suspicion, and scheming. According to Carothers (1954: 15), anxiety caused by social change and manipulation by 'sophisticated egotists' gave rise to Mau Mau. Such concepts revealed how little Carothers and his sponsors understood about the Gikuyu.

Mau Mau and the forest

David Hutchins (1907) proved prophetic in pointing out the strategic value of
the forest to Africans during an uprising. Waruhiu Itote (1967: 43–62) and a
small number of Mau Mau members entered the forest in August 1952 to prepare for guerrilla warfare. Lacking knowledge about Mount Kenya and how to
survive in the remote woods, Itote and others sought out old men to teach 'forest
lore, in the thousand and one details . . . to know to remain alive'. Several elders
not only provided 'much practical advice, they also shared . . . some beliefs
based more on superstition than fact'. Included among the latter by Itote was the
belief that heavy rains or hail would fall if trees or bamboo were cut without
appropriate rituals. At first the guerrillas followed the prescribed rites, but they
gradually abandoned them.

Itote and his allies were joined by others, especially after the Emergency
declaration and increased colonial raids on the homes of suspected insurgents.
The movement into the forest took place in trickles and spurts, with Nyeri
supplying a large share. According to Donald Barnett and Karari Njama (1966:
150–1), the Mount Kenya and Nyandarua forests eventually contained several
distinct groups: the early organizers; fighters recruited directly into forest-based
units; guerrilla bands that moved into the forest from adjacent farms; urban and
White Highland repatriates seeking food and protection; and refugees from the
counter-insurgency campaign waged in the African districts. Thus, not everyone
who entered the forest intended to become combatants (Maloba 1993: 114).
Women served as fighters, but their main role often involved providing provisions and information from the settled areas into the forest (see Kanogo 1987;
Presley 1992). The Mau Mau forces and sympathizers in the Mount Kenya
region probably numbered several thousands at their peak (Itote 1967;
Wachanga 1975).

Among the South Kenya forest-dwelling population, pit-sawyers were most
closely linked to Mau Mau. Several master sawyers and their employees engaged
in recruiting Forest Department labourers through 'oathing' in October and
November 1952. This oathing involved a ritual pledge of support and secrecy. It
lacked the element of ritual defilement contained in more complex versions of
the rites (Kershaw 1991). Colonial officials greatly exaggerated the symbolic
power of recruitment oathing, assuming it exercised a sort of cultural and moral
determinism over the Gikuyu (for example, see Leakey 1954; Corfield 1960).

Government reports and memoirs of Mau Mau participants from other parts
of Gikuyu country showed that pit-sawyers and forest labourers were among the
earliest supporters of Mau Mau (Barnett and Njama 1966: 116; Wachanga 1975:
19). The top military leaders of Mau Mau — Didan Kimathi in Nyandarua and
Itote in Mount Kenya — both had close connections to forestry. As mentioned
in Chapter 6, Itote was a frustrated fuelwood merchant, while Kimathi collected
seeds for the Forest Department. According to a colonial policeman,
'[Kimathi's] seed-collecting forays gave him an early experience of forest life,
which he never forgot' (Henderson and Goodhart 1958: 22).

The involvement of pit-sawyers and forest workers in Mau Mau was not
surprising. They were often landless Gikuyu immigrants, victims of colonial land
appropriation in their home districts. Louis Leakey anticipated the probable
receptiveness of forest labourers to Mau Mau. He observed that many of them
were young men 'who are restless because they know there is no security, nor
any prospect of owning part of the land' (Leakey 1952: 72–3). Besides long-
standing land grievances, the rise of pit-sawing in the reserve had increased local

interest in commercial forest exploitation. A provincial report in 1948 claimed that the Gikuyu increasingly 'cast covetous eyes on the Crown Forests'. Government restrictions on pit-sawing and other local uses of the forest long irked the people of southern Mount Kenya.

Not every pit-sawyer or forest labourer sided with Mau Mau. Several people were killed in the Mount Kenya reserve because they refused to join the anti-colonial movement. Others explicitly aligned themselves as 'loyalists' to the colonial government. Thus, assumptions about the political unity of the sawyers and forest workers can only go so far. There were long-standing divisions between local and outside pit-sawyers, as well as between 'lawless' types and those presumed to be 'law-abiding'. Whether distinctions such as the size and scale of pit-sawing operations (the number of saws or employees), employer or employee status, or the origin of the person (local or outside the district) actually influenced involvement was unclear from archival sources or local interviews (see Kershaw 1991, for a brilliant account of the problems of trying to reconstruct participation in Mau Mau). What is evident is that Mau Mau attracted widespread support and sympathy in the early 1950s, and pit-sawyers, with their intimate knowledge of the remote forest, were in a strategic position for aiding and participating in opposition to colonial rule.

Life in the forest for the guerrilla bands initially took on 'a quality of excitement and challenge' (Itote 1967: 80). The movement encountered widespread, though not universal, support throughout Kirinyaga, especially in Ndia. During 1953 Mau Mau was in ascendancy, and officials admitted that large sections of the district were out of control. As late as August 1954, Kiine location remained in a state of 'complete anarchy'. By that time, however, the government's massive military campaign had taken a substantial toll on the guerrillas and their supporters, including forced resettlement of the Ndia and Gichugu Gikuyu into centralized and guarded villages (see Castro and Ettenger 1994). The forest fighters were increasingly overwhelmed by the superior numbers and firepower of the colonial forces. They also suffered from the erosion of support among the increasingly war-weary rural population.

Only a few forest fighters were left by the end of 1956, when Didan Kimathi was captured and executed. Government figures showed that Mau Mau suffered 1315 deaths in Kirinyaga and Embu between 1953 and 1956, compared to 251 deaths for colonial forces and 'civilians'. Over 700 insurgents surrendered in the district, and several times that number were detained as suspected Mau Mau supporters. The survival of the remaining guerrillas was threatened by specialized squads composed of former forest fighters.

A small number of Mau Mau guerrillas continued to elude the police and military until the end of the colonial era. On several occasions troops were deployed in the Mount Kenya forest in search of the insurgents. Although poorly armed and hardly posing a military threat to the administration, the remaining forest fighters served as symbols of the government's inability to restore the old colonial order. A few of them stayed in the forest after Kenya became independent in 1963, causing much embarrassment for the new regime of Jomo Kenyatta. The Kirinyaga district commissioner declared them 'outlaws' who threatened public security. Their numbers were substantially reduced after 32 forest fighters were captured in July 1964 while seeking food at Kamweti station. Official forestry reports indicated that a handful of people eluded the police as late as 1967.

Itote (1967), who negotiated with the holdouts on behalf of the Kenyatta administration, suggested that they were mainly interested in obtaining land in the former White Highlands. Some present-day informants in Kirinyaga suggested that the forest fighters were dissatisfied with the Kenyatta government. According to the informants, the holdouts wanted the country's president to come from slain leader Didan Kimathi's home district of Nyeri (Kenyatta was a Kiambu Gikuyu). An elderly man stated, 'Kimathi had been a field marshall. With a rank so high, how could he not have been president?' Others mentioned rumours about Kenyatta's possible complicity in Kimathi's execution. The sentiment against Kenyatta was not widespread, however, as most people regarded him as the father of independence.

Warfare and state forestry: 1952 to 1953

Because British officials were unaware of the extent of Mau Mau forces on Mount Kenya, they slowly imposed restrictions over forestry activities. Local access to the reserve was curtailed in the early days of the Emergency. A special permit was needed to enter the reserve. Night-time or overnight trips into the forest by beekeepers were prohibited. Pit-sawing and reafforestation continued as usual. However, officials discussed contingency plans in case of trouble. Douglas G.B. Leakey, the divisional forester, discussed the possibility of suspending pit-sawing in mid-November 1952. Leakey instructed the assistant conservator of forests in Embu to 'preserve the status quo' and to check up on the pit-sawyers 'as we don't want the forest to acquire a bad name'. He urged the assistant conservator: 'Don't hesitate to eject yourself any undesirable pit-sawyers or pit-saw employees.' Leakey felt that repatriating forest labourers, though, was 'most undesirable and highly unlikely' (Embu District Archives).

Events on Mount Kenya were already beyond the control of the assistant conservator or any other local official by the end of 1952. The forest was increasingly viewed by administrators as 'a lair' for Mau Mau, and they added new restrictions. South Kenya was declared a 'Special Area' in January 1953, requiring Africans to obtain a permit before entering the reserve. Forest workers and pit-sawyers were placed under police guard. Still, violence escalated, including the killing of the wife and child of the Yacoob Deen sawmill mechanic near Ragati. They were two of only thirty-two noncombatant Europeans whose deaths were attributed to Mau Mau (Clayton 1976: 54). In July 1953 the Forest Department agreed to move its South Kenya plantation labourers outside the reserve.

Massive amounts of forced labour were used by officials to clear a mile-wide strip along the southern forest boundary in mid-1953 (Castro and Ettenger 1994). This *cordon sanitaire* displaced large numbers of people and caused the abandonment of extensive tracts of farmland. A fortified ditch was added along the perimeter. These actions were aimed at restricting movement of Mau Mau fighters from the forest to agricultural lands. Although most of the vegetation was cleared in the mile zone, pit-sawyers were allowed to salvage valuable timber trees.

Most of South Kenya was declared a Prohibited Area in August 1953, allowing colonial forests to shoot unauthorized persons without first issuing a challenge. Pit-sawing came to a complete halt by September. The department received permission to maintain forest plantations at Thiba and Kamweti in Kirinyaga and Irangi and Sambana in Embu. Its employees could work in designated parts of the forest during the day, but they needed to leave before nightfall. The Royal Air Force had been instructed to bomb any fires or other signs of human activities during night-time. As fighting increased, the department found it difficult to continue work. A lorry filled with forest labourers was attacked and burned in September, for example, its occupants abducted, beaten, and left naked by a band of Mau Mau fighters. State forestry activities soon ceased altogether.

The East Africa Royal Commission

In the midst of the Mau Mau War, the secretary of state for the colonies convened a commission in 1953 to examine political and economic affairs in East Africa. A royal warrant empowered the commission to consider land, labour, and development issues, including ones related to forestry. Influenced by contemporary views of liberal western capitalism, the commissioners wanted to carry out significant social and economic reforms, including an end to racial dualism. According to Anthony Clayton and Donald Savage (1974: 351), '[They] wished to banish traditionalism and paternalism in so far as it was possible to do so and to introduce into East Africa the modern economic arrangements and practices of the western world'.

The commission's final report severely criticized the handling of African land grievances during the 1930s. It also attacked the colonial administration for failing to follow the recommendations of the Kenya Land Commission regarding the potential allocation of excised forest lands. The Kenya Land Commission had proposed placing forest reserves located entirely in the White Highlands under the control of the Highlands Board. This board's function was to protect the economic interests of the European farmers. Thus, any land excised from forest reserves in the White Highlands was potentially opened to European settlement. In contrast, forest reserves bordering both the White Highlands and the African lands were supposed to come under government review when excision took place. The East Africa Royal Commission discovered that Mount Kenya and other forest reserves bordering on both African- and European-owned land had been included as part of the White Highlands. This policy meant that land excised from such forest reserves had been the exclusive concern of the European-controlled Highland Boards. The commissioners wrote: 'We can see no justification for this, and when any areas are excised from the forests, their disposal should be a matter for government decision on the merits of each case'. Ironically, the Gikuyu had argued before the Kenya Land Commission that the administration's appropriation of the forest had been a ploy for setting aside land for white settlement.

The commission also voiced concerns about the Forest Department's resident labour policies, suggesting higher wages, greater security of tenure, and provision of public services for workers and squatters. British officials in Kenya protested against these proposals, stating that they would make plantation forestry unprofitable. In spite of its resistance, the Forest Department was compelled to modify some aspects of the *shamba* labour system. Limited public services such as schools and dispensaries were provided at large forest stations. However, the department often obtained funds for such services by levying a cess on the value of the food crops grown by the resident labour force. Further changes in their terms of employment occurred after independence.

Reopening the Forest

The Forest Department resumed operations in southern Mount Kenya by late 1956. Some local administrative changes accompanied the resumption of state forests. Castle station became its own forest district, covering over 20 000 ha in Kirinyaga. A sub-station was opened in 1959 for the new district at Kamweti, located on the southern edge of the bamboo zone roughly 10 km north of Castle. The Kirinyaga stations were placed in the Fort Hall-Embu forest division, but they were eventually transferred to Nyeri conservancy.

The immediate goal of the department was to repair the neglect and damage sustained by facilities during the war years. In contrast to the Java counter-insurgency of the 1950s, where government forces deliberately burned large tracts of forests in pursuit of Muslim rebels (Peluso 1992: 103), the South Kenya reserve was generally spared such scorched-earth tactics. Nevertheless, small fires, aerial bombings, sabotage, wildlife damage, and years of inattention caused a marked decline in the condition of forest stations and plantations.

The resumption of state forestry was hindered by a shortage of low-paid African workers. In the past foresters often relied on *kuni* labour — informal groups of women and men who lived near the forest and provided their services on an occasional basis in exchange for firewood — to perform such tasks as boundary clearance or road maintenance. However, the reopening of the mile strip after years of closure furnished ample deadwood for nearby families. The colonial-sponsored land tenure reform, which consolidated and privatized farm-land, absorbed the attention of the people of Ndia and Gichugu. Thus, foresters encountered difficulties trying to obtain day labourers.

Local fuel contractors relieved some of the pressure caused by labour shor-tages. They purchased licences to collect deadwood from certain sites, including areas vacated by sawmills. They often sold the wood in advance to shops or schools, and used the advance payments to hire workers, arrange transport, and cover other costs. One of the contractors at Castle regularly sold wood in local markets. An official report from May 1957 observed that near Castle there seemed to be 'someone to buy every stick out of every size and kind'. Foresters encouraged the clearing of certain areas, particularly those slated for plantations, by discounting the stumpage charge for stacked wood.

The sawmills in southern Mount Kenya were slow to resume operation. The colony's timber industry was in a recession, which deepened following the 1960 announcement of Kenya's coming independence. The Yacoob Deen Company continued to harvest trees near Chehe, but its sawmill ran at less than half capacity. Although it held a timber licence for the forest near Castle station, the company made no attempt to work the area by the early 1960s. There was a turnover in the company's management in 1959, as it tried to cope with tough times. That same year Timsalos Ltd. sold its sawmill at Ragati to Keith Timber Co., which became known as South Kenya Timbers. The firm focused its ac-tivities in the south-western portion of the reserve. Small sawmills opened in Kutus and Embu, but they purchased baulk timber from pit-sawyers instead of cutting their own wood in the forest.

The Forest Department announced in 1955 that only pit-sawyers loyal to the colonial administration would be granted timber licences. By the time sawyers returned to the forest in 1957, however, officials had renounced the use of term 'loyalist'. They did so as part of the 'rehabilitation' process — the belief among government officials that the Gikuyu had to be guided back from the trauma of Mau Mau (see Kershaw 1991; Maloba 1993). Still, only pit-sawyers from the district received licences. Irangi was the first site reopened, and by the end of 1957 sawyers operated at Castle, southern Kamweti, and Chehe. Northern Kam-weti remained closed through 1958 as a security precaution.

The Embu forester complained that the sawyers at Irangi were 'extremely disappointing workers' who showed little interest in the quality or quantity of their output. Similar complaints were lodged about the Castle pit-sawyers. The forester recognized that the sawyers were worried about land privatization. A total of 21 master sawyers sold baulk timber in 1958 to the Kutus and Embu sawmills. Each sawyer reportedly averaged between 60 and 80 tons of timber, usually camphor and podo. By 1961, officials recorded 40 pit-sawyers and employees at Castle and 18 master sawyers and 57 employees at Irangi. The Forest Department tried to revive the pit-sawyer co-operative, but low timber prices made it difficult for members to sustain interest. The co-operative was formally dissolved in 1962.

Because of the nationally depressed timber prices, the pit-sawyers tapped into the local market for inexpensive sawn wood. Families were moving out of the Emergency villages and back to their homesteads by the late 1950s. They required wood for dwellings, granaries, and fencing. The foresters in Kirinyaga and Embu allowed local families to purchase individual trees and make arrangements with pit-sawyers to cut and transport the timber. In contrast, the Chehe forester curtailed the number of pit-sawing licences in an effort to reduce wood supplies and thus raise prices. As the Emergency travel restrictions were lifted, pit-sawyers in Fort Hall encountered difficulties retaining employees. It is likely that Kirinyaga sawyers had similar problems.

British officials expected land tenure reform in Kirinyaga to leave one-fifth of the adult male population as landless. They also thought that a large number of the Gikuyu immigrants in Kirinyaga would end up without land. Thus, resettlement as resident forest labourers was seen as an option for absorbing the landless. The Kikuyu Reabsorption Scheme called for displaced persons to be employed in expanding plantation forestry. In southern Mount Kenya this meant re-establishing and increasing the forest villages. The Embu District Emergency Committee, the civil-military body that governed local counter-insurgency affairs, insisted that forestry villages contain no more than 40 per cent immigrant Gikuyus. Officials felt that the immigrant Gikuyu were too politically volatile. A new anti-colonial secret society, *Kiama kia Muingi*, had been detected in some of their lowland villages.

The department resettled 200 families as *shamba* labourers near Chehe along the Nyeri-Ndia border in late 1956. Castle and Kamweti stations had a total of about 200 resident families as well. Retaining the labourers became a major problem in the cool, damp conditions prevailing in the upland forest. The resumption of forest *shamba* labour in 1957 coincided with one of the wettest periods in years (Moris 1973: 24). A report by a South Kenya forester in August 1957 indicated the general mood: 'The cold wet weather continued to depress labour and staff alike. No food grows in the shambas, everyone is hungry and has a cold or flu and the outlook remained extremely bleak throughout the month'. Elephants, buffaloes, and other game were troublesome, attacking crops and sending workers scurrying up trees for protection. By 1958 only 140 were left at Chehe. Meanwhile, the forester at Castle decided that soil conditions were not conducive to agriculture in several of the proposed plantation sites. He shifted some plantation sites northwards to Kamweti. Attracting resident labourers to the remote forest station proved difficult.

Foresters continuously complained about low worker morale and poor discipline. Problems controlling labourers intensified as independence approached. Some workers refused to pay taxes, and a few engaged in such illicit activities as growing marijuana or stealing department property. By 1961 the standard of labour at Castle and Kamweti was characterized as 'rock bottom', with a widespread anti-disciplinary feeling. There was also problems with high turnover. Whenever the forest became irksome, the workers moved away. On the eve of independence the district commissioner observed that the forest villages were clearly 'not prospering'.

In spite of these difficulties, the department proceeded with its reafforestation plans. Different afforestation strategies were used at each forest station. Exotic species such as pine and eucalyptus were planted at Castle and Kamweti, while enrichment planting of indigenous species was carried out at Irangi. About 140 ha of plantation forests were established at Castle and Kamweti between 1959 and 1961. By the beginning of 1962 nearly 240 ha of land had been used for reafforestation at the Kirinyaga stations. Over 90 per cent of it consisted of exotic plantations, mainly pine and cypress. Fewer than two hectares were dedicated to natural regeneration of camphor and other native hardwoods. The emphasis on exotic species would continue after independence.

The Forest Department explored other economic opportunities beyond wood production. In 1958 it experimented with harvesting bamboo shoots for oriental-style foods. Over 9000 kg of bamboo shoots were collected in the Nyandarua forest of Fort Hall and shipped to Kenya Canners for processing. A Chinese woman who tested the final product declared it 'rubbish'. The project was abandoned. Somewhat more successful, yet still controversial, was the building of a small fishing camp on the edge of the forest at Thiba. It consisted of a few sparse cabins along a very scenic part of the Kamweti River. The upland streams were long known for their fishing. Several colonial officers had introduced trout into them during the early days of British rule (Hutchins 1912). The camp opened in late 1958. There were 152 booking in its first full year. Other fishing-minded Europeans visited only for the day. Competition for fish soon emerged with local people, who were called 'poachers' by officials. The Africans, now possessing privately owned land, complained that Europeans often trespassed on their property while fishing. Although the camp still operated in the early 1980s, it remained little used.

Local access to the forest

Reopening the forest to the public took place gradually. Small numbers of Mau Mau guerrillas remained in the forest. A few beekeepers were allowed back into the forest in early 1958. The divisional forest officer initially allowed 25 beekeepers to be licensed per station. Certain conditions had to be followed: beekeepers needed to check-in with a guard before entering; only day trips were allowed; and the beekeepers had to inform the guard when they returned. Officials believed that the beekeepers might provide information about illicit activities in the forest, including the movements of the remaining Mau Mau bands.

The move out of the Emergency villages and back to the homesteads stimulated a demand for timber, poles, posts, building sticks, and thatch. The people of Kirinyaga and Embu were encouraged to upgrade their standard of housing. Provincial officials requested Forest Department assistance in making inexpensive building materials available, particularly in places experiencing wood and thatch shortages. The Gichugu district officer, for example, wanted the foresters to allow people to cut thatching grass without charge. The department looked upon forest products as a source of revenue, however, and it refused to offer free issues. The administrators were advised to use the forests held in trust by the Embu African District Council to supply local needs free of charge.

Mount Kenya remained a prohibited area until at least 1958, and entry controls remained in effect even after independence. Still, people violated forest regulations. Along the forest in Nyeri officials detected 1422 violations in 1959, but most of the cases were minor and resulted in fines averaging three Kenyan Shillings. Recorded offences in Nyeri actually decreased over the next two years: 675 compounded offences in 1960 and 342 cases in 1961. Once again, they were usually petty violations, such as unauthorized removal of firewood. However, Nyeri forest guards reported several cases of threats and intimidation in 1961, as local people realized that independence was imminent. District officers provided assistance to the beleaguered forest sentries.

The situation appeared calmer along the forest in Kirinyaga and Embu. District records are less precise about the number of offences, they indicate that very few violations took place. At Castle station in 1961, for example, the only recorded offence was illegal grazing, with the violator fined 10 Kenyan Shillings. The small number of offences was attributed by the foresters to 'the relatively short length of boundary and the relatively low development of the Native Land Unit adjacent to the Crown Forests'.

The hunting and trapping of wildlife emerged as serious problems in the forest not only during the Emergency years but later as well. According to Itote (167: 76), the forest fighters relied on antelopes, elephants, buffaloes, and other animals for meat. Trapping was preferred, since the guerrilla forces suffered from an acute lack of ammunition (Maloba 1993: 85). Interviews with present-day elders indicated that furs and animal skins were occasionally used for clothing.

As the fighting died down, some individuals and groups engaged in illicit hunting and trapping in the reserve. Bush meat was not a major part of traditional Gikuyu diets; indeed, some people believed that game meat was ritually unclean (Crawshay 1902). Given the hunger that prevailed in the Emergency villages (see Sluiter 1956), it is not inconceivable that obtaining meat was a motive. Much of the game poaching that occurred by 1959, however, was aimed at procuring saleable game trophies. Highly organized groups of poachers operated in the southern part of Embu and Kirinyaga. Perhaps they spread their activities northwards. In 1961, forest guards occasionally reported 'gangs' of 40 to 50 men, some of them using hunting dogs, poaching in the reserve. Several times the guards were threatened by them. British troops shortly afterwards carried out operations in the region.

Local poachers were not the only ones killing game in the reserve. Foresters regarded animals such as elephants, buffalo, monkeys, and pigs to be troublesome. Moats and fences were built in certain areas to contain the movement of elephants and other large game. Game wardens also shot animals seen as threats to forestry activities or farmland adjacent to the reserve. Some crop damage still continued.

The end of the colonial era

When the forest reopened in 1956, very few Europeans imagined that independence was imminent. Mau Mau was largely defeated, and the colonial government was carrying out some political and economic reforms aimed at addressing African grievances. A short time later the Forest Department issued its first formal policy statement of the colonial era. Over 50 years had passed since the founding of the department. Its status as a colonial bureaucracy would last less than seven more years. Yet, the fundamental assumptions and organizational structures of its custodial management strategy would serve as the basis for public forestry in independent Kenya.

Uncertainty pervaded the Forest Department as independence approached. Staff turnover increased, and plans were made to close some forest stations. In 1961 foresters in Kirinyaga and Embu reported success in carrying out their activities despite unpleasant working conditions and doubts about 'what the future had in store'. As things turned out, there was much more continuity than change in state forestry after independence.

On 12 December 1963, Kisoi Munyao raised the flag of independent Kenya on the summit of the nation's highest mountain. Two decades later some residents still recalled the excitement that accompanied the planting of the new nation's flag by an African on the top of Mount Kenya. Colonialism ended, but its policies and administrative structures would live on.

8. Southern Mount Kenya since independence: the first quarter century, 1963 to 1988

THIS CHAPTER EXAMINES the management and use of the southern Mount Kenya reserve in the periods between independence in 1963 and 1988. These years spanned the governments of Jomo Kenyatta (1963 to 1978) and Daniel arap Moi (1978 to the present). As will be seen, the end of colonial rule resulted in the Africanization of the forestry bureaucracy. Yet, the policies and organizational structures of custodial forestry remained in place. State forest administration continued to be based on the premise that local households, pit-sawyers, and other small-scale forest enterprises posed the most serious threat to sustained management of the reserve. This chapter, however, argues that official mismanagement and government-sanctioned development activities generated or instigated substantial forest degradation. It shows that the Forest Department long encountered difficulties in managing fuelwood production for local tea factories and, to a lesser extent, timber harvesting on any sort of sustained yield basis. Indeed, there remained no specific operational guidelines for sustained-yield management of the forest. The chapter will suggest that both planned and spontaneous conversion of forest accelerated in the mid-1980s largely because of the muddled implementation of government plans to establish extensive forest plantations. Proposals by the local and national government to convert part of the reserve into tea revenue farms are also discussed. Although local tea-growing households, pit-sawyers, and sawmills often benefited from, or participated in, forest clearance, government policies and programmes strongly influenced their actions.

Change and continuity in forestry management

The Regional Boundary Commission included 308 km² of the Mount Kenya forest within newly-created Kirinyaga district. This land stayed under the control of the Forest Department, now part of the Ministry of Environment and Natural Resources. The department maintained its centralized and top-down administrative structure. A custodial forest management policy was reiterated in Sessional Paper Number One of 1968. The policy emphasized environmental protection and economic development on a nominally sustained-yield basis. The professed goal remained balancing the use and replenishing of forest resources. Ideally, working plans based on current inventories of standing timber were to regulate multiple-use exploitation of the reserve. The department continued to be run on a semi-commercial basis, with the price of forest products based on their value. Guards remained in place to protect the forest from unauthorized use.

In reality, sustainable forest management proved as elusive to foresters in independent Kenya as it did to their colonial predecessors. Although parts of Mount Kenya had management plans devised by the early 1980s, the department lacked operational guidelines for sustained-yield management. Indeed, as late as 1989, no research had been conducted on the sustained-yield capacity of the forests on Mount Kenya (Beentje 1990a). In spite of the importance of the forest as a source of revenue, the fees and royalties charged by the department failed to keep pace with inflation. A World Bank (1986a) review of Kenya's forestry sector complained that stumpage rates furnished only a fraction of the production or replacement costs for timber and industrial fuelwood. Ironically, funds from the World Bank now supplied a significant share of the department's expenditures. Other international donors supported forestry activities as well, including the United Nations Development Programme, the European Economic Community, Finland, Norway, Australia, Canada, the United States, and, of course, the United Kingdom through its Overseas Development Administration. Quite clearly, the end of colonial rule opened Kenya's forestry sector to an unprecedented flow of international financiers and technical experts. Low stumpage fees increased the accessibility of forest products to local households, but it also caused the department to subsidize large-scale consumption of wood fuel by tea factories, resulting in accelerated forest clearing. Overall, the appropriateness of the custodial forestry became even more questionable in the quarter century after independence.

The department continued dividing the forest into management blocks run by self-accounting stations and satellite substations. Kamweti forest, the department's largest administrative unit in the district, covered over 200 km^2 from the Kiringa River eastwards to Irangi block in Embu. It was initially supervised by a forester posted at Castle station. From the mid-1960s to the mid-1970s Kamweti was overseen by the Irangi station in Embu Forest Division. It re-emerged as a self-accounting station in 1976, supervised by a district forester at Castle. In 1981 Kamweti was transferred to Nyeri division when the department realigned forestry borders to coincide with provincial ones. Chehe and Ragati stations in Nyeri were responsible for the forest reserve located west of the Kiringa. Thus, Kirinyaga's tract of Mount Kenya reserve was united into a single forest conservancy unit only in the early 1980s, and it remained subdivided between stations in different districts. Some local officials claimed that state forestry managerial arrangements divorced Mount Kenya from the rest of Kirinyaga.

Interviewed members of the department claimed that the ambience of forest administration changed after independence. An official said, 'In the time of the *mzungu* [white man], people were beaten. There was a fear of entering the forest. Today, people don't worry about this.' Several district residents agreed with this assessment. It was widely believed in colonial times that the whites had usurped the forest for their own use. Independence eliminated racial competition as a source of tension regarding state management of the reserve. Africanization of the bureaucracy further reduced the socio-cultural distance between forest officers and district inhabitants. Some Europeans stayed in the department after independence, but by the early 1980s it was almost completely Africanized. The foresters assigned to Kirinyaga in the early 1980s, for example, were Gikuyus from Central Province. Despite these changes in personnel, households and small-scale forest users continued to be viewed by administrators as the most serious threat to the reserve.

The forest reserve and district households

The belief that 'man' constituted the most dangerous threat to the reserve remained a central tenet of forest policy. 'Man' largely referred to district households, whose use of the reserve remained regulated by the Forest Department's personnel and policies. In 1983 the district forester commanded 11 guards posted along the edge of the reserve. Dressed in green uniforms and armed with *pangas* (machetes), these guards patrolled 'beats' whose boundaries were defined by rivers. They kept ledgers with the names of monthly fuel ticket and grazing permit holders. Violators of forest regulations were subject to fines or imprisonment. Forest officers retained the power to compound offences, charging up to five times the value of damage inflicted or produce taken. Serious offenders were prosecuted in court.

The government of Jomo Kenyatta gradually eased restrictions on local forest access. In February 1965 it rescinded the rule requiring a permit to enter the forest. This regulation had been on the books since the Emergency in 1952. Other rules dating back to the Mau Mau era still applied. The public was allowed access to the reserve only during daylight hours, and people were supposed to limit their travel to roads and main tracks. The permanent secretary for the Ministry of Natural Resources and Wildlife admitted that those rules were maintained to prevent unauthorized political meetings in the forest. The government also retained long-standing restrictions on removing forest products, grazing, and other uses of the reserve.

Relatively few violations of forest rules were recorded in the first two decades of independence, continuing the pattern established during most of the colonial era. Only six cases were compounded at Kamweti in 1978, yielding 1020 Kenya Shillings in fines. In 1981, 19 offenders were assessed 2599 Kenya Shillings. Illicit cultivation, grazing, or fires sometimes occurred in the reserve. Once again, the incidence of encroachment by local households was low. For example, only one case was handled in 1981.

The lack of encroachment along the forest line and in the interior of the reserve in 1983 was surprising given the pressing demand for farmland in Kirinyaga. There was a striking contrast between the reserve and adjacent homesteads. It was especially noteworthy because most forest boundary markers were intended as symbols instead of barriers: wooden-rail fences, game moats spanned by logs, or a line of eucalyptus trees planted along a three-metre wide strip of cleared land. Wire fencing was used near Kangaita tea factory, but seldom elsewhere. Several field visits on footpaths through the interior of the reserve revealed little clearing for agricultural purposes outside of the areas set aside for department labourers. The situation in Kirinyaga differed from that occurring in some other parts of the country, particularly Western Kenya, where local encroachment in forest reserves was often endemic.

The land adjacent to the forest underwent considerable economic and demographic growth after independence. In 1961 the area was described as largely undeveloped. It was regarded by officials as the poorest part of the district. Two decades later the upper zone was densely settled and generally prosperous. Some places along the forest often exceeded 400 people per km^2 in 1979. Tea, which flourished in the cool, moist climate and slightly acidic soils near the forest, propelled this transformation. The process started slowly. The crop was introduced on a small-scale and closely-supervised basis in 1955. It was not very popular initially: people complained about the start-up costs, the four-year wait for a harvest, and the labour-intensiveness of plucking tea leaves. At the time coffee was the preferred cash crop among Kirinyaga households, though it was not suitable in the tea-dairy agro-ecological zone. Around independence the district had less than 330 ha of tea planted, and it suffered from low yields because of what officials described as 'plucker apathy'. Some families illegally sun-dried their tea and sold it on the black market, rather than shipping the green leaf to the government's processing factory at Ragati in Nyeri.

The Kenya Tea Development Authority (KTDA), a parastatal responsible for supervising smallholder production, processing, and marketing, contributed to the crop's rising popularity (Lamb and Muller 1982; Grosh 1991). It skilfully used incentives, including a monthly pay system, and a sparse but efficient bureaucracy to raise morale about the crop. KTDA reports showed that Kirinyaga achieved some of the highest yields in the country by the early 1970s, and the district's teas commanded a premium price on the world market. Between 1963 and 1984 the tea-growing areas in Ndia and Gichugu increased nearly ten-fold. By 1988, Kirinyaga's 9060 licensed tea growers had over 3600 ha planted. They produced more than 37 million kg of green leaf worth 185 million Kenya Shillings. The tea-growing zone was known locally as 'a land of stone and timber houses', a reference to widespread (but by no means ubiquitous) material indicators of local prosperity.

Increasing agricultural development along the forest edge led to some confrontations between local households and wildlife, particularly in the 1960s and early 1970s. Elephants, buffaloes, monkeys, and other animals occasionally inflicted heavy crop damage in northern Gichugu and near Kangaita in Ndia. The game warden was called from neighbouring districts to eradicate troublesome animals. In 1964, for example, the warden shot 35 monkeys, 10 elephants, and a rhinoceros. As late as 1975, the warden killed three elephants and two buffaloes. Deep moats were dug along the forest edge in some areas to keep large game out of farmland. The Kirinyaga County Council, which supplanted the Embu council at independence, was supposed to compensate households for serious crop and property damage caused by wildlife. Such funds came from the central government, but they were often in short supply. At times councillors sought to divert the funds for other purposes, including establishing a school for disabled children. The issue of unpaid game compensation continued into the mid-1970s. By that time, however, the moats and a decline in wildlife because of poaching for game trophies reduced the incidence of crop damage. A very small number of women and men engaged in illicit trapping and hunting for commercial purposes in the early 1980s. One poacher, who offered a leopard skin and a rhinoceros horn for sale, told of selling such items on an irregular basis to Asians and Europeans in Nyeri and Nairobi.

Several factors contributed to the relatively low level of recorded forestry offences. Importantly, many forest products, such as firewood (the main household fuel) were available to the public at low prices. A monthly fuel ticket in 1983, which allowed a woman to collect 30 head loads of firewood a month, usually cost four Kenya Shillings. Its price had increased by only two Shillings during the past 50 years! In a few places women reported that monthly fuel tickets had been discounted to one or two Shillings because the department wanted deadwood removed from areas newly cleared for plantations. Even at its regular price, the fuel ticket was a bargain compared to the cost of fuelwood elsewhere in the district, where a single head load might sell for four Kenya Shillings. Even a landless family that earned only 10 Kenya Shillings a day in wages could easily afford to buy a ticket.

Restrictive access rules, the presence of guards, and fear of prosecution fostered compliance among forest users. Only women could purchase monthly fuel tickets. They usually went into the forest in groups, bringing *pangas* to cut deadwood into convenient sizes for carrying. Their bundles generally included a variety a species. In the forest north of Kabare location in Gichugu, for example, two groups of women had collected *muthiringu (Strombosia scheffleri)*, *mukaragati (Macaranga kilimandscharica)*, *mutundu (Neoboutonia macrocalyx)*, *mwerere (Tabernaemontana stapfiana)*, *wakarigo (Rytigynia friesiorum)*, *mungo-*

nyoni (*Apodytes dimidiata*), *muriru* (*Syzygium guineense*), *wakabuyu* (unidentified), *mucai* (an unidentified tall timber tree], and *wainyakamure* (unidentified).

Women were allowed to take more than one head load per day as long as they did not exceed their monthly total. They often accumulated several loads at a time, stacking them outside the reserve boundary. Ox carts were not allowed into the reserve to haul loads belonging to fuel ticket holders, but carts waited at the forest line to be hired by them. Teamsters sometimes asked women to show their fuel ticket before carting wood. As an oxcart driver told a woman near the Kiringa River, 'I won't go to jail for you'. That is, he faced penalties if caught hauling wood taken illegally.

Men could buy firewood by the stack, with an annual limit of 50 m^3 per person. Making charcoal in the reserve was restricted to a few areas where trees had been contaminated by a heartwood borer, *Oemida gahani*. A monthly grazing permit cost one Shilling per head of cattle and 20 pence per sheep (goats were excluded). Other forest products were also available, including poles, posts, withies, and bookings at the Kamweti fishing camp. The total revenue in Kamweti from minor forest products amounted to 117 300 Kenya Shillings in 1981.

The level of vigilance among Forest Department staff, including guards, varied widely. In general, guards did not check every person leaving the forest. Record keeping at some guard posts was very casual. It was not uncommon for monthly ledgers of fuelwood and livestock permit holders to be poorly maintained. Interviews with, and observations of, forest users indicated that some illicit activities, such as unauthorized cutting or game poaching to obtain trophies for sale, took place. There was undoubtedly under-reporting of violations among staff who pocketed payments for ignoring violations. Nevertheless, the impression gained from observations and interviews with local forest users and forestry staff in 1982–3 was that the incidence of violations by district households was not serious.

Many forestry staff members felt confident that their performance maintained the integrity of the reserve. A guard stated in 1982, 'Tell the people in Nairobi the Mount Kenya forest is safe.' Within a couple of years, however, there would be serious doubts about the department's effectiveness in managing the forest reserve.

Timber

Although the Mount Kenya forest may have been 'safe' from local households, it was under considerable pressure from commercial users. Officials noted in 1980 that the high demand for timber, woodfuel, and other forest products depleted supplies faster than they could be replenished. An official confirmed in December 1982, 'We do not have enough raw materials to supply demand.' Such shortfalls seemed minor compared to the controversies about forest degradation that erupted later in the decade.

Sharp conflicts arose about logging and deforestation in the southern Mount Kenya forest during the 1980s. A small-scale woodfuel and timber contractor said in October 1982, 'Last year some people said we [licence holders with small-scale operations] were spoiling the forest.' He disputed these charges, arguing that 'big contractors' — sawmills and the tea factories — were responsible for deforestation. Complaints in Kirinyaga about loggers in the Mount Kenya reserve 'wantonly destroying trees' made national headlines in July 1984. Members of the county council offered to take television camera crews into the forest to show the damage. Mwea tenants blamed deforestation for decreased water flow in the streams feeding their irrigation canals. It was a time of severe drought throughout the country. The notion that deforestation affects rainfall is long-standing among the Gikuyu (Routledge and Routledge 1910: 6–8). Ironically, concern that deforestation might impair water supplies was used to justify the appropriation of the forest in the colonial era. The provincial commissioner intervened, ordering local officials to evict the loggers.

More drastic measures were eventually introduced. The central government closed much of the reserve to exploitation, and a presidential ban was placed on harvesting indigenous trees. Such restrictions on forest use in peacetime were unprecedented. A 1986 World Bank mission that carried out a comprehensive review of Kenya's forestry sector in 1986 endorsed the complete closure of Mount Kenya as a protection measure. Only during the Mau Mau Emergency had local access to Mount Kenya been so limited.

Reports about overcutting in the mid-1980s seemed incongruous with official statistics of wood supply and timber production in Kamweti forest during the 1970s and early 1980s. It should be noted that the figures discussed below represented the best available information in Kirinyaga, and that their limitations were indicative of shortcomings in government forest management. According to the World Bank (1986b: 20) forestry sector review, for example, excessive timber cutting licences were issued in the Mount Kenya area, including some granted without the authorization of the national licensing board. Unfortunately, however, the mission offered no quantitative measure, or detailed qualitative accounts, to back up its claim.

Sources of ambiguity and error in official statistics at the district level were not difficult to locate in the early 1980s. An official interviewed in Kirinyaga in late 1982 admitted that the forest statistics were approximations, that no recent inventories had occurred, including surveys of plantation sites. In some areas lax supervision or illicit wood sales by forestry staff caused the amount of timber harvesting to be under-reported. It is impossible to estimate with any precision the extent to which the figures varied with reality. The interviewed official claimed that the statistics were reasonably accurate. Still, it must be emphasized that the figures be treated with caution and regarded as artefacts of a particular style of state resource management.

In 1971 the Forest Department reported about 800 000 m³ of 'potential commercial species' available in Kamweti forest. It is unclear whether this figure included nearly 450 ha of plantation forests, mainly pines and cypress for timber and eucalyptus for fuel existing at the time. Almost half of the plantations were established before 1962, and some trees were ready for harvesting by the 1970s.

Available Kamweti timber production statistics revealed a downward trend during this period: 5123 m³ in 1976; 3516 m³ in 1978; and 1416 m³ in 1981. This decline, however, preceded the ban on the harvest of indigenous timber. Until the mid-1980s, exploitation of native trees occurred on a selection basis. The decline in recorded timber production at Kamweti coincided with a time of increased local demand for building material. High coffee prices in the mid-1970s set off a construction boom, causing timber to be in short supply. Increased incomes in the tea zone also fueled the demand for timber. People often grumbled about the high price of sawn wood in the early 1980s. Thus, ample incentives existed for commercial timber suppliers.

A combination of circumstantial and structural factors can be identified to explain the pattern of declining timber exploitation at Kamweti during the late

1970s and early 1980s. Exceptionally wet conditions obstructed logging in 1978, 1979, and possibly other years as well. Prolonged wet and misty periods ruined roads and tracks, often making them impassable for days. The owner of a local sawmill stated, 'You can never say how many days until the roads dry.' The relatively large timber harvest in 1976 coincided with an unusually dry year in the forest. But weather alone did not explain Kamweti timber trends. Conditions for logging were more favourable in 1981 than in 1978, yet timber extraction dropped.

The felling of easily accessible indigenous timber trees in earlier years proba-bly contributed to the decline in production. As described in Chapter 6, timber exploitation in the southern Mount Kenya forest was not very extensive during colonial times. Few sawmills operated in the area prior to 1950, and Gikuyu pit-sawyers worked only on a tightly supervised basis.

Competition from other supply sources often reduced the demand for Kamweti timber. Njukiine forest, which is managed for the Kirinyaga and Embu County Councils by the department, emerged as a major supplier of pine and cypress (see Chapter 10). Located on the border with Embu, Njukiine is easily accessible by road, and its distinctly drier climate makes forest tracks less prone to closure during the wet season. Nearly all of its native forest had been replaced by exotics for timber and fuel purposes. Local sawmills and sawyers also sought out trees from local farms, as well as from plantation forests near Nyeri and Naro Moru.

Many production constraints were encountered by very small-scale timber contractors. They obtained wood on a salvage basis, working deadwood and trees rejected by sawmills. Their operations were seasonal and labour intensive, usually relying on axes and handsaws. Few figures were available on their output. During 1978 they harvested 864 m³ of timber at Kamweti, a larger amount than some local sawmills. Still, the small-scale contractors only removed one-quarter of the logs reportedly taken from Kamweti that year. In general, they lacked the equipment, transport, and operating capital necessary to engage in timber pro-duction and marketing on a substantial basis. Some felt hard pressed to meet royalty fees for trees and business permits. There was some unlicensed produc-tion, but not all contractors or pit-sawyers engaged in illegal harvesting.

The district's timber industry also suffered from the lacklustre performance of many local sawmills. Kirinyaga's mills were small-scale operations. None of the three sawmills licensed to exploit Kamweti forest in 1975 were prospering at the end of the decade. Nyamindi Sawmill, which cropped 467 m³ of logs in 1975 and 175 m³ in 1977, closed in 1979. It experienced chronic management and transport problems. Kamugi Sawmill, the leading harvester at Kamweti during the mid-1970s, severely curtailed operations by the end of the decade. In 1978 it had removed nearly 1200 m³ of indigenous logs. Despite taking 663 m³ in 1975, Irangi Sawmill 'did not do well'. It closed two years later. Kutus Sawmill became a Kamweti licence holder in the late 1970s. It harvested 238 m³ from Kamweti in 1977 and 445 m³ in 1978. Recent figures on timber extraction by individual sawmills are unavailable.

Kirinyaga's sawmills were generally undercapitalized. Sawmills often lacked money for necessary fixed investments: power saws, vehicles, business premises, electrical hook-ups, and so on. Chronic shortages of working capital also under-mined productivity. The mills often had trouble meeting basic obligations: equip-ment maintenance, timber royalties, utility bills, business licences, labour, and other requirements. Rough roads and poorly maintained lumber trucks led to numerous problems. Lorries incapacitated by flat tires, mechanical breakdowns, or punctured sumps were common sights along forest roads. Inadequate or insufficient training in sawmill practices and business management were serious obstacles in some cases.

Not every sawmill was on the brink of collapse. A sawmill owned by a Kenyan citizen of Asian descent seemed well-equipped and prosperous by local standards. According to its owner, the mill could handle up to eight lorry loads of logs a day, although the actual amount handled by the mill fluctuated. Besides planks and boards, the sawmill sold wood scraps and shavings, offering them in two-Shilling and 10-Shilling piles. Sawdust was free to anyone wanting it, and the owner pointed out, 'Many come to get it.' Both sawdust and wood scraps were used as fuel. This sawmill also had a *posho* (grain) mill on its premises.

Yacoob Deen Company, a long-standing sawmill in Karatina township in Nyeri, continued to harvest both indigenous and exotic species from the forest near Chehe. It processed camphor and podo, as well as cypress obtained from plantations. A brief illustrated account of its wood-processing operations is presented in J.A. Ojiambo's (1978) book on Kenyan forests.

The Kirinyaga Timber Co-operative Society

A case study of the Kirinyaga Timber Co-operative Society (KTCS) illustrates problems faced by a significant number of small-scale timber producers. It was organized by the government in 1967 to co-ordinate and to improve production by pit-sawyers. Similar societies were established in Embu and Meru. Like the small-scale fuel contractors, the sawyers cleared worked-out sawmill concessions, taking logs which could not be profitably removed by the mills. They also worked in areas regarded as inaccessible by the mills.

A local timber shortage in 1966, which officials blamed largely on 'the bad management' of pit-sawyers, prompted the effort to organize the co-operative. To encourage membership in the society, forest officers selected trees only for KTCS members. Pit-sawyers who refused to join the society were forced to abandon the reserve. By 1977 the co-operative reportedly had 463 members and 15 staff members.

The new co-operative was quickly immersed in political factionalism. Financial and management disputes led to new elections for society officers in August 1967, only months after the first ones had been selected. The struggle for leadership was split along Gichugu-Ndia territorial lines. By 1970 the co-operative was in a crisis. Its licence had not been renewed, nor had its officers discussed logging needs with foresters. The government intervened in an effort to unite the factions, and an investigation uncovered some misappropriation of funds.

In spite of difficulties, the Forest Department encouraged the society to expand its operations. The KTCS had been allowed to harvest up to 1000 m³ of wood, but the government offered to triple this if the co-operative set up a sawmill. As part of the deal, the department would have managerial control of the sawmill. The KTCS approved, requesting a foreign expert to assist it in planning the new unit. The mill was eventually built near Kianyaga Township in Gichugu. The KTCS also applied for a 30 000 Kenya Shillings loan to provide members with working capital.

The society failed to achieve its intended production goals. For example, recorded harvests at Kamweti were only 323 m³ in 1977 and 739 m³ in 1978. In addition, the co-operative experienced chronic financial problems. By 1980 the KTCS had accumulated nearly 500 000 Kenya Shillings in unpaid commissions and fees to the District Co-operative Union. This debt represented a large sum, especially compared to the society's reported yearly turnover: 120 000 Kenya Shillings in 1976, 635 000 Kenya Shillings in 1977, and 750 975 Kenya Shillings in 1978. Low payouts were said to be a problem, but figures on net income were unavailable except for 1977. That year members received 281 260 Kenya Shillings, only 44 per cent of gross sales.

The problems experienced by the KTCS, many sawmills, and small-scale wood and fuel contractors generally during the 1970s and early 1980s contrasted with the account of heavy logging in 1984. As will be discussed below, the deforestation reported that year was related to plans for accelerated conversion of indigenous woodland into plantation forests, particularly for fuelwood purposes. According to informants, such plans had existed since early in the decade. This wood was to be used primarily by two of the district's tea factories.

Tea factories

In many ways tea, through its consumption of fuelwood in processing and its potential as an alternative land use, posed the most serious threat to the forest. The leaves of *Camellia sinensis* need to be processed within a few hours after plucking to maintain their commercial quality. A high priority is attached to the operation and efficiency of local tea-processing facilities or 'factories' managed by the Kenya Tea Development Authority. There are four factories in Kirinyaga: Kangaita (opened in 1965), Thumaita (1975), Kimunye (1977), and Ndima (1982). The latter factory is located on the Ndia-Mathira boundary and receives green leaf from both Kirinyaga and Nyeri. Each factory is set up as a separate firm, and local growers can purchase shares in them at a cost of five Kenya Shillings apiece. Because of the steady increase in the area under production since independence, the factories have been asked to handle larger and larger volumes of the crop. In the 1983/84 fiscal year the four factories processed 28 729 445 kg of green leaf, and by 1987/88 this rose to 38 112 627 kg, a 33 per cent increase. Kangaita often processed more green leaf than any of the other 30-plus KTDA factories in the early 1980s, while Ndima ranked second in the country during 1983/84. Indeed, the Kirinyaga factories were at times on the verge of being swamped by green leaf from local smallholders.

As mentioned earlier, Kirinyaga's smallholders produce some of the most commercially valuable tea in the country. In 1983/84, when global tea prices reached record levels, Kirinyaga growers earned over 179 million Kenya Shillings. Although world market prices sharply declined in subsequent years, local growers still received a total payout of more than 185 million Kenya Shillings in 1987/88. The money generated by tea was warmly welcomed at the national and local levels. Tea emerged as a major source of foreign exchange, 'delivering the golden eggs the treasury so badly need[ed]' (*Farming Review*, July 1985: 5). Families in the upper zone of Kirinyaga relied on income or daily wages to purchase such necessities as food or fuel, to pay school fees or related expenses, or to make investments in land and shops. The payout method for tea made it especially popular. Growers received two types of returns from the KTDA: a monthly payout based on a fixed rate for green leaf delivered to buying centres, and a yearly lump payment based on the remaining value of their output at a price determined by their factory's performance in world and national markets.

The KTDA has become known as one of Africa's most efficient agrarian bureaucracies (Lamb and Muller 1982; Grosh 1991). The cost-conscious agency has tried to reduce factory operating expenses through a number of strategies, including substituting furnace oil with fuelwood for drying processed tea. Two of Kirinyaga's factories used wood fuel by the early 1980s: Kangaita, which had switch to fuelwood apparently in the late 1970s, and Thumaita, a recent convert. The two facilities were the largest single consumers of wood fuel in the district. An official report in 1980 estimated that the factories would burn 10 000 m³ and 7500 m³ of wood per year, respectively (Akinga 1980: 21). A KTDA official interviewed in late 1983, however, revealed that annual fuelwood use was higher: 12 000 m³ for Kangaita and 9000 m³ for Thumaita. Ragati factory, to the west of Ndima in Nyeri, also relied on fuelwood for drying tea.

According to local KTDA officials, the use of fuelwood greatly reduced energy costs. Kenya depends on imported petroleum because it lacks reserves of its own. In the 1970s and early 1980s rising petroleum prices contributed to the country's severe balance of payment problems. The fossil fuel 'famine' of late 1982 was indicative of the nation's difficulty in paying for imported fuel. In contrast, the royalty charged for stacked firewood from forest plantations was said to be very low. According to a World Bank report (1986c: 29), the stumpage rate only recovered one-third to one-half of the department's production costs. Thus, by switching to fuelwood, the factories would be subsidized by the low rate. A KTDA official estimated that the price of wood fuel per unit of energy in 1982 was half that of furnace oil. Fuelwood had other advantages. Tea is processed year-round, placing a premium on continuity of supply. Furnace oil deliveries were sometimes delayed, particularly when tankers broke down or the wet season made roads impassable. Roads in tea areas throughout the country went 'from bad to worse' in the early 1980s, adding to the difficulties. Kangaita and Thumaita were able to maintain large stockpiles of wood obtained from the nearby forest reserve.

In theory, 21 000 m³ of roundwood for the tea factories is equivalent to the harvest from approximately 120 ha of plantations or 70 ha of closed forest. It was unclear, however, how much land was actually harvested on an annual basis in the Mount Kenya plantations and forest to supply the tea factories. Eucalyptus plantations near Kangaita, Chehe, and elsewhere in the reserve provided some of the tea factories' needs. Information was not available for review on the output of these plantations. However, an official admitted in 1982, 'We don't have enough exotics, so we are cutting indigenous trees.' Sizeable tracts of indigenous forest were being clear-cut, though exact figures were unavailable.

The KTDA planned in the early 1980s to increase the use of fuelwood and alternative energy sources in the factories. It regarded fuel substitution as necessary given the rising cost of imported oil and the programme to increase factory capacity. Officials wanted to substitute wood for furnace oil for withering green leaf at Kangaita and Thumaita. They also intended to switch Kimunye and Ndima to fuelwood, raising wood consumption in Kirinyaga a minimum of 15 000 m³ per annum (Akinga 1980: 21). In fact, the KTDA intended to convert 22 factories in Central Province and adjacent parts of Eastern Province to wood use, raising total consumption to an estimated of 167 500 m³ per annum. Officials acknowledged that forest resources would be hard pressed to meet such a large and continuous demand (Akinga 1980: 24). There was no attempt to develop a wood-supply source for the tea industry among local smallholders, even though many families readily planted trees for commercial and home use (see Castro 1983; Brokensha *et al.* 1983).

Local KTDA officers stated in 1982 and 1983 that proposed fuel conversions in Kirinyaga were constrained by the already substantial demand on wood supplies. The situation was similar at other tea factories throughout the country. By the late 1980s most processing facilities, apparently including Kangaita and Thumaita, reverted at least partly to furnace oil for drying tea because of wood scarcity. By 1988, only four factories in the country relied on fuelwood as the sole source of energy to dry tea, including Ragati, compared to seven facilities a few years earlier.

Reforestation and deforestation

The need to supply large amounts of wood for tea processing had been long anticipated by the Forest Department. As early as 1961, local foresters looked forward to selling as much as 1000 tons of stacked fuelwood per month from Kamweti for a soon-to-be-constructed tea factory in the district, presumably at Kangaita. The sale of so much wood on a regular basis seemed a blessing, offering a steady source of revenue.

With financial support from the World Bank, the department for years maintained its strategy of meeting prospective fuelwood and timber demand through the expansion of industrial plantations. As in the past, exotic species were favoured because they were regarded as faster growing, hardier, and more commercially valuable than indigenous species. The financial returns for exotic plantations were seen as much higher per unit of land than for indigenous forest (World Bank 1986b: 51). In Kirinyaga the department replaced indigenous forest with plantations of pine and cypress for timber and eucalyptus for fuelwood.

The *shamba* (*taungya*) system of reafforestation continued to be used, combining tree planting and temporary farming in cleared areas (FAO 1978). For many years the colonial pattern remained intact: workers and their families received a small wage, housing, access to land for growing food crops, and the right to pasture up to 15 sheep in return for nine-months service for the department. The workers and their households expected to clear land, plant trees, and keep the plantations weeded. Other duties included road construction and nursery work. In 1976, though, full-time department labourers were absorbed into the civil service. The resident forest workers now received a higher wage, but they were forced to pay a small rent of 70 Kenya Shillings per year for temporary access to land for farming. According to a World Bank report (1986b), this labour force was poorly supervised, lacked incentives for performance, and suffered from low productivity. Nevertheless, such workers remained indispensable for carrying out, however ineffectively, the department's annual planting programme. Clusters of *shamba* labourer settlements were located near long-established plantation sites such as Chehe and Castle, while some workers resided in recently cleared areas. There was also a growing number of retirees, forest workers of the late 1950s, who had been allowed to remain in the forest as part of their original terms of employment. The World Bank mission (1986b: 19) blamed much of the 'encroachment' problem in the Mount Kenya region on the retirees. In contrast, forest workers and retirees interviewed in 1982 and 1983 regarded the provisioning of housing to be one of the main inducements for their jobs.

The yearly target for plantation expansion at Kamweti was 30 ha in the mid-1970s. It was increased in the latter part of the decade. In 1978, 20 ha of Mexican pine (*Pinus patula*) and 18 ha of *Eucalyptus saligna* were established at Kamweti. Even higher annual targets were set by 1980: 50 ha of eucalyptus plantations to meet the energy needs of Kangaita and Thumaita factories; and 30 ha of timber species. Local records indicated that tree planting lagged behind the department's afforestation schedule in the early 1980s. Only 21.5 ha of eucalyptus and 19.6 ha of cypress, for example, were reportedly planted at Kamweti in 1981. These figures, an official cautioned in late 1982, were estimates, pending a survey of the plantations. Meanwhile, large areas of forest continued to be cut to meet the demand for fuelwood from the tea factories.

Several informants mentioned plans in 1983 to accelerate and expand the planting of exotics, particularly eucalyptus for fuel plantations. Large areas adjacent to the forest edge were already slated for conversion. This activity was connected to a national development and environmental strategy devised in conjuction with two United Nations agencies. The strategy called for converting one-fifth of the country's gazetted forests and woodland into industrial plantations. It sought to make Kenya self-sufficient in sawn wood and to generate a surplus of timber for export. In some places buffer zones of plantations were to be established between the forest and settled areas to reduce encroachment.

Many potentially negative consequences of forest conversion had been considered in government planning and were felt to be either negligible, as in the case of stream flow, or otherwise acceptable, such as the loss of some wildlife habitat. Several studies in the highlands indicated, for example, that the replacement of native forest by exotic plantations had no adverse impacts on the hydrological balance or soil erosion (Dunne and Aubry 1981: 49; Ministry of Environment and Natural Resources 1981: 209). In terms of biological diversity, planners apparently assumed that the southern Mount Kenya forest was not an especially unique biome. There was concern that monocultural plantations were susceptible to pests. However, it was felt that ecologically balanced exotic forest plantations could be developed.

Unfortunately, there was no ongoing monitoring in the early 1980s of how the components and processes of the southern Mount Kenya ecosystem were affected by forest conversion. The compatibility of forest clearing and plantation expansion with diverse local uses of the reserve, such as watershed or collection of medicinal plants, was not discussed with district residents. Only in the late 1980s and early 1990s would the still substantial gaps in knowledge about the ecology and land use of southern Mount Kenya forest be identified by outside researchers (see Winiger et al. 1990; Castro 1991).

Much of the forest degradation in southern Mount Kenya during the early 1980s derived from clearing to supply fuel for tea factories and the plan to expand plantation forestry. As clearing took place, Forest Department employees often were unable, or at times unwilling, to maintain control over the reserve. Loggers, pit-sawyers, and others took advantage of the situation, and parts of the forest reportedly suffered heavy encroachment (*Daily Nation*, 23 July 1984: 16). A Kenyan periodical claimed that forests throughout the country were 'indiscriminately felled because of the enticing lure of a tea boom' (*Farming Review*, July 1985: 5). Still, large areas of indigenous forest remained intact in southern Mount Kenya (Agatsiva 1990). Meanwhile, the *shamba* system unravelled to some extent, when only 25 ha of cypress and 8 ha of eucalyptus were planted in 1985, far below the department's targets. Cleared areas were not promptly replanted, and labourers were reportedly more interested in growing their own food crops than protecting tree seedlings (World Bank 1986b). By the middle of the decade the Forest Department abandoned its plans to convert massive tracts of indigenous forests, stating that plantations would be established only in already cleared areas.

The limitations of state management were also manifested in official statistics about the Mount Kenya forest area in Kirinyaga. The *Kenya Statistical Abstract* of 1991 still listed the government forest area as 308 km². The Kenya Rangeland Ecological Monitoring Unit in the Ministry of Planning used remote sensing in 1981 to estimate its area as 29 365 ha (World Bank 1986b: 4). The Forest Department showed the government forest area in 1985 as covering 29 215 ha. The 1984 *District Development Plan* prepared by local officials listed the forest area as 27 621 ha, though no source was provided.

The Forest Department reported that 1117 ha of industrial plantations had been established in Kirinyaga by 1985, over four times the amount in 1961. Most of the current plantations consisted of exotic softwoods for timber: pines (422 ha) and cypress (361 ha). Eucalyptus for fuel covered 302 ha, and an unspecified hardwood was grown on 32 ha for timber purposes. Thus, roughly 4 per cent of Kamweti forest had been converted into monocultural plantations of exotic trees. The department did not disclose how much land had been cleared but remained unplanted.

By the mid-1980s the Forest Department was considering innovative approaches to reafforestation in state reserves, including agroforestry strategies (World Bank 1986a). The rise of such interests probably reflected increasing expertise in the department in the field of community forestry. In particular, the Rural Afforestation Extension Scheme (RAES), started in the 1970s, took foresters outside the government forest estate and placed them in contact with district households. Although tree-growing schemes had been directed at rural households since the earliest years of colonial rule, these had usually been the responsibility of administrative or agricultural officers (see Castro, forthcoming). The RAES offered an important avenue for rethinking forestry in Kenya. An extension forester in Kirinyaga interviewed in the early 1980s admitted that he felt initially his posting to RAES had been 'a punishment'. Serious forestry, he thought at the time, meant working in plantations of exotic species. After several years in RAES, however, the forester now regarded working with rural households as very effective and personally rewarding.

Still, strong support remained in some quarters for custodial forestry. An annex in a 1986 World Bank review of Kenyan forestry contained the following recommendations about harvesting in the reserves: 'Tighten supervision . . . [by] increasing inspection in the forest of logging activities, increasing patrols for illegal cutting, improving supervision of foresters and forest guards, and supplying adequate vehicles and other resources to carry out these expanded activities' (World Bank 1986b: 55). One wonders whether the 'other resources' included night-vision goggles for paramilitary forestry squads. Such thinking remained frozen in the 'man is the enemy' mode, instead of seeking out innovative ways to interact with local forest users as partners in resource management.

Revenue farms

The administrations of Kenyatta and Moi often pledged their support for the continued conservation of Kenya's forests. Yet, there have been mounting demographic and economic pressures to excise state forest lands for agricultural purposes. The conversion of forests into farmland offers only limited possibilities for meeting the country's land scarcity problem. Because of steep terrain, high altitudes, and cool, overly damp climates, the potential for agricultural production is probably more limited than suggested by a review of soils and agro-ecological zones (World Bank 1986b: 49–53). In addition, the magnitude of Kenya's rapidly growing population is such that only a small fraction of it could be accommodated on forest lands suitable for farming. In spite of such limitations, some forest areas are very capable of sustaining intensive agriculture, including tea. According to the World Bank (1986b: 50), tea furnished the highest financial rate of return per unit of land in suitable parts of the highlands. Whether to maintain forest cover or convert such areas to other purposes has been a major issue since independence.

The Kangaita Tea Nursery was founded in the mid-1950s to supply seedlings and cuttings for the region's budding tea industry. Nowadays run by the KTDA, it expanded to become one of the country's largest tea nurseries. Part of this growth included the clearance of 80 ha of forest in 1966. By the late 1980s Kangaita nursery contained 167 ha of tea plantations, plus additional land for offices and staff housing. One-fifth of its tea fields were used in 1988 to produce planting stock for smallholders and the Office of the President's new Nyayo Tea Zones. The rest of the tea bushes furnished over 553 000 kg of green leaf for processing into black tea valued at 2.4 million Kenya Shillings. The highly productive tea gardens of the nursery and nearby smallholders demonstrated what money could be earned by converting the forest, if the government allowed it.

There have been numerous proposals since independence for converting part of the reserve into tea estates. The Kirinyaga County Council, a local governing body composed of elected and appointed members from different parts of the district, served as the local forum for discussing such ideas. Its first request came in 1967, shortly after the expansion of Kangaita nursery. A councillor proposed that a strip of state forest lands be handed over to the local landless for growing tea. Another council member added that undeveloped forest land should be made to serve 'a useful purpose'. The council soon reconsidered the request. Two councillors emphasized the watershed value of the forest, stating that the flow of several rivers in the district had decreased 'due to lack of trees'. The council not only withdrew its request, it called on local families to plant more trees around their homesteads.

The Kenyatta government excised 65 ha of the Mount Kenya forest in 1969 for a KTDA experimental farm at Kagochi near Ragati station. The Kagochi estate not only served as a research facility, it provided a substantial sum for KTDA through tea sales. In the 1987/8 crop season, for example, its 47 ha of plantations produced 535 000 kg of green leaf worth more than three million Kenya Shillings. Once again, the conversion of forest into tea fields by the central government revealed the agro-economic potential of the forest reserve.

Coinciding with the Kagochi excision was the revival of the proposed Kirinyaga council tea farm for the landless. Once again, the council asked for forest land from the Ministry of Natural Resources. This time the central government explicitly rejected the request. The permanent secretary in the ministry told them the forest was needed to maintain the country's water supply. He advised the council to seek room for its landless in the resettlement schemes scattered throughout the nation. Councillors noted the contents of the letter with 'regret'. However, the government eventually returned 100 ha of Nyagithuci Forest it had managed on the council's behalf since colonial times. The land was used to resettle families displaced by the expansion of public schools.

The Kirinyaga councillors made another proposal to the central government for a tea farm in 1981. They offered to relinquish half of the council's share of Njukiine forest, trust land consisting mainly of exotic plantations straddling the

Gichugu-Embu border. In return, the council wanted land in the Mount Kenya forest for growing tea. Proponents of the trade wanted to establish a tea farm so the council could generate more revenue. The Kirinyaga County Council was in financial trouble, having ended 1980 with a deficit of 1 250 000 Kenya Shillings. To meet its financial obligations the council had been forced to withdraw 1 750 000 Kenya Shillings held in reserve. At the time tea had emerged as the most popular cash crop in the district, offering councillors a strong financial incentive. The landless were not mentioned in the council minutes describing the proposed property exchange. Presumably they were to benefit by serving as employees of the council, planting and plucking the tea. The central government apparently rejected the offer.

A brief visit to Kirinyaga in 1988 revealed that a tea farm has been established within the Mount Kenya reserve. However, it was unlike the County Council's proposal. The strip of land was part of the central government's new Nyayo Tea Zone. In February 1985 the Ministry of Environment and Natural Resources announced a plan to grow tea in the nation's forest reserves. The scheme was reportedly the 'brainchild' of President Daniel arap Moi, a Kalenjin who constitutionally succeeded Jomo Kenyatta following the Gikuyu leader's death from natural causes in 1978 (*Daily Nation*, 17 Oct. 1985). Although Moi entered office a nominal reformer, he ended up much like Kenyatta: an authoritarian leader who favoured his own ethnic group and close political allies (see Widner 1992).

The Nyayo scheme called for creating a 100-metre belt of tea on gazetted land along the rim of forest reserves in Kirinyaga, Meru, Nandi Hills, Marakwet, Elgeyo, and other places. There were varying accounts in the press of the total amount of land to be involved, ranging from 6000 ha to 17 000 ha (*Weekly Review*, 25 Apr. 1985: 23; 1 Sept. 1986: 19; *Farming Review*, July 1985: 5). The tea belt was announced as a conservation measure: to protect reserves from encroachment by creating buffers between forests and settled areas. The strips of low-lying tea would create a space in which forest guards could readily detect the movement of 'trespassers' (Widner 1992: 186). Soil stability would be restored by growing tea on degraded lands. The scheme was also supposed to increase tea output (its announcement occurred in the midst of a price boom), generate foreign exchange, and create jobs locally.

The Ministry of Agriculture initially ran the scheme, but the Office of the President soon took control of the Nyayo Tea Zones Development Corporation. Kalenjin supporters of Moi were placed in charge of the new parastatal agency (Widner 1992: 180). President Moi ordered the district commissioners to organize the tea zones in conjunction with forestry and agriculture officials. Throughout the nation much of the land used in the project was wooded rather than deforested, with forest clearing at times stretching 'a mile wide' (Widner 1992: 187). Officials tried to reduce planting costs by allowing workers to harvest the wood in exchange for land preparation (World Bank 1986b). The KTDA, including Kangaita tea nursery, supplied over 41 million cuttings in 1987/8 alone for the project. About 15 000 workers were employed nation-wide to tend to the fields and harvest the crop (Widner 1992: 187). Information was not available on the extent of the scheme in Kirinyaga, though a quick visit to the area in 1988 revealed that a strip of land along a sizeable length of reserve boundary had been converted.

No new factories were planned in the late 1980s to handle the Nyayo scheme's tea harvest. The KTDA was assigned the task of processing its output. Some accounts indicated that increased green leaf production from the scheme flooded transport and factory facilities in Central Province, including Kirinyaga, and other smallholder areas. KTDA leaf carriers were told to give priority to the Nyayo zone tea, and local growers experienced crop losses because of lack of transport or insufficient factory capacity.

According to Jennifer Widner (1992: 187), events in the tea sector were connected to wider political strategies by the Moi regime aimed at consolidating political control over the export crop sector. The Nyayo scheme enhanced the government's control over land resources and increased its revenue from tea. At the same time it reduced the economic power of smallholders and contributed to a decline in their political influence. Widner acknowledges that many aspects about the operations of the Nyayo Tea Zones Development Corporation, however, remain unclear.

The World Bank mission (1986b: 54) called the scheme 'a good idea in principle'. Of course the notion of agricultural buffer zones around Mount Kenya was not a new idea: Hutchins proposed it as early as 1907 as a colonial forest control measure. However, World Bank analysts refused to endorse the tea belts because of the lack of information about the scheme's costs, benefits, and management. In fact, the Nyayo Tea Development Corporation has continued to possess an aura of mystery since its placement in the Office of the President.

While many aspects of the Nyayo scheme remain uncertain, one general conclusion can be drawn: the genuineness of government's policy of creating better barriers to protect the forest reserve was very questionable. This chapter has argued throughout that forest degradation in southern Mount Kenya during the 1980s was largely attributable to state policies and officially sanctioned development activities. Calling the scheme a conservation measure was unfair to the local population. Quite clearly, the tea zones were chiefly a mechanism for promoting the economic and political interests of the Moi regime. In the realities of Kenyan politics, appropriation of state forest lands in Gikuyu country for the benefit of the Kalenjin-dominated Moi administration could have been viewed as too provocative an act. Thus, promotion of environmental protection and rural development served as guises, just as they had in the colonial past, for outsiders to enhance their control over the resources and people of Mount Kenya.

Conclusion

Despite independence and the Africanization of government administration, there has been much continuity in the state management of the Mount Kenya forest reserve. Government policies and practices assumed that district households and small-scale forest users posed the greatest threat to the reserve. Yet, in the first two decades after independence, official records, field observations, and interviews indicated that the incidence of forest offences in Kirinyaga was relatively minor. It should be pointed out that the situation in the district between the 1960s and early 1980s differed from that occurring in some other parts of the country, especially Western Kenya, where local encroachment in the forest reserves was often endemic. Indeed, officials with experience elsewhere in Kenya commented on this during interviews in 1982 and early 1983.

Although local encroachment was not a serious problem in the early 1980s, the district forestry staff acknowledged that the reserve was not managed on a sustained-yield basis. In fact, there were no guidelines for balancing the use and replenishing of forest resources in southern Mount Kenya. Two tea factories, which were operated by a parastatal and partially owned by local tea-growing households, were the largest consumers of wood in the district. In contrast, timber harvesting in the reserve appeared to be on the decline, at least according to official records. Sawmills, rather than pit-sawyers, cut the largest amount of timber, although both small- and medium-scale producers often encountered difficulties remaining in business.

A major turning-point was reached in the mid-1980s, associated with the implementation of government plans to convert large tracts of indigenous woodland into forest plantations. The system of forest supervision, as well as reafforestation, broke down. Much uncontrolled cutting and cultivating occurred. Some groups within the district, including county councillors and Mwea–Tebere irrigation tenants who depended on the reserve for watershed, protested about the situation. There was significant intervention by provincial administration and central government, with severe restrictions placed on forest use. The Forest Department abandoned its plans to convert large tracts of reserve into monocultural plantations comprised of exotic species. In addition, a narrow belt of government tea was planted along the reserve boundary as a buffer zone.

The government's emphasis on curtailing local use of the forest and setting up buffer zones deflected attention from the state's role in deforestation. It has been argued throughout this chapter that much of the forest degradation in southern Mount Kenya during the 1980s was attributable to government policies and officially sanctioned development activities. This conclusion is not to minimize the ever-increasing subsistence pressures in the country and region, or the role that local people have played in damaging the reserve. However, the pattern of forest degradation should not be seen simply as the outcome of population growth in a resource-scarce economy, or the result of short-sighted land use practices by impoverished rural dwellers. Rather, the events in southern Mount Kenya must be understood in the context of state resource-management policies and practices, as well as national politics.

9. Sacred groves and social change in Kirinyaga: the decline of communal bonds

SACRED GROVES OFFER a window for understanding social change in Kirinyaga Gikuyu society. Such trees were once key cultural institutions associated with rites and ceremonies that fostered a sense of community among dispersed homesteads. Many sacred groves were associated with the generation-set holding ritual power over the land, while others were part of lineage or family affairs. The decline in the religious and social value of sacred groves during the twentieth century derived from, and was indicative of, emerging social divisions among the people of Kirinyaga. Thus, the purpose of this chapter is to analyse the links between religious ideology, socio-economic and political change, and shifts in the use and management of a particular and locally significant form of communal property: sacred groves. Although the chapter focuses on Ndia and Gichugu, comparative information is included from other parts of central Kenya.

The sacred groves

The Kirinyaga Gikuyu and their neighbours customarily used selected trees and groves as places of worship and sacrifice. Individual families made offerings to Ngai (addressed in prayer as Mwene Nyaga, 'The Bright One') and ancestral spirits at a tree or shrub near their homestead (Hobley 1967: 48; Leakey 1977c: 1081–1101). Sometimes a tree was planted for this purpose in the homestead's yard. In other cases a tree or bush used in a ceremony was not specially dedicated beforehand. After the ceremony it was not treated as possessing any extraordinary spiritual significance. Lineage elders occasionally picked particular copses to serve as regular *mbari* sacrificial sites (Leakey 1977c: 1078–81). These trees were deliberately protected and often used from generation to generation. The extent to which lineages recognized one another as members of the same clan was partly defined by shared participation in such ceremonies (Maxwell *et al.* 1929b: 7).

The most important sacred groves were those designated by the people of a particular locality as places of communal worship and sacrifice (Routledge and Routledge 1910; Barlow 1913; Bēech 1913a, 1913b; Dundas 1915; Kenyatta 1938; Lambert 1956; Hobley 1967; Mwaniki 1974; Leakey 1977c). Indeed, the extent of local or neighbourhood identity was essentially defined, and certainly reinforced, by shared worship at sacred groves. Such trees were called *matiiri* or *miti wa Ngai* ('trees of God'). They were regarded as communal property under the control of the local generation-set (*rika* or *nduki*) elders. Members of the Aithaiga clan also acted as guardians of sacred groves (Baker 1931: 196–7). In a few cases these trees were associated with a renowned healer or prophet, but no exclusive ownership was implied (Hobley 1967: 40). Where the local territorial groups such as the *itura* ('parish') consisted primarily of people from the same lineage, the *mbari's* and community's sacred groves were probably one and the same. In addition, the local territorial or descent group council (*kiama*) and *rika* were not entirely distinct entities because many of their members overlapped.

Selected elders performed ceremonies in the sacred groves to nurture newly planted crops, offer thanksgiving for harvests, induce rain, protect warriors, and ritually cleanse the land. An informant from Nduini in Inoi, Ndia, recalled a ceremony to invoke rainfall:

108

Irungu [generation-set] . . . met when there was no rain. They offered a sheep or goat as sacrifice. When they completed the slaughtering, rain would automatically fall. The slaughtered goat was eaten by Irungu, not taken home. If they were unable to finish it, they burnt it to ashes.

Important sacrifices were conducted in times of disaster, such as crop failures, epidemics, epizootics, and locust infestations. People also held special dances in the groves.

The trees were also involved in ceremonies marking group rites of passage — initiation into age-sets and advancement to senior elder status. (Barlow 1913; Kenyatta 1938; Mwaniki 1974; Leakey 1977b; Davison 1989: 96). Initiation was particularly important, since it bestowed rights of marriage and procreation. The ceremony occurred annually for girls and over a cycle of years for boys. The various ceremonies held in the groves were important for neighbourhoods because they cut across kin groups and occurred with enough regularity to instil a sense of communal identity. The *ituika* ceremony, a very important yet rare event involving the transfer of ritual power from one *rika* to another, also took place in the groves. It occurred roughly once a generation, involving extensive co-ordination of activities throughout Ndia and Gichugu. Shared participation in *ituika* rites defined multi-community territorial identities (Dundas 1915: 239–41). The handing-over ceremonies in Ndia and Gichugu, for example, were held separately from those in Embu and Mbeere, or Mathira and Tetu (Lambert 1956).

The sacred groves were widely distributed. H.S.K. Mwaniki (1974: 258–9, 282) was told by Kirinyaga elders, 'Every ridge had at least one of these groves', and, 'Every locality had a sacred grove, like a church, for such sacrifices'. In the early 1930s each of Kirinyaga's administrative *itura* (pl. *matura*), a cluster of homesteads based to some extent on the pre-colonial social unit of the same name, had at least one sacred grove. At the time 202 sacred groves were recorded by the Embu Local Native Council in Ndia's and Gichugu's nearly 160 *matura*. Not everyone who occupied land near a particular sacred grove worshipped at it. The Mbeere had two sacred groves in lower Mwea that were not used by the Ndia Gikuyu, for example, even though the latter spent much of the year in the area herding cattle.

In the midst of thickly cultivated countryside, the sacred trees stood out as landmarks (Stigand 1913: 242). They were often located on the top of hills and ridges. The groves varied in size and composition. The sacred groves seen by Colin Maher (1938a: 153) in Kirinyaga during the late 1930s ranged from .04 ha to 1.20 ha. The groves usually consisted of several tall trees with spreading branches, plus a dense understorey of smaller trees, woody shrubs, and bush. The Gikuyu preferred huge trees because they resembled the abode of Ngai (Beech 1913a; Kenyatta 1938: 236). Some of the big trees were more than 30 metres high. A single tree within a grove often formed the focal point of ceremonies, but the entire grove itself was considered sacred. Large wild figs with spreading branches were the sacred tree *par excellence*: *Ficus natalensis* (*mugumo*), and to a lesser extent, *Ficus wakefieldii* (*muumbo*) in moist northern and central Kirinyaga; and *Ficus capensis* (*mukuyu*) in the drier southern lowlands. Figs which started as epiphytes and eventually engulfed their hosts were particularly preferred. Not every fig tree was sacred, nor were figs always found in the groves. Maher (1938a: 153) saw a Ndia sacred grove, for example, composed almost exclusively of *Syzygium guineense* (*mukui*) and *Albizzia gummifera* (*mukurue*). Other tree species noted in present-day groves included *Pygeum africanum* (*mweria*), *Cordia abyssinica* (*muringa*), *Bridelia micanthra*, *Trichilia emetica* (*mururi*), *Phoenix reclinata* (*mukindu*), and *Markhamia hildebrandtii* (*muu*). Bernard Riley and David Brokensha (1988a: 199–200) identified over 30 tree species in neighbouring Mbeere's still well-preserved sacred groves during the 1970s.

With few exceptions the sacred groves were inviolable. No one was allowed to live within them (Orde-Browne 1925: 205). Cutting or clearing the trees and bush was considered 'sacrilege and treated as a serious anti-social act requiring expiation' (Lambert 1949: 21). Elders in present-day Ndia confirmed the sanctions against interfering with the groves. An old man from Nduine sublocation in Inoi, for example, stated emphatically, 'No one was to disturb a grove.' Another elder stated, 'The leaf could not be picked from such a tree.' Death, disease, drought, and other disasters, plus the wrath of neighbours and kinfolk, awaited those who violated the groves. Satish Saberwal (1967: 66) recorded in Embu that excessive rain was attributed to tampering with sacred groves. If no one confessed to such an act, the Embu elders responsible for the trees placed a public curse on the culprit. Ndia informants said that a person who encroached on a sacred grove was supposed to pay one or more goats to the generation-set elders in order to undergo ritual cleansing. The concerned *rika* elders and the grove itself also needed to be ritually purified after the desecration.

There were socially sanctioned uses of the trees and plants in the groves. Sometimes a tree was pruned by elders to cause it to fork. Prior to circumcision ceremonies the smaller branches of the forked tree were removed to create a space in its middle (Barlow 1913). The boys to be circumcised often had the task of trimming such a tree. The day before initiation they raced to their local grove and climbed the tree, breaking off branches and throwing them on the ground (Beech 1913a; Kenyatta 1938). These were collected by girl-initiates for use in sacred fires. As part of the initiation ceremony, the boys tested their physical ability by attempting to throw a spear through the clearing in the forked tree. A stick taken from a sacred tree was also used by children in rituals associated with the crop-planting ceremony (Kenyatta 1938: 240).

There were other ritual uses of the groves. The sacred figs were often associated with increasing fertility in people and livestock (Beech 1913b). Men sometimes collected the fig leaves and slept on them, while women rubbed the tree sap on themselves, to order to improve their ability to have children. *Rika* elders were permitted to take cuttings of the figs and other appropriate species in the groves to propagate new sacred trees. Prominent men and their wives were sometimes buried in sacred groves (Stigand 1913: 243). This was considered a great honour, considering that the corpses of most people were left in the bush to be devoured by the hyenas and other carrion feeders (Orde-Browne 1925: 93–4; Hobley 1967: 98–9). A few sacred groves in eastern Gichugu in the 1930s were not regarded as permanent. They could be opened by local elders for general use. Removing the ritual status from a long-time sacred grove, however, was not common. It mainly occurred with the change-over in ruling generation-sets associated with the *ituika* ceremony. Each new *rika* could establish its own sites for worship and sacrifice, but most groves were used from generation to generation.

Some of contemporary Kirinyaga's most beautiful trees owe their survival to their reputation as customary shrines and ceremonial sites. As mentioned previously, there is a small grove along the Gakoigo–Ithareni road in Nduini, Inoi, dominated by a tall *mururi* (*Trichilia emetica*) tree with a thick bole. Once surrounded by 'lots of bush', the tree now has a thin understory of *mukindu* (*Phoenix reclinata*) and woody shrubs. An elderly resident of that area recalled the tree's colourful history:

> Years ago Gikuyu warriors used to measure their strength by throwing clubs and spears over this tree. Then, some people, the old men called Irungu, saw it wise to pray to God here.

God is said to have spoken to the Gikuyu through a prophet who climbed the tree in pre-colonial times. Another elder from the area stated:

> Githuku, a well-known seer, told people to come to the tree. After they gathered, he climbed the tree. Ngai spoke through him, and he came down to say what he had been told. First, Ngai said people different from us would come, and they would have different skin color from us. Also, when the newcomers arrived, they would not stay a long time. If the people saw a place called Kiamucue being built with metal sheets, they would know the strangers were ready to return to their own country . . . [And] at the time when they would leave, the power of Irungu would be finished.

The old man who retold the prophecy claimed it had been accurate. Corrugated metal sheets appeared at Kiamucue around the time of the Emergency, while independence happened near the end of Irungu generation. Other accounts say that the prophets mentioned the coming of 'an iron snake' — a reference to the railway. For many people, the *mururi* tree was a significant link with their pre-colonial past.

The generational system and the *ituika* ceremony

The *ituika* ceremony involved the transfer of ritual power from one generation-set to another. Occurring every few decades, the ceremony marked a fundamental shift in the organization of local authority. There are many differing accounts of the generational system and *ituika* in Gikuyu country, reflecting local cultural variations as well as contrasting interpretations by ethnographers (see Middleton and Kershaw 1965; Kershaw 1972; Lonsdale 1992b). The description presented is based on written sources on Kirinyaga and environs, including reports in the Kenya National Archives, plus interviews with contemporary Ndia elders (see Lambert 1956; Saberwal 1970; Mwaniki 1974; Muriuki 1974; Leakey 1977c; Lonsdale 1992b).

Fathers and sons belonged to successive generational-sets called Mwangi and Irungu. Informants emphasized that, 'People in different clans were able to be in the same group.' That is, the generation-set was another social mechanism for integrating people across kinship boundaries. At any given time *rika* was recognized as ruling the countryside. Its elders were responsible for making sacrifices at the groves, settling disputes involving different clans, proclaiming or sanctioning changes in custom, and organizing ceremonies and dances. Because of the wide age span of siblings in polygynous households, the membership of a generation-set always consisted of males of varying ages, only a fraction of whom had attained senior elder status. Each retired *rika* became known by a name based on its reputation.

The ceremony was expected to occur once every generation, with elderly fathers turning the countryside over to their mature sons after an interval of decades. It is unclear what exactly triggered the *ituika* to take place at a specific time. H.E. Lambert (1956: 41) believed succession took place at regular intervals based on a seven generation cycle. C.F. Watkins, the chief native commissioner in the 1920s, recorded, 'when the ruling group gets old, pressure of public opinion and weariness of affairs, force it to relinquish control'. One of Mwaniki's (1974: 280) Gichugu elders said it occurred when the ruling *rika* 'judged that the children were mature and they themselves were old enough to retire from active service'. Two of his Ndia interviewees said that *ituika* was prompted by the members of the junior *rika* feeling increasingly 'troubled' by their lack of ritual position and prerogatives (Mwaniki 1974: 295). They said succession was a way of getting 'the rights for things'. In an insightful essay, John Lonsdale (1992b: 346) suggests that *ituika* was prompted by famine or other economic upheaval and the need to cleanse ritually the countryside of accumulated sorcery accusations. The impression gained from interviews with present-day elders was that both generation-sets understood that the ruling group must relinquish control after governing for a sufficient interval. The process involved long and complex negotiations between the leadership of each *rika*.

One of the most impressive aspects about *ituika* was the co-ordination it required over space and through time. Mwaniki (1974: 62) recorded, 'All Ndia and Gichugu bribed [held ceremonies] at the same time starting from the lowlands upward ridge by ridge.' The first step in the ceremony was to collect the customary fee of one or more goats from members of the incoming *rika*. Most of the goats were eaten at ritual feasts, but some of them were killed as sacrifices, and others were used to purchase sacrificial bulls. Having a goat selected for sacrifice was regarded by the Kirinyaga Gikuyu as an honour. All families were expected to participate. The payment of goats to the outgoing *rika* occurred in installments over several years. The last *ituika* ceremony in Ndia and neighbouring Nyeri occurred in the early 1890s, before the advent of colonial rule. Yet, two decades later, Mwangi elders were still collecting goats from its members to pay off the outgoing *rika* known as Maina. The pattern of delayed payments was preferred because it permitted the retiring *rika* to retain a presence in local rituals and other affairs until its successor was in turn replaced. The incoming *rika* also provided specially brewed beer and honey as part of the transfer.

A series of public rites involving men and sometimes women culminated in exclusive ceremonies involving a few selected elders (for published accounts, Kenyatta 1938: 187–94; Lambert 1956: 59–63; Saberwal 1970: 47–68; Leakey 1977c: 1279–1284; the Kenya National Archives also contains detailed descriptions). These individuals were chosen to obtain secret ritual knowledge and to serve as the *rika's* sacrificers in the groves. They were usually prosperous individuals, possessing large herds. Many animals were needed for paying the customary fees required of those seeking to attain the highest ranks of seniorhood and to maintain a state of ritual purity. The trade of the *mundu mugo* was said to be a profitable one because there were so many ways of becoming ritually unclean (*thahu*), ranging from touching a corpse to eating from a cracked pot. The traditional pattern of leadership by the prosperous was common throughout Gikuyu country, reflecting local sensibilities about the nature of wealth and civic virtue (see Lonsdale 1992b). Two of the earliest ethnographers of the Nyeri Gikuyu noted, 'Wealth is held in immense respect amongst the Akikuyu, in a manner which is, it must be confessed, somewhat depressing, when the simple life appears to have been reached' (Routledge and Routledge 1910: 142). The aim of such wealth, they added, was the influence it brought.

Ituika combined the conspicuous exchange and consumption of wealth with a secretive ritual rich in symbolism (Lonsdale 1992b: 345). According to Lonsdale, the ceremony emphasized to its participants the costs and dangers of revivifying power, as well as the need for 'a fortitude tempered by years of self-mastery and virtuous production'. Jomo Kenyatta (1938: 196) points out that *ituika* celebrated peaceful succession based on widespread participation and common values. The power and legitimacy of the ruling *rika* was reflected in its control of the sacred groves.

The sacred grove as a symbol of pre-colonial unity

The sacred grove was a fundamental part of traditional life. Kenyatta (1938: 250) called the sacred grove a key institution of the Gikuyu people. He added:

> It marks at once their unity as a people, their close contact with the soil, the rain and the rest of Nature, and, to crown all, their most vital communion with the High God of the tribe.

Of course one must bear in mind that Kenyatta's *Facing Mount Kenya* exaggerated the cultural, socio-economic, and political homogeneity of the Gikuyu peoples (see Lonsdale 1992b). He sought to convey an idyllic and patriotic account of the Gikuyu as a response to prevailing colonial ideologies. In some ways sacred groves actually reflected traditional divisions among the Gikuyu peoples: their fragmentation into localized groups, the dominance of elders over juniors and men over women, and distinctions accorded to the prosperous over the poor or ordinary.

Yet, Kenyatta was undoubtedly correct in identifying the groves and their associated rituals as a vital part of the local social fabric, bonding together diverse strands of traditional life. Perhaps the most important aspect of the sacred groves was their role as a focal point for the shared concerns of the local community — families that were in regular interaction with one another. These people did not identify themselves as members of a tribe *per se*, but as neighbours who possessed common values and problems. The sacred groves were places for communities to worship God and for marking their own passage of ritual time.

Colonialism and political authority

British colonialism undermined through direct and indirect means the indigenous socio-cultural system which had supported the sacred groves. Many groves in southern and western Gikuyu country were lost through land appropriation by the administration or white settlers. In Kenyatta's (1938: 245) Kiambu neighbourhood, for example, only one sacred tree reportedly survived. The rest were cut down by, or otherwise lost to, European planters who seized the land. Cuttings were taken from some of the sacred trees situated on land alienated by white settlers (Lambert 1949: 22). They were planted inside the remaining parts of Gikuyu country, providing some spiritual continuity for a people undergoing dislocation and forced socio-economic change.

Relatively few sacred trees were lost by the Ndia and Gichugu through European land appropriation. The declaration of Kirinyaga and Embu as closed districts in the early days of colonial rule protected them from the initial waves of white land acquisition (Ross 1927: 60). Still, they lost several ceremonial sites when the upper slopes and summit of Mount Kenya were alienated in 1910 as a state forest reserve. In Kirinyaga the decline of the sacred groves mostly came about through subtle yet pervasive processes of cultural change, especially the emergence of significant internal socio-economic divisions. As Marshall Clough (1990: xx) writes, 'The colonial situation oppressed all the people of central Kenya, but it also divided them into antagonistic groups.'

The erosion of traditional authority, including the generation-sets, diminished the cultural significance of the sacred groves. The colonial government regarded customary political organization as too diffuse for administrative purposes (Dundas 1915; Muriuki 1974). It quickly initiated its own local hierarchy of appointed chiefs, headmen, and other functionaries, supervised by white officials. In some cases the individuals who filled these posts, such as Njega wa Gioko in Ndia and Gutu wa Kibetu in Gichugu, had been prominent leaders in pre-colonial times (see Moris 1973). However, their political authority now derived from the British regime, rather than from the respect of their peers. Yet, some chiefs and headmen, such as Njega, proved very capable of remaining staunch advocates of local land and political rights while serving the colonial state. They also used their posts to enhance the economic standing of themselves and their close followers. Official reports showed that men such as Njega, Gutu, and Naaman Ikahu became even more prosperous after their appointments, controlling large tracts of land, having big herds, and owning businesses.

Other colonial institutions encroached on the authority of the ruling *rika*. The customary elders' *kiama* (council) was supplanted by a government tribunal of the same name. The new *kiama* was actually set up to restore some political influence to the elders. By 1910 British administrators recognized that chiefs and headmen had assumed or usurped more political and economic power than had been intended (Mungeam 1966: 246). The tribunals were organized on a divisional basis and empowered to handle selected judicial functions, including adjudicating certain civil and criminal cases. In the past some of these cases would have been adjudicated by the ruling *rika*. Colonial officials tried to model some aspects of the tribunals on the indigenous *kiama* and *rika*. Membership, for example, was initially limited to men who were fathers of circumcised children, and they needed to pay entry and ceremonial fees. *Kiama* members were picked at public meetings. Chiefs in Kirinyaga and Embu attempted to control the tribunals, however, by serving as *ex officio* members and influencing the selection of elders. Over the years the *kiamas* were reorganized several times because of local dissatisfaction with their composition and rulings, as well as colonial concerns about their efficiency (Glazier 1985). Public outcry about the 'oppression and corruption' of the Embu *kiama* members, for example, led to their replacement in 1923. The Embu and Kirinyaga *kiamas* were reconstituted in the 1930s because British officials and much of the local population felt that the chiefs and missions were over-represented.

The creation of the local native council — first as an advisory body in Nyeri in 1917 and as a formal administrative entity in 1925 — also encroached on the authority of the *rika*. The council exercised authority over customs ranging from the disposal of the dead to the practice of clitoridectomy in female initiation rites (see Chapter 5). The power of the colonial institutions and the corresponding erosion of authority of the ruling *rika* was evident by the early 1930s, when Irungu elders appealed to the council to stop the tribunals from collecting fees in matrimonial and other cases that were once their prerogative.

Voluntary associations also emerged as new arenas of politics. The emergence of Christian missions and the rise of Gikuyu cultural nationalism contributed to the spread of these institutions. The anti-colonial activities of Harry Thuku after the First World War generated some interest in national political affairs, especially among the young. A small branch of the Kikuyu Central Association opened in Kirinyaga by the 1920s. The South Nyeri Progressive Kikuyu Party, with connections to Protestant missions, was formed that same decade.

The British administration was not entirely opposed to indigenous political organization. On the contrary, district officials tended to be sympathetic toward traditional authorities and the 'tribal' discipline they supposedly imposed on the local population. However, the colonial regime viewed its own political apparatus as more efficient for the key tasks of maintaining order, collecting taxes, and promoting labour migration.

Missionaries and early religious change

Religious conversion, mainly to Christianity but also to Islam, reduced the ideological and popular basis of support for the sacred groves. Some people became acquainted with Islam through caravan traders and labour migrations to the coast (Stigand 1913: 254). An informant from Inoi, Ndïa, recalled, 'When people went to the coast, some of them became Muslims. They came back here and influenced others. Before there were only a few here, then their numbers increased.' Despite a spurt of conversions in the first years of colonial rule, Islam was overtaken by Christianity as the major source of religious change. The Anglican Church Missionary Society (CMS) established stations at Kabare, Gichugu, in 1910 and Mutira, Ndia, in 1912 (Cole 1970). Because of the government's zone of influence policy regarding missions, the CMS remained for years the only Christian group allowed to proselytize in Kirinyaga. Although the Roman Catholic Church operated missions in neighbouring Nyeri and Fort Hall since 1902, it was not allowed to seek converts in Ndia and Gichugu until the early 1920s. The Italian Consolata Mission eventually established parishes at Kianyaga in Gichugu and Baricho and Kerugoya in Ndia (Bottignole 1984). Other churches, such as the Salvation Army, were introduced by returning labour migrants.

Religious change occurred gradually in the early years of colonial rule. The CMS missionaries initially encountered resistance from local chiefs (Crawford 1913: 151–3). Informants emphasized that there was much suspicion of the newcomers and their reasons for coming. A Ndia elder recalled, 'At the time the people believed the white man was a great poisoner.' No baptisms took place at CMS Kabare until 1916, while Mutira mission waited another four years before celebrating its first ceremony (Cole 1970: 61–64). Silvana Bottignole (1984: 67) collected the following statement by Roman Catholic elders in Kianyaga recalling local reactions to the early priests:

> when the Europeans came and began to preach it was embarrassing for the African who already knew God . . . The people of Kianyaga . . . were embarrassed when the first Mzungu (white) priest referred to them as 'primitive' and 'pagan' . . . For some missionaries our religion, teaching us kindness, justice and mutual relationship, was no longer the religion of the 'true' God but 'paganism'.

Although their spiritual message sometimes met resistance, the services such as schooling provided by the missions soon developed a receptive following (Crawford 1913; Cagnolo 1933; Cole 1970). In the first decades of colonial rule the government relied on the churches almost exclusively to provide such public services to Africans. Thus, people had little choice but to co-operate with the missions if they wanted to partake of these innovations.

Religious conversion, adoption of Western material culture, and increased socio-economic differentiation were closely related. Missionaries encouraged people to adopt a package of Western culture. The Church Missionary Society, for example, started the first schools and provided the first public health care in the southern Mount Kenya area (Crawford 1913). People quickly valued schooling as a means for individual advancement in colonial society. Many of those educated at the CMS-Kabare school, for example, obtained jobs such as teachers or government clerks that were regarded locally as well-paying (Sluiter 1956). The churches promoted other aspects of western consumer culture. Photographs taken by the CMS missionaries who opened Embu mission in 1910 showed neophytes wearing khaki clothing. The pictures included in Father Cagnolo's (1933) account of Catholic activities in Nyeri showed Gikuyu children being taught to eat with plates and spoons while sitting at a table. The missionaries also strongly encouraged people to abandon customs that went against Western values and cultural practices, including infanticide, polygyny, bridewealth, leaving corpses unburied, and, among the Protestant churches, clitoridectomy (Murray 1974; Sandgren 1982). A distinct mission community emerged by the early 1920s, vocally separating itself from adherents of the indigenous religion.

The sustained presence of particular missionaries, especially at the CMS stations, was important in the formation of the local Christian community. The Rev. W.J. Rampley and family occupied Kabare station for much of the time between 1918 and 1933, and the Rev. H.J. Butcher and family worked at Mutira mission from 1919 to 1926 (Cole 1970: 61–64). Rampley was especially known for promoting a self-governing and self-supporting local church, thus fostering the formation of a cadre of local leaders (Murray 1974: 212–35). By 1928, Kabare was a large and prosperous mission, with nearly 2000 members (Rosberg and Nottingham 1970: 120; Cole 1970). Mutira lagged behind, but it still developed an active church community.

Religious conversion affected local politics. Rampley, Butcher, and the other missionaries not only provided spiritual guidance, they influenced the political and social outlook of their parish. In 1931, one district officer in Kerugoya accused the CMS missionaries of 'a love of powers temporal'. Church followers were very active in the new political institutions. In spite of their small numbers, Christians were appointed by district officials to the local advisory council and tribunals as early as 1917. Local adherents of Islam sought similar representation, but they lacked the political support from the administration and sheer numbers needed to prevail. As the Christian ranks grew in the 1920s, they contested elections for council and *kiama* posts. By 1934, nearly half the members of the Embu and Kirinyaga *kiamas* were mission members, even though their share of the total population was significantly smaller. The proselytes sought preferential treatment from the administration, including exemption from poll tax and communal labour obligations. This contributed to a rift between the Christians and their neighbours. Thus, the missions emerged as a distinct political force, willing to pursue their perceived interests.

Economic change and social divisions

Other processes of socio-economic change influenced events in Kirinyaga. The imposition of taxes shortly after the advent of colonial rule prompted labour migration as people sought money to pay their obligation (see Clayton and Savage 1974; Kitching 1980; Stichter 1982). Thus, a substantial number of people were absent from the district for varying periods during the year. Initially it was men who migrated, but by the late 1920s women also travelled to Nairobi and other outlying places. Some Ndia and Gichugu settled year-round in Nairobi, Mombasa, and other distant areas. Although most occasionally returned home, some of them lost interest in local affairs.

Land clearing increased in response to demographic pressures and the commercialization of agriculture (Maher 1938a). Much of the population growth in the 1920s and, especially, the 1930s, derived from Kiambu and Nyeri Gikuyus, plus Kambas from Kitui and Machakos, who immigrated into the district. There was a tendency for land tenure to become individualized, as well as clashing interpretations regarding customary land rights (Maxwell *et al.* 1929a, 1929b; Moris 1973; also see Kershaw 1972). As already mentioned, people started adopting items of Western consumer culture. Major Granville Orde-Browne (1925: 9), who was stationed in Embu District in 1909, was impressed by the pace of economic change in just the first five years, 'Communities . . . [were] buying and selling in coin, going away to work, and using piece goods, steel tools and matches as if they had known them all their lives.' Economic differentiation became more pronounced as some families started adopting Western consumption patterns. Kenyatta (1938: 252) recorded that the older generation complained that young people were 'individualised and selfish', causing them to turn from Ngai's influence. Officials observed in 1926 that the literate, especially young mission followers, were often impatient with their illiterate elders.

Thus, deep socio-cultural fissures emerged among the people of Kirinyaga. New forms of political organization eroded traditional authority. Religious conversion, labour migration, economic change, and immigration contributed to socio-cultural differentiation. Intergenerational tensions were emerging. The Ndia and Gichugu were no longer united by shared values, customs, and ceremonies. A young man from Kerugoya succinctly summarized the impact of religious change:

> Before as Gikuyus we worshipped one God, Ngai, who stayed on Mount Kenya. Ngai united the people. Today, some say 'Allah' or 'God of Moses', and others worship idols . . . People do not share the same customs.

These profound social changes would be reflected in the controversies that eventually engulfed Kirinyaga's sacred groves.

Early challenges to the sacred groves

Colonial administrators often viewed the sacred groves as ethnographic curiosities (Beech 1913a, 1913b; Dundas 1915; Lambert 1956). In contrast, many missionaries considered them symbols of savagery and darkness. Father C. Cagnolo (1933: 27) of the Roman Catholic mission in Nyeri, for example, called the groves 'temples of the Gikuyu paganism'. He compared the sacrifices held in them to those carried out by the Druids of Gallia. Some elderly Christians in contemporary Kirinyaga recalled being told by missionaries that the sacred groves were bad places.

The sacred trees eventually became targets for missionaries and neophytes attempting to root out pagan superstitions. One of the first recorded challenges in southern Mount Kenya took place around 1911, when an Italian priest desecrated sacred groves in Nyeri. The district commissioner noted that the priest's activities were unpopular with local inhabitants. It was unclear from colonial records whether the priest had any Gikuyu accomplices. Two decades later, however, Father Cagnolo (1933: 28) wrote about early neophytes, 'who having long before rejected the old beliefs, dared to fell some of the [sacred] trees with the purpose of making good firewood'. They, reportedly, 'did not end the year alive, but paid dearly for their boldness'.

Such assaults on the sacred groves were not common in the first two decades of colonial rule. Early colonial records and other accounts suggested that the sacred trees remained untouched. Orde-Browne, an administrator in Embu between 1909 and 1916, recorded that people had considerable respect for the groves, 'no trees being felled and no one living within them'. The threat of supernatural sanction or peer pressure undoubtedly influenced the neophytes to leave the groves alone. They probably felt little need to tamper with such an important cultural symbol. Orde-Browne (1925: 205–6) points out that early converts often selectively practised their chosen faiths. Muslims kept drinking alcoholic beverages, for example, and Christians remained polygynous. Many spheres of local life remained guided by the habits and customs of pre-colonial culture.

CMS and the ituika goats

In the early 1920s, the sacred groves and the ceremonies associated with them faced another challenge from Christians. This time the CMS led the campaign, with the controversy mainly focusing on the *ituika* ceremony. As mentioned previously, the transfer of ritual power from generation-set to another was one of the most important rites held in the groves. The ceremony took place roughly every 30 years. It last occurred before colonial rule began. Everyone was expected to participate in one form or another, including the customary payment of goats by members of the incoming *rika*. Nyeri officials reported that preparations began for the transfer from Mwangi to Irungu generation in 1912. Some colonial administrators in western and southern Gikuyuland attempted to halt the ceremonies, regarding them as seditious (Kenyatta 1938: 196–7; Benson 1964: 467). They were allowed to take place in Fort Hall from 1925 and 1927. There was little official interference with the process in Nyeri and Embu. In fact, their district commissioners strongly encouraged the Africans to perform the ceremony (Saberwal 1970).

Controversy arose in the early 1920s when CMS leaders from Kabare and Mutira refused to contribute the customary *ituika* goats as part of the incoming *rika*. The leaders were identified by the district commissioner in 1925 as Musa, Elijah, Jacobo, and Samuel — their Biblical names underscoring their embrace of the new religion. It was claimed that the payment of goats involved them in a repugnant pagan ceremony. They feared that the goats were used as a sacrifice to a 'heathen Evil Spirit'. This was an unprecedented interpretation of *ituika*, calling into question not only the legitimacy of indigenous authority but the ethical basis of traditional religious beliefs. The influential Rev. Rampley of Kabare was reportedly responsible for introducing this new perspective. According to Arthur M. Champion, the district commissioner in the mid-1920s, the CMS missionary had 'an entirely wrong impression of the matter' Because of his involvement in the affair, Rampley was known locally as 'Muthungu wa Ituika', the *Ituika* White Man (Murray 1974: 217). He was joined in his misunderstanding of the ceremony and its religious context by the Rev. Butcher, pastor of the CMS mission at Mutira. The *ituika* controversy went beyond the meddling of a few missionaries, however. It was indicative of emergent cultural conflicts among a number of overlapping groups: Christians and adherents of the native religion; literate and non-literate; and young and old.

The issue of *ituika* goats was discussed many times in various public forums during the 1920s. It was considered serious enough to be included in the agenda of the first meeting of the Kikuyu Province Council, a body composed of leading elders, chiefs, and colonial officers, in 1922. After a discussion it was decided by the councillors, including CMS-Kabare representative Musa wa Muriithi, that the custom should continue. They stipulated that animals provided by Christians were not to be used for sacrifices but consumed at meat feasts. Any violation of this agreement was to be reported to district officials. Three years later, however, the issue was revived at the South Nyeri Advisory Council in January 1925. Mission neophytes from Mutira and Kabare once again refused to contribute their customary fees. Councillor Musa now objected to the practice, claiming that fat from all goats was placed in sacrificial gourds. Other councillors said the charges were groundless. They pointed out that 'mission boys' from other parts of the district paid their fees without protest. It was argued that non-payment would create 'a rift between Tribal Authority and defaulters', permanently dividing the groups. After further discussion, the vast majority of councillors resolved that the 1922 agreement should be adhered to. Goats had to be paid. Money would not be accepted in lieu of the animals. In return for their contribution, the Christians were reassured that their goats would not be used for sacrifice. They were also exempted from attending the ceremonies. Musa and the CMS followers remained unhappy. The issue carried over a few months later to the first working session of the newly created local native council in July 1925. A resolution introduced by Nyeri Paramount Chief Wambugu and seconded by Ndia Paramount Chief Njega wa Gioko reiterated the principles agreed to earlier. It passed 18 to two, only Musa and another CSM follower from Ndia voting against it.

Champion, the district commissioner, supported the resolution in reports to senior officials. He feared the issue would create a permanent breech and possibly strife between the Christians and the rest of the people. The notion that *ituika* constituted devil worship, Champion argued, was based on missionary ignorance. The ritual was actually directed toward 'the good God', a deity similar to the God of Moses. The indigenous belief was 'a beautiful one', possessing 'the best Christian principles'. He compared *ituika* to ceremonies occurring in the agricultural countries of Europe.

The CMS leaders took their protest to a higher level of the colonial hierarchy. With Rampley on leave, they were accompanied by Butcher to a meeting in July 1925, with key senior officials: O.F. Watkins, the colony's acting chief native commissioner, and R.G. Stone, the acting senior commissioner for the province. After listening to the various arguments, Watkins ruled that there was no basis for the religious or moral objections to paying the fee. It was pointed out that other CMS adherents contributed their goats without controversy. In a January 1926 memorandum, Watkins suggested that the neophytes' refusal largely stemmed from economic, rather than ideological, concerns. He regarded payment as an obligation to traditional authority. Watkins shared the fear that non-payment would divided the Kirinyaga Gikuyu between 'the qualified ruling Rika and the Christian, disenfranchised as it were by his own act, but claiming superior consideration from the European on that account'. His memorandum emphasized, 'This is most undesirable.'

At the July 1925 meeting the elders and chiefs reiterated their invitation for a district officer or missionary to witness the goat killing. The officials encouraged Butcher to promote compromise. Watkins, like Champion, believed the conflict was abetted and inspired by the missionaries. He cautioned Butcher about involvement in an issue likely to prejudice so many people against the missions. It is interesting to note that shortly afterwards Watkins issued a similar warning to all administrators and missionaries regarding efforts to ban female circumcision. The *ituika* issue seemed settled after the South Nyeri resolution was approved by Sir Edward Grigg in late 1925, the acting colonial governor. It had yet to reach its denouement, however.

The return of Rampley in 1926 coincided with another phase of CMS protest about paying *ituika* goats. The South Nyeri councillors allowed a 15 Shilling payment to substitute for payment of the goats. The issue continued late into 1927, when it was discussed by a wider body of CMS (Murray 1974: 216). Champion always claimed that Rampley lacked support on the issue from other missionaries. The lack of controversy about *ituika* at CMS stations outside Kirinyaga and the ultimate solution to the problem in the district suggest that his assessment was correct. Rampley finally agreed to the killing of the animals. He devised a plan approved by the district commissioner to slaughter goats submitted by CMS adherents at a centralized place on a single day. This contrasted with the custom of dispersed ceremonial meat feasts taking place over a long period. With tribal police watching, the animals were killed, their meat eaten and any remains burned. In telling the event over 40 years later to Jocelyn Murray (1974: 217), some CMS leaders recalled the great disappointment of the *rika* elders. After seeing the hurried way in which the animals and feasts were handled, Murray was told, the elders stopped asking the Christians for goats. 'It became a kind of useless thing.' Not surprisingly, there remained much tension between the mission followers and the rest of the population. Officials, however, considered the issue to be settled amicably.

The paying of *ituika* goats became much easier as the decade ended. Kirinyaga was one of few places in central Kenya to escape severe crop failures caused by drought in 1929. So many Kamba fled into the Ndia and Gichugu with livestock that the average price of goats dropped from 15–20 Shillings to 4–5 Shillings. By the early 1930s, the payment of sufficient goats occurred so that the main part of the *ituika* ceremony could begin.

The registration of the *ituika* groves

The *ituika* controversy temporarily died down in the late 1920s. The struggle about indigenous customs in central Kenya intensified, however, with the growing conflict over the practice of clitoridectomy in the female initiation ceremony (Rosberg and Nottingham 1970; Murray 1974; Davison 1989). Perhaps having learned from the *ituika* affair, the CMS–Kabare pastorate committee and Rampley avoided much controversy by refusing to sanction a ban of the practice. Instead, in 1931 they called for a modified operation to be performed by church-sanctioned practitioners. Their compromise had important implications for the sacred groves, since it called for mission followers to have their rite of passage carried out privately. This followed the pattern of reduced Christian participation in the traditional ceremonies held at the sacred trees. They generally refused to attend the crop planting, harvesting, or rainfall ceremonies, associating these ancient rites with witchcraft (Kenyatta 1938: 254).

The transfer of ritual power between Mwangi and Irungu in Kirinyaga took place between 1931 and 1933. While the ceremony was going on, new challenges arose to the sacred groves, with CMS adherents accused of desecration. Elderly informants in present-day Kirinyaga recalled zealous neophytes who challenged tradition by cutting down sacred trees and the surrounding bush. Investigations by officials in Embu (Kirinyaga had been placed in its jurisdiction in a provincial reorganization) revealed the issue to be complex. Some of the accusations were unsupported by law or custom. *Rika* elders apparently manipulated the interpretation of customs about clearing sacred or ritually defiled ground in order to annoy certain individuals. The district commissioner cited the example of people 'prevented from opening up new cultivation because of the death of a dog near the site'. A long-time Anglican Church member from Ndia recalled the still-considerable authority of the ruling *rika* in such matters:

> Irungu had power like government. It could tell someone not to cultivate. If someone ignored [the order], he could be taken away, arrested. If one knew the rule of Irungu and it was not a big offense, then only a goat or lamb would be paid. A big offense required a cow or bull. People paid, they didn't refuse.

The CMS leaders wanted to end prosecution for any supposed desecration. Their proposal was unpopular, however, because destruction of legitimate sacred groves had occurred. Several lawsuits were initiated in the native courts.

Unable to resolve the desecration issue in the tribunals, the matter was brought before the Embu Local Native Council in 1933. It decided on a compromise, ordering the registration of all places of worship, including sacred groves and churches. This proposal was resisted by the CMS, but it eventually relented. The council registered 117 sacred groves in Ndia and 102 groves in Gichugu. The census probably represented a full accounting of the groves involved in the *ituika* rites. Once the sacred groves were registered and protected by the council, the desecration controversy ended.

Powers delegated to the Embu Local Native Council under Section 8 (g) of the Native Authority Ordinance now protected the sacred groves. Once the embodiment of local unity, the sacred trees and their registration now served as symbols of local cultural heterogeneity. The protection once provided by shared values and peer pressure had to be supplanted by state authority. The council's intervention saved the groves from encroachment, but it could not halt their declining cultural significance. Continued religious conversion, increased school attendance, socio-economic and political upheaval associated with the Mau Mau War, the privatization of land during the State of Emergency, and widening economic differences among households and local agro-ecological zones because of the uneven expansion of commercial agriculture undermined even further the socio-cultural solidarity that once sustained the sacred trees.

The decline of the generation-sets and their groves

Irungu elders made their presence felt in local affairs in the years immediately following the *ituika* ceremony. They halted the practice of circumcising boys without their parents' consent, for example, at the Catholic mission in Kerugoya. As late as 1960, *rika* elders in Ndia and Gichugu announced and enforced a ban on the sale of produce at a time of widespread crop failure — much to the surprise of officials. In general, though, their activities were highly localized and focused on traditional aspects of life. Except for trying unsuccessfully to enlist their support against the Mau Mau movement during the early 1950s, the colonial government made little effort to integrate the ruling *rika* as a corporate group into its administrative apparatus. Individual rika elders were appointed to locational and divisional councils established in the 1940s. By the mid-1950s officials believed that the Irungu elders in Ndia and Gichugu did little beyond preserving the sacrificial sites. When land consolidation and privatization were carried out, provisions were made to set aside the Irungu groves.

Some preliminary discussions were held about the transfer of ritual power from Irungu to Mwangi prior to the Mau Mau Emergency in 1952. Negotiations slowly resumed once the war restrictions were lifted in the late 1950s. According to informants, conflict arose between the generation-sets because, 'Mwangi refused to pay.' That is, many potential members of the junior *rika* were uninterested in contributing the customary goats and *marawa* (beer). After years of hardship in the war, including forced resettlement into villages, most households were concerned with rebuilding their lives (see Castro and Ettenger 1994). Irungu elders would not transfer ritual power to Mwangi leaders without the payments. An impasse was reached that could not be resolved. In 1962, chiefs granted the generation-sets received permission to hold ceremonies on a small scale, but no *ituika* rites occurred.

As independence grew nearer, Irungu and Mwangi became enmeshed in local politics. By 1962, administrators accused former Mau Mau supporters of trying to use the *rika* as a medium for promoting extreme ideas such as undoing land consolidation. The relationship between the generation-sets and colonial-appointed chiefs deteriorated. Some tensions continued after the end of British rule. Some Mwangi and Irungu elders associated with Mau Mau were arrested in 1964 at Baricho, the division headquarters for Ndia, for holding an illegal court. The district commissioner for Kirinyaga pointed out that the incident was not typical. Most *rika* elders had focused their efforts on condemning excessive drinking and smoking marijuana by the young. For the most part, he observed, the generation-sets were almost dead. Within a few years they were completely inactive.

Nowadays the sacred groves are not used for ceremonies. An elder remarked, 'People have churches. They don't offer sacrifices under trees any more. The *muratina* [*Kigelia africanum*] has shed its leaf.' Some informants pointed out that many groves and their surrounding bush were severely cut back after land tenure reform. Provisions made for the protection of the groves sometimes lapsed. Landowners gradually cleared the bush and trees. Respect for tradition caused many landowners, including devout Christians, to preserve local groves. Another informant suggested that people still fear the sacred groves, suspecting misfortune if they harm them. They also feared 'backbiting' by their neighbours if the trees were removed completely. The groves often provide practical benefits: catchment protection, windbreaks, shade, seeds, and useful products such as deadwood for fires. Thus community sentiment and utilitarian concerns have protected some groves.

Conclusion

Sacred groves once defined and reinforced local territorial and social identities. They were the sites of communal worship presided over by generation-set elders.

In colonial times the introduction of new religions, political organization, labour migration, and socio-economic differentiation eroded the old communal ethic. Deep cultural, political, and economic fissures emerged. New ideological and socio-cultural commitments led a small number of neophytes to rebel against tradition. Although district officials actually attempted to preserve the groves, the social forces set in motion by colonialism undermined the cultural roles and importance of the sacred trees. The state intervened through the Local Native Council to reinforce the customary management regimes. Thus, the social predictability of pre-colonial life based on shared socio-cultural relations and small-group trust was replaced by the legal predictability of state laws. Despite their diminished cultural status, many of the trees remain protected today by community sentiment and respect for the past. Their preservation sometimes involves utilitarian concerns such as catchment protection, providing shade, or furnishing useful products. Although the sacred groves are a relic of a past society, they are, to quote Riley and Brokensha (1988a: 200), 'environmentally desirable and a pleasing reminder of one aspect of . . . traditional life'.

10. Njukiine and other woodland: the fate of small forests

ABOUT 130 KILOMETRES north-east of Nairobi, on the lower slopes of Mount Kenya, is a large tract of eucalyptus, pine, and cypress plantations known as Njukiine forest. Along the margins of the plantation blocks managed by the Forest Department are scattered indigenous trees, including a *Cordia abyssinica* (*muringa*) from which hangs a traditional beehive. In contrast to the cacophony of bird and animal sounds to be heard in the remaining indigenous moist forest on the upper slopes of the mountain, the plantations of Njukiine are generally silent except for the distant hum of a chain-saw. Surrounding Njukiine are numerous small, privately-owned farms of mainly Gichugu (on the west) and Embu (on the east) families. Embu township also skirts the plantation forest on its eastern side.

The present-day cultural landscape is in sharp contrast to the area's social and ecological setting at the turn of the century. At that time Njukiine consisted of indigenous closed-canopy and open forest spreading over a wider area than the nearly 1000 ha now covered by plantations (Maher 1938a: 154–5; Beentje 1990b: 281). The forest provided habitat for abundant wildlife, including large numbers of buffalo and rhinoceros. For the people of Gichugu and Embu, Njukiine was not an open-access resource, without well-defined property rights, but a communal forest with rules and norms that regulated land use. Rights to Njukiine were vested in kinship and neighbourhood groups, rather than individual owners.

This chapter examines the changing institutional arrangements and management regimes that have governed Njukiine from 1900 to the early 1980s. It argues that colonialism altered the traditional authority and land-use dynamics that maintained forest cover at Njukiine, leading to conflict, negotiation, and eventually accommodation between the indigenous population and the colonial state. By the 1940s Njukiine was held in public trust by the local native council, a governing body set up as part of the colonial policy of indirect rule. The council devised its own system of forestry management combining customary rights with bureaucratic administration. This innovative arrangement ended during the Mau Mau Emergency, when the Forest Department assumed control over Njukiine and other local woodland. The department has continued to manage Njukiine since independence in 1963. Comparisons with the fate of other common-property woodland in Kirinyaga help to set Njukiine's history in perspective.

Indigenous management of Njukiine

Njukiine forest straddles the Kiye and Rubingazi rivers along the Gichugu–Embu border. Located roughly eight kilometres south of the Mount Kenya reserve, it is drier than the upland forest. The area falls within the Main Coffee and Marginal Coffee agro-ecological zones (Jaetzold and Schmidt 1983). The average annual rainfall is probably fewer than 1200 mm near Njukiine forest station at its lower edge, and in drought years it has received fewer than 750 mm. Njukiine lacked the biological diversity characteristic of the wet montane forest. In 1937 the Forest Department estimated that 'about 70 per cent' consisted of a single species: *Croton megalocarpus* (*mukinduri*). Another 15 per cent was comprised of *Cordia abyssinica* (*muringa*), a tree locally valued for its timber and other products. Other species included *Pygeum africanum* (*mueri*), *Markhamia hildebrandtii* (*muu*), *Ekebergia rueppeliana* (*mununga*), *Albizia gummifera* (*mukurue*), *Milletia oblata* (*mwangwa*), and *Trichilia emetica* (*mururi*). Now, almost all of the indigenous forest has been replaced by exotic species grown in industrial plantations.

Around 1900 Njukiine was a common property resource managed by descent and neighbourhood groups on both sides of the rivers. It had been preserved by 'the local elders, in order to provide building timber and wood for beehives' (Maher 1938a: 155). Setting aside small tracts of heavily wooded land for the supply of timber and other products was commonplace in central Kenya (Routledge and Routledge 1910: 39; Hobley 1967: 184; Kenyatta 1938; Leakey 1977a: 42–3, 123). A rightholder (*mwene githaka*) was free to limit felling, and permission of lineage (*mbari*) elders was customarily needed before any large timber tree could be harvested. In many places a curse (*kirumi*) had been placed on a group of trees, adding supernatural protection against encroachment. Unlike sacred groves, Njukiine and other local 'timber reserves' were usually regarded as land banks, to be opened to farming as needed.

Although local kinship groups claimed rights to Njukiine, it was not an exclusive 'clan forest'. Instead, anyone living near Njukiine enjoyed customary rights to certain of the forest's products. People collected deadwood, gathered medicinal and other useful plants, hung beehives, trapped animals, and herded livestock. The forest was also the site of dances and initiation ceremonies (Mwaniki 1974: 260). Restrictions on clearing were enforced through neighbourhood consensus. A person who cleared land without permission had to face the wrath of rightholders and local elders. A fine of one goat, paid to *mbari* or generation-set (*rika*) elders, was the customary punishment for such transgressions.

Other factors helped Njukiine retain its tree cover. The land adjacent to the forest was lightly settled. Pockets of permanent and temporary cultivation existed, but people primarily used the area for seasonal herding of livestock (Maher 1938a: 137). Cattle raids between people living on either side of the Kiye and Rubingazi rivers occasionally turned the forest and nearby fields into a 'no man's land' (Maher 1938a: 29; Mwaniki 1974: 266, 270–1). Contrary to colonial accounts, however, the Gikuyu and Embu were not in a state of perpetual warfare.

An abundance of game reflected and reinforced Njukiine's frontier character. Large numbers of buffalo, rhinoceros, lion, and other animals lived in the forest and glades (Stigand 1913: 254; Maher 1938a: 157). They also occupied the plains, wetlands, and savannah to the south of the forest (Madeira 1909: 86–93). The sporadic presence of tsetse fly near the southern edge of the forest also discouraged settlement.

The commons under siege

Njukiine served as a battleground during the colonial invasions of Kirinyaga and Embu between 1904 and 1906 (see Meinertzhagen 1957; Mwaniki 1973). After the alienation of Mount Kenya in 1910 and 1911, Njukiine remained the largest tract of forest under local African control in the region. In addition, small patches of woodland existed along rivers and on the tops of a few hills and ridges. Such areas were officially protected by the Native Authority Ordinance of 1912, which empowered chiefs and headmen to regulate the cutting of timber and to prohibit the 'wasteful destruction of trees'. However, informants recalled that local authorities seldom restricted the clearing of woodland without prompting from white officials. District administrators showed little interest in Gichugu's and Ndia's woodland until the 1930s. The controversy beginning in that decade reflected changes not only in local society but also in the political economy of the wider colonial state.

A shift in land use at Njukiine was under way by the 1920s. It was largely initiated by Gikuyu immigrants from Kiambu and Nyeri (Maher 1938a: 136–42). Most of them had become landless when their holdings in their home districts were appropriated by the colonial government and white farmers. These displaced Gikuyu saw the sparsely settled and generally fertile lowlands of southern Gichugu and Embu as a land of opportunity. Several Kirinyaga and Embu chiefs encouraged this migration to expand their constituencies. British administrators initially considered Gikuyu immigration to be a positive development because the newcomers brought innovations such as ploughs and wagons. Some Gichugu and Embu descent group elders were less welcoming, afraid the immigrants would not respect local land claims.

Immigration increased during the early 1930s. Several thousand outside Gikuyus reportedly entered the district between 1932 and 1936 (Maher 1938: 136–42). Those who moved near Njukiine were joined by local people, especially from Kirinyaga, seeking work as labourers or trying to stake claims to land. A new road from Embu township to Kiamutugu market in Gichugu skirted Njukiine and thus increased access to the forest.

Some newcomers acknowledged pre-existing claims to Njukiine by being ritually 'reborn' into Kirinyaga or Embu lineages. Others sought permission from local elders to be temporary land users or *ahoi*. Thus local clans and lineages sometimes sanctioned clearing by such individuals in return for recognition of their group's tenure rights. Many settlers, including local people, argued that the forest and nearby unoccupied land were open-access resources, rather than communal property held by particular kin groups. These newcomers claimed exclusive land rights through first clearance. Similar controversies about land tenure occurred elsewhere along the southern frontier of Kirinyaga and Embu (Moris 1973: 38–44).

As the conflict about Njukiine tenure rights intensified, deforestation accelerated. Indeed, uncertainties about land tenure reduced the incentive for conserving the forest. To clear the land, newcomers used both fire and axes. Fires set to remove trees on the outskirts of Njukiine spread 'into the main part of the forest' (Maher 1938a: 156–57). Wildlife, especially buffalo and rhinoceros, remained a constant threat, compelling many pioneer families to built their huts on platforms raised on pilings. Pit-sawyers penetrated Njukiine's interior, attracted by its rich supply of *Cordia abyssinica* and other timber trees. The Embu district commissioner reported in 1936 that companies of pit-sawyers conducted 'a roaring trade there'. Most of them were Gikuyu immigrants from Kiambu and Nyeri. British officials now complained that the sawyers reaped personal gain at the expense of communal resources.

Njukiine's customary status as a timber reserve had lapsed by the mid-1930s. The influx of settlers and sawyers undermined the old combination of low population density and, especially, customary authority based on close kinship and neighbourhood ties. Conditions of social predictability rooted in long-term socio-cultural relations and small-group trust no longer existed. Njukiine now largely housed a community of strangers. In the new social order, land hunger and individual self-interest clashed with communal needs to maintain the forest. British officials in Embu increasingly viewed the situation at Njukiine with alarm. The eastern edge of the forest was located only a few kilometres from their headquarters. The officials contemplated intervening, but awaited instructions from the colonial secretariat.

Colonial plans for African-held forests

As early as 1929, the acting chief native commissioner issued a circular letter to provincial administrators suggesting that the Forest Department take control of 'important' woodland within the African reserves. He proposed two plans for doing so. The first scheme called for woodland to be placed in a Native Forest Trust and managed by the department. In the second plan the department would lease woodland at a fixed price from the local native council. Neither proposal was seriously considered at the time by South Nyeri or Embu officials regarding Njukiine.

A 1931 government report by J.W. Nicholson again raised the issue of colonial control over African-held forests. He criticized the Forest Department for lacking a consistent policy towards such woodland. Nicholson proposed that a central board be established to act as trustee for these areas. Wooded land with major economic and environmental value was to be placed under Forest Department management. Local people would retain some rights to collect deadwood and other products. The Local Native Councils would assume control over smaller forests. Critical in other forestry matters as well, the Nicholson report received a cool response from the Forest Department. It failed (or refused) to implement Nicholson's proposals about African-held woodland.

Deforestation at Njukiine in the mid-1930s coincided with a new period of heightened colonial concern about soil erosion. The fixing of permanent racial boundaries during the early 1930s, plus prolonged drought in parts of the colony, focused attention on the sustainability of African land use (Anderson 1984; Throup 1988). Many officials believed that indigenous agricultural practices were destructive, or were becoming so because of demographic and market pressures (Maher 1938a, 1938b). In 1934, the governor declared soil conservation to be a colony-wide priority. The administration launched several soil conservation and agricultural intensification programmes aimed at Africans. Such activities included planting grass strips to serve as wash stops, terracing, establishing compost pits, and pasturing cattle in paddocks. Thus, the colonial government displayed an unprecedented willingness to interfere with African land use.

In November 1936, the colonial secretariat in Nairobi revived the idea of Forest Department management of 'important' African-held woodland. A circular letter issued by H.G. Pilling proposed that the department take control of all woodland covering more than 240 ha in the native reserves. The foresters were to manage such land 'on businesslike lines'. Pilling recommended charging forest users for all timber and other produce taken, arguing that the Africans would make better use of resources if they had to pay for them. He added that if the local people opposed the policy, they should be allowed to gather deadwood freely. The fees for forest produce were to be set at '25 per cent below the standard rate' — a concession to low African incomes. The department could recover its operating costs from the fees, with any net revenue going to the Local Native Council serving as trustee of the land. The district commissioner and the Local Native Council were to be responsible for the management of woodland covering less than 240 ha.

Negotiations about protecting Njukiine

Pilling's proposal prompted British officials in Embu to take action about Njukiine. In December 1936, District Commissioner K.G. Lindsay expressed concern about the destruction of the forest to the Embu Local Native Council. The council was a legislative body responsible under the 1924 Native Authority Ordinance for a range of African affairs, including agriculture, forestry, and land tenure. In the late 1930s it was composed of eight publicly elected and nine government-appointed members from different parts of Embu district. The membership included chiefs and Christian converts. No women served on the council until 1952. The district commissioner acted as president of the council, which met quarterly at Embu township.

Lindsay told the councillors it was essential to protect the forest. He mentioned the possibility of the Forest Department assuming managerial control over Njukiine. As an alternative, he suggested that Njukiine be placed under the council's direct supervision. The councillors, who were usually cautious in matters relating to land use, appointed a subcommittee to ascertain the views of local rightholders.

Three months later the subcommittee reported that people opposed any intervention. The rightholders vowed to take steps of their own to protect the forest. The new district commissioner, Ivor R. Gillespie, expressed doubts at the meeting about the landholders' promise, pointing out that severe fire damage had occurred during the recent planting season. Nevertheless, Gillespie accepted the rightholders' wishes, requesting that the councillors also 'use their influence get this valuable Tribal asset protected'.

The administration's acquiescence to continued local control of Njukiine reflected several considerations. There was already much apprehension about land rights. District officials had compelled households to adopt several farm practices, including growing cotton, planting fodder grasses as wash stops, and digging compost pits. Many people in Kirinyaga and Embu believed the practices were the colonial government's underhanded way of establishing claim to their property. The suggestion that Njukiine be turned over to the Forest Department only made the administration's motives more suspect. Gillespie thought that anti-soil erosion regulations passed by the council in early 1937 were an effective alternative to direct government management of Njukiine.

The colonial government itself was not of one mind on the future management and use of Njukiine. Despite Lindsay's proposal, the Forest Department initially lacked interest in directly managing Njukiine. Colin Maher, the head of the colony's soil conservation programme, reported in 1937 that the foresters had no wish to control Njukiine as long as the Embu council 'effectually preserved' the area. Instead, the department offered to advise the council on forest management.

Provincial agricultural officials wanted to use 160 ha near it for an African farm training school. Maher argued against the plan in October 1937, on the grounds that 'it would be difficult to preserve this or any native forest if Government neglects the Principles of forest conservation for its own purposes and so gives a handle to argumentative natives who might wish to acquire land by destruction of forest at a later date'. Gichugu clan elders strongly opposed the proposed school site, despite support for it from several councillors. A final decision was delayed by the onset of World War II in 1939.

Deforestation continued during 1937. Officials toured the area, reporting extensive land degradation, including denuded ravines and gullies (Maher 1938a: 88–90, 99–104, 136–44, 154–6). Maher warned that deforestation would adversely affect local humidity and climate. The district commissioner predicted that the temperature would climb in the vicinity of Njukiine if the forest was destroyed. Quite clearly, officials believed that state intervention was needed to control the situation.

Calling local efforts to protect the forest 'a complete failure', Gillespie pressed the council in December 1937 to intervene. He wanted Njukiine declared a reserve and handed over to the Forest Department for management. The councillors strongly opposed relinquishing local control. Yet, they feared that their own refusal to act might provoke the administration to appropriate the forest. Before reaching a decision, they asked for a one-day delay to consult with Njukiine rightholders. Gillespie granted the request.

The next morning Mbeere Chief Kombo 'suggested' and Ndia Chief Njega wa Gioko 'amplified' a plan for designating Njukiine as a protected woodland. A council subcommittee would demarcate the forest, then local chiefs would assume responsibility for it. The proposal was passed unanimously as 'Recommendation 2/37'. Five councillors and six local elders were appointed to mark the boundaries. Gillespie approved it because he thought the plan was similar to one implemented by the neighbouring Meru Local Native Council.

Despite minor disagreements about the boundary, the area was demarcated as recommended by the subcommittee in March 1938. The council's acceptance of the committee's report made Njukiine an officially protected woodland. Thus the forest was transformed from a commons, governed by local social relations and indigenous tenure rights, into a trust, held by the state-sanctioned Embu council in the name of the district's people.

Forest degradation decreased during 1938. However, Assistant Conservator of Forests Douglas G.B. Leakey reported substantial new clearing during his tour of Njukiine in 1939. Responsibility for the forest had fallen on unpaid and therefore largely unmotivated chief assistants. In response the Forest Department argued that stronger measures were needed to maintain the area's woodland.

Leakey met with the Embu council in August 1939 and proposed that Njukiine be proclaimed a Native Forest Reserve under department supervision. The forest would still belong to the council, but its management would change. Leakey pointed out that the Meru council had submitted to a similar arrangement with much success. The most startling aspect of his presentation was the revelation that the Njukiine subcommittee had already agreed to the idea. Its members, which included Chief Kombo and Embu Chief Muruatetu, had met beforehand with Leakey and the new district commissioner, Captain J.E.H. Lambert.

Most councillors were hostile to the proposal, which provoked protracted discussion. Their opposition was heavily based on the experience of the Mount Kenya forest alienation. Several councillors claimed the government used treachery to appropriate the montane forest — telling people that the line being cut to demarcate the reserve was a road to improve local trade. Subsequently, the foresters curtailed local access to the area through a system of strict land-use regulations, user fees, and penalties. The Africans believed there would be little difference between a Crown forest and a Native Forest Reserve. Councillor Johanna from Kirinyaga cited a proverb to express their misgivings, 'Local people had no intention of putting their sheep in the custody of a leopard.' Officials were impressed by the opposition to the proposal by Kirinyaga Chiefs Njega wa Gioko and Jacob Kirei, two key local leaders. As the council minutes noted, 'They represented a large body of people who would never agree to the Forest Department's views'.

Influential Ndia Chief Naaman Ikahu suggested a compromise, proposing that the council directly manage Njukiine. The Forest Department would have an advisory role, including training council employees to serve as guards. Chief Njega and other councillors endorsed the idea, which was similar to the plan proposed by the department in 1937. This time around officials were sceptical of the council's ability to protect the forest. They urged the councillors to visit Meru and see the reserve for themselves. The councillors agreed to go, but the trip was delayed temporarily because of the war.

In January 1940 Njukiine was discussed at a special council meeting. Gillespie, back as district commissioner, expressed disappointment about the failure of Recommendation 2/37. He urged the council to put Njukiine under Forest Department control, emphasizing that in Meru the foresters had reduced unauthorized felling and fire damage, and provided its council with revenue through user fees. Arrangements were made to transport the 17 councillors and five clan elders to the Meru forests.

Chief Muruatetu spoke for the council at the next meeting in April 1940. He said the contingent had been impressed by the Meru reserves. Nevertheless the councillors preferred to retain control over Njukiine. They proposed hiring two guards to supervise forest use. The guards would work with the local chiefs and district commissioner to protect the woods. A committee of six councillors would walk around the perimeter each year to verify that the forest was protected adequately. Muruatetu said the councillors were willing to review the whole matter after two or three years. If the plan failed, they would consider alternatives.

Instead of arguing against the plan, Gillespie made two suggestions. First, the subcommittee ought to inspect the perimeter during the main planting seasons in April and November, 'when encroachment was most likely'. Second, the council must consult with the district commissioner about methods for controlling the area. The councillors agreed and reaffirmed their 1937 decision to keep Njukiine. Gillespie believed the council's proposal might work because it involved only a very small area. His willingness to give the council another chance was not the first time he had supported local forest rights. A year earlier he championed Ndia and Gichugu claims to land excised from the Mount Kenya reserve, despite pressure from the central government to oppose them (see Chapter 5).

The approval of the provincial administration was needed before the plan could be implemented. In June 1940 Provincial Commissioner C. Tomkinson was willing to try the plan on one condition: if it failed, the Forest Department would take control of Njukiine. Tomkinson reiterated that the forest would still belong to the council; only its management would change. He admitted to being sceptical about the scheme. While stationed at Ngong near Nairobi, he observed a similar arrangement to manage woodland. The Maasai had two forests: one was handed over to the Forest Department; the other was left under council control. After a short time, the department's reserve remained intact, but the council's woodland was severely damaged. Tomkinson claimed the same would happen at Njukiine if the council retained control.

Tomkinson's request upset several councillors. Chief Naaman said the council did not want to bind itself or future members to a course of action. He emphasized that councillors resented being told what to do. Finally, Naaman asked if the colonial government had the power to compel the councillors to accept Forest Department management.

In response to Naaman's question, the council was warned that powers vested in the Central Land Board could be used 'to deprive the local people of the control of the area.' The position of the administration was stated clearly: 'Government could not continue to stand by and watch a valuable asset like Njuki-ini being destroyed because local authorities would not exert themselves to protect it.' The debate continued. Several Njukiine subcommittee members supported Tomkinson. For example, Embu Chief Arthur Mairani, a Christian, pointed out that the council was being given its third chance to protect the forest. Other councillors vehemently opposed any outside interference.

The issue was put to vote. Eight councillors agreed to permit Forest Department management if the latest plan failed. Six members defied the administration, voting to postpone any decision about allowing outside intervention. Three councillors were absent. Thus Tomkinson's proposal was accepted by a narrow margin, and he granted permission for the council to be given a last chance to preserve Njukiine. The threat of an immediate government take-over was averted, but only at the cost of opening the door to future Forest Department management.

The new regime at Njukiine

The council's system of forest management combined ancient customary rights with bureaucratic administration. The borders were marked in 1941, and guards were hired to supervise forest use. They received a monthly salary and free housing. In an attempt to keep the guards near their posts, the council specified that they must be married and have their family reside with them. Clearing, cultivation, and herding within the forest were restricted. People from the district could freely collect deadwood and other forest products for subsistence purposes. Outside *ahoi* were denied foraging rights. People who wanted to cut timber left their names with the district commissioner's office in Embu, and the Njukiine subcommittee reviewed their applications. The subcommittee seldom granted pit-sawing rights, except for the removal of diseased trees. Twice a year the subcommittee inspected the forest. In 1942, for example, they encountered a large number of women gathering firewood. The subcommittee reported, 'We were satisfied that they were only taking dead wood, that they were not being hindered in any way and that only natives of this district were taking the firewood'. On another occasion buffalos chased the councillors as they toured the woods. Aside from a few minor infractions, encroachment ended. The council's efforts impressed Gillespie, who thought it displayed a real interest in preserving Njukiine.

The councillors continued to suspect the administration of manoeuvring towards full control of Njukiine. In 1944 the Public Works Department (PWD) applied for four ha of forest to cut firewood. The PWD was finally building the African agricultural training school and needed fuelwood to fire bricks. Officials emphasized that the land would be returned as soon as the wood was cut. They also stressed that the rest of Njukiine would be untouched. The councillors remained sceptical. Some of them suggested that the PWD would be in competition with local firewood collectors. One councillor said that the government planned 'to take the land from the Natives for Europeans'. He wanted the administration to surrender a similar area of Mount Kenya forest to the council. Despite these concerns, the PWD's request was approved. The councillors stipulated that only indigenous species, specifically *Cordia abyssinica, Markhamia hildebrandtii, Pygeum africanum,* and *Bridelia micanthra*, be replanted on the land. These trees were valued locally for timber, poles, and other uses. The councillors also feared that if the government planted exotic species on the property, it might try to claim the land as its own. The PWD paid a royalty for every stack of wood it removed.

The significance of the council's decision to protect Njukiine can be better appreciated by examining the fate of another patch of riverine woodland in Kirinyaga. Near the waterfall at Ngungu on the Mukengeria River separating Ndia and Gichugu is a small but dense stand of trees. An elder from Kimande sublocation in Inoi recalled that the forest used to cover 'many acres' when he was young in the 1930s. Various tree species grew along the banks, including *muringa, muu, mununga, mururi, Phoenix reclinata (mukindu), Blighia unijugata (muikuni), Bridelia micanthra (mukoigo),* and *Cordia ovalis (mukuu).* Living within or near the forest were numerous animals: wart-hogs, bush pigs, porcupines, hyenas, antelopes, monkeys, and leopard. Although the area was claimed by local descent groups, communal controls on forest use broke down by the 1930s. Ngungu became 'a free place for everyone'. Both the forest and wildlife steadily declined as timber was cut and the land brought under cultivation. The 1940s were especially decisive years in the clearance of the forest. 'Most of the animals vanished around 1941, after deforestation, after the bush was cleared.' At the time the administration was preoccupied with promoting increased food production for the war effort, so soil conservation controls were relaxed. People continued to clear the land for years. Nowadays trees are confined to a short but very beautiful stretch along the steep river bank.

The council's activism regarding Njukiine contrasted with its largely *laissez faire* attitude toward Nyagithuci forest, the tract of Mount Kenya reserve returned as part of the Gikuyu land claims (see Chapter 5). Several hundred hectares were left unoccupied following local resettlement. The district administration temporarily posted tribal police along the forest edge to halt encroachment in 1939. Three years later, however, Gillespie complained that Nyagithuci was damaged by illicit cutting for timber and firewood. Chiefs Justin of Mutira and Mugera of Inoi, plus the local councillor, were appointed to monitor forest use. The council agreed to fund a permanent guard starting in 1943, but three years passed before one was hired. Sporadic encroachment continued.

The conflict about Njukiine largely died down between 1940 and early 1946. Not coincidentally, this period was marked by the tenure of a single district commissioner, Ivor R. Gillespie, who took a special interest in the forest. His appreciation of local sensitivity regarding forestry matters was reflected in the district's five-year-plan drawn up in 1945. The plan emphasized that when the Africans were ready — 'and not before' — the council should receive Forest Department assistance to reforest its trust lands. During his retirement speech to the council in February 1946, Gillespie warned the members against easing up on the protection of Njukiine.

The return of controversy

With the end of World War II, the Forest Department revived its interest in managing woodland in the African reserve. Records in the Kenya National Archives showed that administrative officers throughout the province welcomed the department's involvement. Tomkinson wrote to the assistant conservator of forests, however, stating that the district commissioners asked that compulsion not be used by the government to obtain forest for the department. Officials such as Gillespie who had spent long periods in their assigned districts were aware of the conflict likely to arise if compulsion were threatened. A major turnover in administrative personnel occurred between late 1945 and early 1946, including the departures of Gillespie and Tomkinson. Subsequent events suggest that their successors were not aware of the deep local mistrust of the Forest Department and its management plans.

Controversy erupted again in 1946, when the department again proposed taking over management of local woodland. It not only wanted Njukiine and Nyagithuci, but other forested land still under indigenous control. The department planned to incorporate them into a green belt scheme to prevent desert encroachment. The councillors opposed relinquishing control over Njukiine and Nyagithuci at a meeting in May 1946. They referred the issue of protecting other woodland to the local generation-set elders: Irungu *rika* in Kirinyaga, and Kimanthi *rika* in Embu. At the next meeting the elders strongly objected to any additional woodland being removed from their authority. The elders argued that local rightholders were capable of caring for their own trees without outside intervention. D.W. Hall, the interim district commissioner, explained that the goal was not only to protect existing woodland but to extend them. The council recommended that the elders and rightholders be given a chance to show they could protect and increase their own forests. Although Hall expressed grave doubts, he agreed to give them a reasonable period to prove themselves.

The issue was far from resolved. Officials and councillors debated forest management at the next council meeting in November 1946. P. Wyn Harris, the new provincial commissioner, asked that Njukiine and other local woodland be turned over to the Forest Department, 'the only real experts on forest management'. Embu Chief Muruatetu replied sharply to the request, pointing out that the government had long promised to establish a primary school in the district, yet had failed to do so. If the government's unfulfilled pledge to provide adequate education was to be taken as a guide, then, 'no promises to look after their forests properly on their behalf could be believed with safety'. His speech swayed the councillors, who defeated the proposal. R.E. Wainwright, the new district commissioner, claimed it was not so much the councillors as the public at large that rejected Forest Department management.

Negotiations about the area's other remaining large tracts of woodland continued during the late 1940s and early 1950s. In the case of Mount Kiang'ombe in nearby Mbeere, the government threatened to set apart its forest compulsorily unless the council and local people took steps to halt deforestation. Officials generally attempted to use persuasion, however, rather than open intimidation. Nevertheless the councillors were always aware of the colonial government's power to appropriate land.

The prospect of losing territory to either the foresters or the council had little appeal to descent-group elders and land occupants. Yet, immigration, increased individualism, and other social changes weakened communal controls, threatening to unravel the landholding rights of the *mbari* and *muhiriga*. In the negotiations for Kirimiri Hill in Embu division, the local clans tried to use council trusteeship to their advantage. With the hilltop forest experiencing outside encroachment, clan elders proposed surrendering control to the council as long as they received a document confirming their ownership of the land. The elders also sought the right for clan members to cut timber without charge once sufficient trees were available. The Embu clans relinquished their rights to Kirimiri in 1949 under less favourable terms.

After considerable prompting, the council appointed a subcommittee to inves-
tigate forest destruction at Nyagithuci in 1947. They were asked to clarify
whether Nyagithuci should remain under the control of local clans or placed in
trust by the council. The subcommittee reported back seven months later, recommending that the local clan be entrusted to replant the land. Ndia councillor
Lukas attacked their idea, arguing instead for council trusteeship. Following
much discussion, his proposal was passed unanimously. The council set up a
strong subcommittee of Ndia and Gichugu councillors to determine the boundaries. Support was provided for two guards and a tree planting programme. A
few weeks later the new subcommittee reported that the borders had been
demarcated without local opposition. *Ficus natalensis* (*mugumo*) trees, a species
rich in symbolism for the Gikuyu people, were planted as boundary markers.
Families evicted from the new council forest received no compensation. They
were, however, allowed eight months to relocate. Wainwright called the action 'a
great step forward'.

By-laws and collaboration

By 1950 the Embu African District Council, as it was now called, was trustee of
four large tracts of woodland: Njukiine (1070 ha), Nyagithuci (410 ha),
Kiang'ombe (280 ha), and Kirimiri (145 ha). Except for Njukiine, the wooded
trust lands underwent substantial changes in boundaries during the remaining
years of colonial rule. Over 300 ha were excised from Nyagithuci in 1957 for
agriculture. Kirimiri lost land as well, shrinking to 100 ha by 1961. In contrast,
the council assumed management of an additional 1830 ha on Mount
Kiang'ombe. Five other hilltop and riverine forests were declared council trust
lands in the 1950s, including two in Kirinyaga: Murinduko Hill (190 ha) in north-
western Mwea; and Karaini Forest on Kamurdwana Hill (24 ha) in north-central
Ndia. Karaini was turned over to the council in compensation for the large
amount of land excised from Nyagithuci.

The acquisition of wooded trust lands marked a new phase in council forest
management. It increasingly sought to develop the commercial potential of its
forests. The new policy compelled the council to seek a close working relationship with its former adversaries in the Forest Department. As early as 1947, the
councillors and foresters collabourated in planning a small-scale tree planting
project for Njukiine. Only indigenous species were supposed to be grown, but
the project soon grew more ambitious. The Forest Department drafted a long-
term plan in 1948 for establishing plantations of fast-growing, commercially
valued exotics such as cypress. A year later 15 ha were cleared at Njukiine for
plantations of cypress and *Grevillea robusta*. A local contractor was hired to
carry out the work. His employees used the *shamba* (*taungya*) system, allowing
food crops to be interplanted with trees for the first few years in each newly
reforested site. Pines were planted at Nyagithuci using a similar method.

The foresters used their technical collaboration with the council as leverage to
modify its policies. The department made the promulgation of forest-use by-laws
and the declaration of reserve status for the wooded trust lands preconditions for
providing additional support for the council's activities. The councillors initially
rejected the proposals in 1949. Before leaving the district in 1951, however,
Wainwright persuaded them to agree to the terms. By this time the council had
increased to 26 members, 15 elected by the public and 11 nominated by district
officials. The resolution establishing the by-laws and forest reserves was spon-

sored by Chief Muruatetu and Richard Githae, a councillor from Ndia and a leader in the local branch of the Kenya African Union. Both men were regarded by their peers as political moderates but staunch defenders of local land rights.

The forest by-laws codified many of the practices in use at Njukiine. People originally from the district could freely collect deadwood, gather wild berries or fruits, cut thatching grass, take certain vines, and hang beehives. 'Genuine tribal ceremonies' were permitted, but were limited to four days. Local schools were allowed to cut building timber free of charge. The rules restricted clearing, farming, herding, and construction. The district commissioner's office retained exclusive rights to grant timber-cutting permits. Violators of these rules could be arrested or fined.

The Forest Department now assumed advisory management of the council's by-law reserves. A forest ranger was appointed for the council and posted to Njukiine. Besides supervising the expansion of plantation forestry, the ranger was responsible for the network of tree nurseries in the district. There were 22 nurseries scattered throughout Kirinyaga, Embu, and Mbeere in the early 1950s. Funds for reforestation were obtained through the Agricultural Betterment Fund. The council maintained an active forestry subcommittee, though it eventually merged with a larger one that handled agricultural and veterinary affairs. The new forest management regime was soon overwhelmed by national and local political events. In October 1952 the governor declared a State of Emergency in response to the growing anticolonial Mau Mau movement.

The Emergency years

Council forestry activities in Kirinyaga were disrupted by the Mau Mau War in the 1950s. Some of the key issues that ignited the widespread Mau Mau movement and led to years of bitter conflict have been touched on elsewhere: colonial land grievances, displaced landless Gikuyu, conflicts about land tenure, increased local sociocultural differentiation, and the frustration of Africans with their limited role in decision making under the colonial state. There were numerous connections between the anticolonial movement and local forestry issues. Pit-sawyers, forest labourers, and people living along forest boundaries, including outsider *ahoi*, were among the staunchest supporters of Mau Mau in the district. Indeed, approximately 700 Gikuyu *ahoi* who resided near Njukiine were among the first people involuntarily resettled as part of the government's villagization programme during 1954.

Njukiine served as a depot and reassembly point for Mau Mau. It was also the site of an arms factory. In October 1953 officials declared the forest a prohibited area. The tree-planting contractor was forced to abandon his work without compensation. Njukiine remained closed for four years, as the government carried out its counter-insurgency campaign. Access to Nyagithuci was restricted for years as well because of its proximity to the Mount Kenya forest.

The Mau Mau War led to widespread deforestation (see Castro and Ettenger 1994). Officials ordered land clearing to take place to reduce the vegetation cover for anticolonial guerrillas and their local supporters. Forced resettlement of Kirinyaga's population into guarded villages also led to massive cutting for housing, cattle sheds, granaries, fencing, and military posts. In addition, uncontrolled cutting for commercial timber and fuelwood sales occurred. The wooded savannah of sparsely settled Mwea and southern Gichugu were especially hard hit. Communal controls broke down in the midst of warfare and population dislocation. The council passed a by-law regulating timber sales in late 1956, but its main purpose was to limit the purchase of trees by local Asian sawmill owners. The council sponsored some public works reafforestation during the war years. It was partly a response to deforestation, but mainly a means for keeping 'youths out of mischief as well as providing them with employment'.

As part of its counter-insurgency programme, the colonial government adopted an ambitious scheme of social engineering. A British official in Ndia wrote that the policy sought to create 'a stabilised, prosperous Kikuyu middle class'. It called for modifying Gikuyu agriculture by consolidating scattered farm plots, privatizing landholding, and expanding commercial agriculture (Swynnerton 1954). Land tenure reform started in Kirinyaga in late 1954, and it was largely completed in Gichugu and Ndia by 1960 (the process continued in Mwea after independence). An examination of land tenure reform is beyond the scope of this study (see Huxley 1961; Sorrenson 1967; Shipton 1988; Haugerud 1989). The profound impact of privatization on access to forest products on descent-group lands, however, must be mentioned. In the early 1980s many people throughout the district contended that their problems with fuelwood scarcity started with land tenure reform. Privatization not only enclosed the 'bush' or other communal lands, but it curtailed the rights of commonality that had allowed people to gather deadwood on the holdings of neighbours. Several informants stressed that access to land became restricted immediately with the handing out of title deeds. A Gichugu woman in Nyangeni, Ngariama location, said, 'Each got his own piece of land which he was supposed to take care of. People did not want intruders on their land'. An elderly landless woman near Sagana stated, 'No one could go on another's shamba. It was trespassing'. An old woman from Mathigaini village in Mwea commented, 'If I go to the places where I used to collect firewood I can be chased out by the owners'. All farmland in Kirinyaga was demarcated by the early 1970s, creating a permanent class of landless. In the early 1980s over one-fifth of the district households were said to be landless, though precise figures were difficult to determine. The landless constituted the poorest sector of the population.

With the counter-insurgency campaign nearly completed, the council slowly resumed its forestry programme. The Embu councillors faced severe financial constraints. Years of warfare and economic upheaval had reduced the council's revenue from taxes, crop cesses, marketing fees, and other sources. By 1956 its account was overdrawn by 500 000 Kenya Shillings. The council was unable to do more than maintain essential public services. Austerity measures included the introduction of fees for medical services at its dispensaries, causing attendance to drop sharply. Not surprisingly, councillors looked to the forest reserves to provide revenue. A first step was the decision to sell to contractors large quantities of fuelwood from Njukiine. They also planned to charge royalties for timber once the forest was reopened for pit-sawing.

The administration offered in 1957 to take over full maintenance of the council's reserves. It proposed expanding the afforestation programme, especially at Njukiine, using funds available from the African Land Development Board. Extensive plantations of commercial timber trees were to be established. The council would receive any profits from their sale. However, councillors were told the government would only provide such financial support for forestry development if it received some 'security of tenure'. The administration's plan was twofold: gazetting the woodland as forest reserves, thus creating a legal barrier to other uses of the land; and transferring total managerial control to the Forest

Department. The council was reassured that it would remain trustee of the forests and receive financial benefits from their commercial development.

By 1957 the council had lost many of its long-time stalwarts of local land rights. In particular, Chiefs Muruatetu, Naaman, and Richard Githae had been deposed or detained because of their Mau Mau sympathies. The council was now composed entirely of appointees selected because of their loyalty to the colonial regime. Yet, these 'loyalists' initially refused to give up control of the by-law forests. The divisional forest officer commented, 'I don't think they will agree [to the plan] unless financial stringency forces them to it'.

The forester and the district commissioner decided not to press the council on the issue. Instead, they proposed that the department resume its limited financial assistance to the council to run its forest. Much work needed to be done immediately to protect some of the by-law forests after the upheaval of war. The forester believed that the enticement of 'gold injections' to expand commercial forestry activities would induce the councillors to relinquish control. Thus, both the Forest Department and the district administration took a low-key approach, assuming that the council's financial crisis would weaken its resolve. They were correct.

After nearly two years the council approved the Forest Department's plan by a 14 to 10 vote in July 1959. The close margin and long delay revealed the deep misgivings felt by many councillors and the public at large. The decision to relinquish managerial control of the forests was unprecedented, particularly given the longstanding resentment of colonial land appropriation. Yet it also contained elements of continuity. For years the councillors and foresters had collaborated in managing the reserves. The decision was not a major source of controversy. Other critical land issues absorbed local attention, particularly the consolidation and privatization of farmland.

The Forest Department took over Njukiine and other local forests in July 1960. It announced a large-scale scheme to demarcate, gazette, and develop them. The reserves were never formally gazetted, though new boundaries were marked. Njukiine, Karaini, and Nyagithuci forests were designated for intensive plantation development. Murinduko was considered too steep and dry for commercial plantations. It was set aside for environmental protection. The department's reafforestation plans were plagued by labour shortages, troublesome workers, and occasional acts of sabotage such as fires. Foresters estimated that the average cost of tree planting in the council reserves in 1961 was at least six times higher per acre than in the Mount Kenya plantations. As independence approached, it was unclear how the reserves would be managed. The 1962 Regional Boundary Commission announced that Kirinyaga and Embu would be split into two districts, complicating an already complex situation.

The Kirinyaga council forests

Kirinyaga district was officially established in 1963, the year of Kenyan independence. Its council assumed trusteeship of Murinduko, Nyagithuci, Karaini, and the western portion of Njukiine. Forestry matters were handled up to 1974 by the Agriculture, Land, and Forest Committee, and thereafter by the Town, Planning, Markets, and Housing Committee. One of the first tasks facing the committee was whether it wanted to manage the reserves or to retain the services of the Forest Department. The Ministry of Natural Resources permitted the return of the forests to local authorities provided sufficient resources were

available for their protection and development. The councillors sought information on the cost of running the reserves from the Nyeri divisional forester in
1965. He estimated that over 40 000 Kenya Shillings were spent annually on
forest maintenance and afforestation, compared to only 2000 Shillings per annum in revenue. This figure did not include the salary of the Njukiine ranger,
which the council would be partly responsible for if it altered the arrangement.
Little immediate revenue could be expected from Njukiine, the forester added,
because the timber trees already planted by the department needed 15 years
before maturing for harvest. In spite of the purported high costs, the committee
recommended reclaiming full management of the reserves. The full council disagreed, however, and the Forest Department was left in charge.

With its managerial control confirmed, the department continued its reafforestation programme for Njukiine. Charcoal and firewood licences were
offered for areas slated for plantation development. The annual planting target
for plantations on the Gichugu side of the reserve was set at 16 ha in the 1960s
and nearly double that amount during the 1970s. The department used the
shamba system of reafforestation, with trees interplanted with food crops. By the
early 1980s most of the forest had been converted into vast industrial plantation
blocks of cypress, pine, and eucalyptus. Only a few stands of indigenous woodland were left on the margins of the plantation.

The decline in Njukiine's wildlife population was a major indicator of ecological and economic change in the forest. Buffalo, rhinoceros, and other animals
had hindered the first reafforestation efforts in the early 1950s. Officials sought
to reduce greatly the buffalo population. A few buffalo and rhinoceros remained
as late as 1961, but poaching and forest clearing soon eliminated them. Smaller
animals, especially monkeys and wild pigs, inhabited the forest and surrounding
bush into the early 1970s, damaging plantations and nearby farms. Land clearing
and trapping soon eradicated them as well. By the early 1980s local residents
reported that the wildlife population had substantially declined. Some small
animals such as porcupines were left, and crested cranes and other birds remained in nearby wetlands. The presence of large herds of buffalo and other
large game in Njukiine was now only a distant memory among older adults.

Extensive plantation development also took place at Karaini forest in northern Inoi. Its remaining indigenous woodland was cleared and replaced by a
dense stand of pines. The tall pines on top of Kamurdwana Hill stood out as a
landmark in Ndia during the early 1980s. Pines and other exotics were
established at Nyagithuci, but the forest was excised in June 1973 to compensate
people displaced by the building of new schools. Expanding educational facilities
was a major priority in the district following independence. To clear the land for
resettlement, the council offered sawmills and fuelwood contractors its pines and
other trees by acre lots.

Tree planting for environmental protection took place at Murinduko. The
District Development Committee and the Rural Works Programmeme provided
funding for establishing eucalyptus and other species. A guard was hired to
protect the newly planted 50 ha of young trees, but the major threat to the young
trees appeared to be termites. The council sponsored small shelter-belt and
block plantings to serve as green belts in Mwea.

Harvesting in Njukiine's plantation forests was under way by the 1970s. Thin-
ning operations were initially carried out for pine and cypress, while the fast-
growing eucalyptus soon became available. The proximity of Njukiine's plantations to local trade centres made them especially attractive to the area's small-

scale sawmills and timber merchants. Local sawmills preferred Njukiine to less accessible plantations in the Mount Kenya reserve. By 1978, revenue from the sale of plantation thinnings exceeded 75 000 Kenya Shillings. The share of this, if any, provided by the department to the council was unclear from available records. Timber and fuelwood from Njukiine was readily purchased by local households and businesses who had benefited from the expansion of cash cropping since independence. Rising material prosperity for such families led to the increasing adoption of Western styles of housing, furniture, desks for schooling, and other items. Rapid population growth also fueled the demand for forest products.

The management regime for the council's trust forests was indistinguishable from that occurring in the central government's reserves. The emphasis had been placed on industrial plantations in areas regarded as suitable for such intensive development, while drier areas were set aside for environmental protection. Very few forest violations were recorded in the council's reserve in the early 1980s, and field observations and interviews indicated that such incidents were not common. As in Mount Kenya, however, the situation was capable of rapidly changing in some places. In 1987 district officials closed Karaini to local fuelwood collection, excluding even those holding valid permits (*The Standard* 23 Feb. 1987: 4). Local residents claimed over a year later that unauthorized removal of firewood had been triggered by timber cutting. It was felt that the pines benefited only sawmills and the government, so some people tried to take what they could before the trees were removed.

As described in Chapter 8, the issue of Forest Department management over Njukiine resurfaced in the early 1980s. Njukiine had never been gazetted as a trust forest, and the central government proposed to the council that the action finally take place. As in the past, councillors were reluctant to make such a commitment. However, the council faced severe financial problems at the time, running deficits and drawing money from its capital reserves. Some councillors proposed trading part of Njukiine to the central government in return for a strip of undeveloped forest along the edge of the Mount Kenya reserve. The purpose was to establish a tea plantation to generate income for the council. The central government rejected the offer, although it eventually established its own tea plots in the forest.

Conclusion

Colonialism undermined the communal property rights regime that governed use of Njukiine and other small forests at the beginning of the century. The influx of outsiders into the sparsely inhabited woodland and colonial pressures led to the conversion of the forests into local native council trust lands. Years of negotiations took place about the management of such forests, and for a short time — 1941 to 1952 — the council established an innovative property rights regime that combined customary rights with state management. Ultimately, however, the state gained exclusive control over the forests.

11. Conclusion

The contested commons

Garrett Hardin's account of 'The Tragedy of the Commons' presents a simple yet powerful explanation for much of the deforestation occurring worldwide. According to Hardin's analysis, the problem is that forest commons are by their very nature prone to environmental degradation. This outcome occurs because the commons are characterized by free and unmanaged access. Everyone has the ability to use the commons, yet no one has an incentive to control their own exploitation. When conditions arise for individuals to maximize their use of the commons, they do so, passing on the costs to the resource and to society as a whole. Even when people understand the consequences of their actions, Hardin argues, they will continue to act in the same manner as long as the resource remains under communal management. The only way to avoid catastrophic resource over-exploitation is to delegate responsibility for the commons to individuals (privatize) or bureaucrats (socialize). The image of the inevitably 'tragic commons' has been a compelling and appealing one, widely influencing environmental and social policy.

This book has offered another image of forest commons, one rooted in a specific place and time: Kirinyaga, Kenya, in the twentieth century. It has presented an in-depth account of changes in the use and management of the district's forest commons: the vast Mount Kenya forest, sacred groves, and small patches of woodland. The purpose has been to construct a more complex and detailed image of common property resources and regimes that better represents social and historical realities than Hardin's version. Indeed, there are extreme differences between the two images.

Hardin's image of the 'tragic commons' assumes that traditional resource use is typified by an open-access regime, lacking well-defined property rights or social controls. In contrast, the institutional arrangements for managing common property resources in pre-colonial Ndia and Gichugu were explicit, sophisticated, and effective in maintaining trees on the land. These communal controls were based on conditions of social predictability rooted in kinship, neighbourhood relations, and religious customs. The arrangements ensured widespread access to forests, as well as farmland and pasture, but also entailed individual obligations regarding resource use. Social and supernatural sanctions served as means of enforcing communal controls.

The pre-colonial Ndia and Gichugu Gikuyu engaged in practical conservation based on their specific cultural, socio-economic, and environmental circumstances. Communal forest management and agroforestry techniques were not aimed at reversing deforestation. The Gikuyu were not trying 'to save' the tropical forest. Rather, they sought to mitigate the impact of land clearing that took place as agriculture and settlements expanded. Their forest management and agroforestry strategies were means of incorporating valued woodland and trees into local socio-cultural and household production systems. People's willingness and ability to keep trees on the land varied. A significant amount of clearing, for example, took place in the nineteenth century in response to opportunities offered for supplying food to caravans from the coast. Deforestation was not necessarily synonymous with increased land degradation, however, because households used numerous techniques to expand farmland without undermining soil management.

The transformation of the indigenous forest commons in Kirinyaga occurred in a very different manner from that envisaged by Hardin. To borrow from Robert Brightman's (1987: 134) insightful case study of Algonquian hunters, the decline of communal controls were 'less tragedies of the commons than tragedies of invasions'. Great Britain declared Kenya a protectorate in 1895, and colonial forces seized control of Kirinyaga in a series of violent expeditions in 1904–05. Political, socio-economic, and cultural changes set in motion by British colonialism undermined the communal bonds, traditional authority, and in some cases low population density that maintained the indigenous common property regimes.

Two patterns were evident in the transformation of Kirinyaga's forest commons. First, the specific reasons for the decline of the indigenous management regimes varied with the different types of forest resources. Mount Kenya, sacred groves, Njukiine, and other woodland were taken over by the colonial state or its local agency at different times and for specific reasons. Second, when the administration intervened, its actions were strongly influenced by the perceived commercial value of the particular resource. Mount Kenya, the most commercially valuable of the forests, was appropriated by the colonial government by 1911. In contrast, the small forest patches and groves in the district received little official attention for over two decades.

The appropriation of the vast southern Mount Kenya forest was justified by the colonial administration as a conservation measure, but it was prompted by the possibility of European timber and agricultural development. The debate among prospective entrepreneurs, the Colonial Office, protectorate officials, and forester David Hutchins about the use and management of Mount Kenya demonstrated the diversity of colonial interests. Although they possessed different visions of how to develop the forest, the various parties were all of one mind about taking the forest from the Gikuyu. The imposition of state forestry, including the eviction of African families and the criminalization of customary forest use, led to long-standing tensions. The people of Ndia and Gichugu used several strategies to protest colonial forest appropriation: informal forms of resistance such as wood theft; the public meetings of the Local Native Council; and the 1932 Kenya Land Commission. The return of Nyagithuci tract as part of the land claims revealed many of the misconceptions by colonial officials. The subsequent controversy about resettlement at Nyagithuci forest also demonstrated conflicting interpretations of colonial interests by central government, provincial, and district officials. The inability of the administration to satisfy the land grievances ultimately contributed to the Mau Mau War of the 1950s.

After independence, the central government retained control over the Mount Kenya forest. In spite of the Africanization of the forest bureaucracy, the department retained its custodial policies. Recent forest degradation mainly resulted from official mismanagement and government-sanctioned development activities, instead of local encroachment. Large areas of indigenous forest, however, still remain intact on the southern slopes. The use of tea buffer zones to protect the reserve from further damage seemed dubious and misguided. The motives behind the Nyayo Tea Scheme were rooted in national politics and economic concerns, rather than forest conservation.

Government intervention to protect over 200 sacred groves in the early 1930s revealed the decline (though by no means the collapse) of social predictability among the Ndia and Gichugu Gikuyu. Significant socio-economic and cultural divisions had emerged, eroding neighbourhood and kinship ties and obligations. In particular, there were growing tensions between Christian neophytes and the followers of the indigenous religion. Other aspects of social change were important as well: the supplanting of the generation-sets' authority by colonial functionaries; the individualization of land tenure; increasing economic differences among households; and the political influence of missionaries. When Christian neophytes no longer participated in customary communal rituals nor respected the sanctity of the sacred groves, a protracted dispute occurred involving colonial officials, missionaries, Gikuyu colonial and traditional authorities, and the neophytes. Ultimately, the sacred groves were placed under the control of the Local Native Council, a colonial entity. Thus, legal predictability based on state-sanctioned institutions and regulations formally supplanted social predictability. However, social predictability in the form of customary controls also continued to protect the groves in many places.

The collapse of communal controls at Njukiine forest in the 1930s resembled some aspects of Hardin's 'tragic commons'. Competing individuals tried to clear the forest as fast as possible to stake claim to farmland. Once again, though, one must view this event in the context of political and socio-economic change in the district and the wider society. The indigenous common property regime at Njukiine was overwhelmed by the influx of Gikuyu immigrants from Kiambu and Nyeri, themselves the victims of colonial land appropriation in their home districts. As in the case of the sacred groves, internal socio-cultural and economic differentiation propelled by colonialism also helped to erode traditional regulations about land use. Uncertainty about tenure rights fueled the destruction of the forest, as competing groups attempted to occupy the land. Shifts in national policy and the potential commercial value of Njukiine led to efforts by the colonial state to assume management. The political framework of colonial rule established by the 1930s, however, restrained the central government from acting unilaterally. Instead it was compelled to negotiate with the Local Native Council, which officially represented the people of the district. The result was that the council assumed control over Njukiine in 1937, and, in the context of contentious negotiations, eventually developed its own system of community-resource management that blended customary rights with bureaucratic administration. Thus, legal predictability based on colonial institutions was combined with social predictability rooted in local socio-cultural relations. This innovative arrangement lasted successfully for 11 years. In 1952, the council's growing interest in commercial forest plantations as a source of revenue led it to grant advisory management of the reserves to the Forest Department. The Mau Mau Emergency (1952–60) interrupted the department's activities.

In the late 1950s, a financially drained and politically neutered council turned over control of its woodland reserves to the Forest Department. Following independence, the Kirinyaga council remained trustee of the reserves, and the department retained exclusive management over them. Njukiine was converted into a huge industrial forest plantation to meet the rising local demand for timber and fuel. Its fate was neither inevitable nor necessarily the optimal resource-use strategy under existing conditions. Rather, it was the result of long-term state policies that promoted centrally managed commercial forestry development.

Thus, the 'tragedy' of Kirinyaga's forest commons involved colonial conquest, evictions, the criminalization of local forest use, the emergence of significant local socio-cultural and political divisions, the bitter Mau Mau movement, and the brutal counter-insurgency campaigns. By independence in 1963, communal controls over forestry and state resources had been almost completely replaced by state management or private property. Only a few tracts of land in the southern part of the district had yet to be divided into individually owned farms. Within a decade that process would be finished.

Meanwhile, the Forest Department's custodial management proved more problematic and less effective than anticipated by its proponents. Although large tracts of forests remain intact on Mount Kenya to the present day, the absence of viable wood markets, rather than state management, played a decisive role. Kenya's formal-sector timber market remained fairly limited during most of colonial rule, and sawmills never developed a significant export capacity. The historical experience with fuelwood-burning agro-industries in Kirinyaga — the dried vegetable factories of World War II and the tea factories of recent times — showed that forest exploitation could quickly and substantially exceed the ability of the department to engage in local reafforestation. Forest use on a nominally sustained-yield basis could be very difficult to attain. Indeed, in the first eight decades of state forestry, spanning British and Kenyan rule, no research had been carried out on the sustained-yield capacity of the forests of Mount Kenya (Beentje 1990a: 50).

Sadly, the case of Kirinyaga is hardly unique. A World Bank study of common property resources points out the world-wide failure of 'nationalized land and state-centralized management control' (Bromley and Cernea 1989: 25). Such failures, the authors state, might be 'one of the most important development lessons of the last half-century'.

A few lessons

Much of the foregoing discussion has emphasized themes of conflict and historical change. As an applied anthropologist, I also try to draw practical lessons from the long experience of community-state conflicts over the Kirinyaga forests. A few key lessons emerge from this contentious history.

The present study has shown that communities can possess long-standing rules and institutions for the management of forest resources. These arrangements often offer a sophisticated, utilitarian, and durable mechanism for conserving woodland and trees. However, it would be mistaken to interpret indigenous communal controls in terms of contemporary Western notions of forest conservation. The Ndia and Gichugu Gikuyu, for example, were not trying 'to save' the forest as an end in itself. Rather, they were attempting to maintain a convenient supply of valued woodland and trees. Their protection of forests and trees was based on practical and religious considerations, given their specific cultural, socio-economic, and environmental circumstances.

To what extent can local strategies for managing forest resources be combined with global conservationist strategies for 'saving' tropical forests? In many ways this is a trick question. Community-based resource management strategies vary tremendously (Klee 1980; Brokensha et al. 1980; Milton 1993), and conservationists exist in very different varieties (see Adams 1990; Merchant 1992; Simmons 1993). Thus, one needs to deal in specific situations. In a very perceptive paper on Mende communities in Sierra Leone, though, Paul Richards (n.d.) points out the enormous 'cognitive gap' that often exists in the way villagers and conservationists conceptualize the use and management of forest resources. The conservationists view themselves as keepers of the forest, while the Mende perceive themselves as under its protection. Before trying to involve communities in conservation initiatives, Richards argues, outsiders need to gain an appreciation of 'local understandings' of the forest.

The experience from Kirinyaga shows that even where communal controls are breaking down, they can often form the foundation for innovative managerial regimes that are locally responsive and environmentally sustainable. A major element in the continuation or revival of such local strategies is that land tenure rights be retained by, or be returned to, the local community (see Colchester 1992). The Embu council's management of Njukiine from 1941 to 1952 offers a prime example. Despite duress from colonial officials, the councillors maintained an active trusteeship over the forest. They combined ancient customary rights with contemporary bureaucratic control. Not surprisingly, the most innovative and dynamic contemporary forestry programmes are ones based on a significant measure of local control (Chambers *et al.* 1989; Kerkhof 1990; Poffenberger 1990; Arnold 1991; Thomson 1992; Messerschmidt 1993).

A major obstacle in many places is likely to be the reluctance of public forest administrations to recognise community control over commercially valued woodland resources, especially timber. In any society, control over land conveys economic and political power. In many cases, including Kirinyaga, the Forest Department may be the largest local controller of land. Such resources often provide a significant revenue to the department. Various activities carried out on such land — protection by guards, road construction and maintenance, re-afforestation — create budgetary needs and justify the department's presence. Individual forestry employees may also use government forest lands for personal gain. Thus, the possible devolution of responsibility for woodland to local communities can pose a direct threat to the economic and power political of forest departments and their individual members.

Another major stumbling block is the propensity for foresters, administrators, and other outsiders to disregard local knowledge of, and rights to, forest resources. It would be misleading to characterize the ignoring or denigrating of indigenous forest use as a problem of miscommunication between 'experts' and the local community. Rather, the problem is often the 'experts' themselves. As Louise Fortmann and Sally Fairfax (1989: 1 839) observe about conventional forestry training:

> Rigid adherence to the fundamental tenets of professional forestry — technical expertise, macro-level planning, promotion of commercial fibre production, and a narrow biological perception of forestry — has led to a blinkered world view that ignores relevant social factors.

Foresters are not alone in having a socially myopic outlook. Robert Chambers (1993: 1) argues that 'normal professionalism' in all development disciplines, professions, and bureaucracies generates a similar world view:

> It values and rewards 'first' biases which are urban, industrial, high technology, male, quantifying, and concerned with things and the needs and interests of the rich.

He calls for a 'new professionalism' based on a 'last-first' paradigm that reverses conventional values, roles, and power relations:

> It puts people first and poor people first of all. The 'last-first' paradigm includes learning from the poor, decentralization, empowerment, local initiative, and diversity. Development is not by blueprint but by a flexible and adaptive learning process.

Obviously, moving beyond 'normal professionalism' will be a major challenge for everyone engaged in development activities.

References

Adams. W., 1990. *Green Development*. Routledge, London.

The African Standard, various dates.

Agatsiva, J., 1990. Cover Estimates in a Typical Afro-Alpine Environment: Mount Kenya Observed from Space. In: M. Winiger *et al.* (ed.), *Mount Kenya Area*. Berne, Georaphica Bernensia, 15–20.

Akinga, W., 1980. Woodfuel Survey Project in Kenya 1979–1980. Unpublished report for the Ministry of Environment and Natural Resources, Nairobi.

Allan, W., 1965. *The African Husbandman*. Oliver and Boyd. London.

Ambler, C., 1988. *Kenyan Communities in the Age of Imperialism*. Yale University Press, New Haven.

Anderson, D., 1984. Depression, Dust Bowl, Demography, and Drought: The Colonial State and Soil Conservation in East Africa during the 1930s. *African Affairs* 83: 321–43.

Anderson, J., Moore, F., Davies, J., and J. Crosskill (ed.), 1962. *They Made It Their Home*. The East Africa Women's League, Nairobi.

Anderson, R. and W. Huber, 1988. *The Hour of the Fox*. University of Washington Press, Seattle.

Arkell—Hardwick, A., 1903. *An Ivory Trader in North Kenia*. Longman, Green, London.

Arnold, J., 1991. *Community Forestry*. Food and Agriculture Organization of the United Nations, Rome.

Atieno-Odhiambo, E., 1991. The Production of History in Kenya: The Mau Mau Debate. *Canadian Journal of African Studies* 25: 308–21.

Ayiemba, E., 1990. The Ecology of Human Settlement in Mount Kenya Region: A Study on Population Growth Consequences on Land Use. In: M. Winiger *et al.* (ed.), *Mount Kenya Area*. Berne, Georaphica Bernensia, 33–40.

Baker, R., 1931. *Men of the Trees*. Dial Press, New York.

Barlow, A., 1913. The 'Mugumo' Tree in Connection with Kikuyu Circumcision Ceremonies. *Journal of East Africa and Uganda Natural History Society* 3: 41–4.

Barnes, C., 1976. An Experiment with Coffee Production by Kenyans: 1933–49. *African Economic History* 8: 198–209.

Barnett, D. and K. Njama, 1966. *Mau Mau from Within*. Monthly Review Press, New York.

Barraclough, S. and K. Ghimire, 1990. The Social Dynamics of Deforestation in Developing Countries. Discussion Paper 16. United Nations Research Institute for Social Development, Geneva.

Battiscombe, E., 1926. *Common Trees and Woody Plants of Kenya Colony*. Crown Agents for the Colonies, London.

Beachey, R., 1967. The East African Ivory Trade in the Nineteenth Century. *Journal of African History* 8: 269–90.

Beachey, R., 1976. *The Slave Trade of Eastern Africa*. Barnes and Noble, New York.

Bechmann, R., 1990. *Trees and Man*. Paragon House, New York.

Beck, E., Rheder, H., and J. Kokwaro, 1990. Classification and Mapping of the Vegetation of the Alpine Zone of Mount Kenya (Kenya). In: M. Winiger *et al.* (ed.), *Mount Kenya Area*. Berne, Georaphica Bernensia, 41–6.

Beech, M., 1913a. The Sacred Fig-tree of the A'Kikuyu of East Africa. *Man* 13: 4–6.

Beech, M., 1913b. A Ceremony of the Mugumu or Sacred Fig-tree of the A'kikuyu of East Africa. *Man* 13: 86–9.

Beentje, H., 1990a. Forests of Mount Kenya – Vegetation and Human Uses. In: M. Winiger *et al.* (eds), *Mount Kenya Area*. Berne, Georaphica Bernensia, 47–57.

Beentje, H.. 1990b. The Forest of Kenya. *Proceedings of the 12th Plenary Meeting of AETFAT*, 265–82.

Benson, T., 1964. *Kikuyu-English Dictionary*. Clarendon, Oxford.

Berkes, F., 1987. Common-Property Resource Management and Cree Indian Fisheries in Subarctic Canada. In: B. McCay and J. Acheson (ed.), *The Question of the Commons*. University of Arizona Press, Tucson, 66–91.

Berkes, F. (ed.), 1989. *Common Property Resources*. Belhaven, London.

Berman, B., 1990. *Control and Crisis in Colonial Kenya*. Currey, London.

Berman, B., 1991. Nationalism, Ethnicity, and Modernity: The Paradox of Mau Mau. *Canadian Journal of African Studies* 25: 181–206.

Berman, B. and J. Lonsdale, 1992. *Unhappy Valley*. Currey, London.

Blackburn, R., 1982. In the Land of Milk and Honey: Okiek Adaptations to Their Forests and Neighbors. In: E. Leacock and R. Lee (ed.), *Politics and History in Band Societies*. Cambridge University Press, Cambridge, 283–306.

Bodley, J., 1990. *Victims of Progress*, 3rd edn. Mayfield, Palo Alto.

Bottignole, S., 1984. *Kikuyu Traditional Culture and Christianity*. Heinemann, Nairobi.

Boyes. J., 1912. *King of the Wa-Kikuyu*. Metheun, London.

Brightman, R., 1987. Conservation and Resource Depletion: The Case of the Boreal Forest Algonquians. In: B. McCay and J. Acheson (ed.), *The Question of the Commons*. University of Arizona Press, Tucson, 121–40.

Brokensha, D., Warren, D., and O. Werner (ed.), 1980. *Indigenous Knowledge Systems and Development*. University Press of America, Lanham.

Brokensha, D. , Riley, B., and A. Castro, 1983. *Fuelwood Use in Rural Kenya*. Institute for Development Anthropology, Binghamton.

Bromley, D. and Cernea, M. 1989. *The Management of Common Property Natural Resources*. World Bank, Washington, D. C.

Brookfield, H., 1988. The New Great Age of Clearance and Beyond. In: J. Denslow and C. Padoch (ed.), 1988. *People of the Tropical Rain Forest*. University of California Press, 209- 24.

Buijtenhuijs, R., 1973. *Mau Mau Twenty Years After*. Mouton, The Hague.

Cagnolo, C., 1933. *The Akikuyu*. Catholic Mission Press, Nyeri.

Carothers, J., 1954. *The Psychology of Mau Mau*. Government Printers, Nairobi.

Castro, A., 1983. Household Energy Use and Tree Planting in Kirinyaga. Working Paper No. 397, Institute of Development Studies, University of Nairobi, Nairobi.

Castro, A., 1991. The Southern Mount Kenya Forest since Independence: A Social Analysis of Resource Competition. *World Development* 19: 1695–1704.

Castro, A., 1993. Kikuyu Agroforestry: An Historical Analysis. *Agriculture, Ecosystems and Environment* 46: 45–54.

Castro, A., forthcoming. The Political Economy of Farm Forestry in Colonial Kenya: The View from Kirinyaga. In: L. Sponsel, T. Headland, and R. Bailey (ed.). *Tropical Deforestation* Columbia University Press, New York.

Castro A. and K. Ettenger, 1994. Counter-insurgency and Socio- economic Change: The Mau Mau War in Kirinyaga, Kenya. *Research in Economic Anthropology*, Vol. 15.

Caufield, C., 1985. *In the Rainforest*. Knopf, New York.

Cavicchi, E., 1977. *Problems of Change in Kikuyu Society*. EMI, Bologna.

Cernea, M., 1989. *User Groups as Producers in Participatory Afforestation Schemes*. Washington, D.C.: The Work Bank.

Chambers, R., 1991. In Search of Professionalism, Bureaucracy and Sustainable Livelihoods for the 21st Century. *IDS Bulletin* 22: 5–11.

Chambers, R., 1993. *Challenging the Professions*. Intermediate Technology Publications, London.

Chambers, R. and J. Moris (ed.), 1973. *Mwea*. Weltforum Verlag, Munich.

Chambers, R., Saxena, N., and T. Shah, 1989. *To the Hands of the Poor*. Intermediate Technology Publications, London.

Churchill, W., 1908. *My African Journey*. Hodder and Stoughton, London.

Ciriacy-Wantrup, S. and R. Bishop, 1975, 'Common Property' as a Concept in Natural Resources Policy. *Natural Resources Journal* 15: 713–27.

Clayton, A., 1976. *Counter-Insurgency in Kenya 1952–1960*. Transafrica, Nairobi.

Clayton, A. and D. Savage, 1974. *Government and Labour in Kenya*. Cass, London.

Clough, M., 1990. *Fighting Two Sides*. University of Colorado Press, Niwot.

Colchester, M., 1992. Sustaining the Forests. Discussion Paper 35. United Nations Research Institute for Social Development, Geneva.

Cole, K., 1970. *The Cross over Mount Kenya*. Church Missionary Historical Publications, Nairobi.

Corfield, I., 1960. *Historical Survey of the Origins and Growth of Mau Mau*. Her Majesty's Stationery Office, London.

Cranworth, L. 1912. *A Colony in the Making*. Macmillan, London.

Cranworth, L. 1919. *Profit and Sport in British East Africa*. Macmillan, London.

Cranworth, L. 1939. *Kenya Chronicles*. Macmillan, London.

Crawford, E., 1913. *By the Equator's Snowy Peaks*. Church Missionary Society, London.

Crawshay, R., 1902. Kikuyu: Notes on the Country, People, Fauna and Flora. *Geographical Journal* 20: 24–49.

Cultural Survival Quarterly, 1993. Resource and Sanctuary. 17: 1- 64.

The Daily Nation, (various dates).

Dale, I. and P. Greenway, 1961. *Kenya Trees and Shrubs*. Buchanan's Kenya Estates, Nairobi.

Davison, J., 1989. *Women of Mutira*. Reiner, Boulder.

Denslow, J. and C. Padoch (eds), 1988. *People of the Tropical Rain Forest*. University of California Press, Berkeley.

Dewees, P., no date. *Social and Economic Incentives for Smallholder Tree Growing*. Food and Agriculture Organization, Rome.

Dickson, B., 1903. The Eastern Borderlands of Kikuyu. *Geographical Journal* 22: 36–9.

Dilley, M., 1966. *British Policy in Kenya Colony*. Barnes and Noble, New York (reprint of 1937 edn).

Dove, M., 1983. Theories of Swidden Agriculture and the Political Economy of Ignorance. *Agroforestry Systems* 1: 85–99.

Dundas, C., 1915. The Organisation and Laws of Some Bantu Tribes in East Africa. *Journal of the Royal Anthropological Society* 45: 234–306.

Dundas, C., 1955. *African Crossroads*. Macmillan, London.

Dunne, T. and F. Aubry, 1981. Effect of Woodfuel Harvest on Soil Erosion in Kenya. Unpublished report for the Beijer Institute and the Ministry of Energy, Nairobi.

The East African Standard, various dates.

The East African Standard, 1925. *Kenya Manual*. The East African Standard, Nairobi.

The Ecologist, 1992. Whose Common Future? 22: 122–210.

Edgerton, R., 1991. *Mau Mau*. Ballantine, New York.

Eliot, C., 1905. *The East Africa Protectorate*. Arnold, London.

Ellen, R., 1993. Rhetoric, Practice and Incentive in the Face of the Changing Times: A Case Study in Nuaulu Attitudes to Conservation and Deforestation. In: K. Milton (ed.), *Environmentalism*. Routledge, London, 126–143.

Erasmus, C., 1977. *In Search of the Common Good*. Basic Books, New York.

Fadiman, J., 1979. *The Moment of Conquest*. Ohio University Center for International Studies, Athens.

Fadiman, J., 1982. *An Oral History of Tribal Warfare*. Ohio University Press, Athens.

Farming Review, 1985.

Feeney, D., Berkes, F., McCay, B., and J. Acheson, 1990. The Tragedy of the Commmons: Twenty-Two Years Later. *Human Ecology* 18: 1–19.

Fitzgerald, W., 1970. *Travels in the Coastlands of British East Africa and the Islands of Zanzibar and Pemba*. Folkestone, Kent (reprint of 1898 ed).

Food and Agriculture Organization (FAO), 1978. *Forestry for Local Community Development*. Rome.

Fortmann, L. and S. Fairfax, 1989. American Forestry Professionalism in the Third World: Some Preliminary Observations. *Economic and Political Weekly*, 12 August.

Furedi, F., 1989. *The Mau Mau War in Perspective*. Currey, London.

Gedge, E., 1892. A Recent Exploration of the River Tana to Mount Kenya. *Geographical Society Proceedings* 14: 513–33.

Glazier, J., 1985. *Land and the Uses of Tradition among the Mbeere of Kenya*. University Press of America, Lanham.

Gradwohl, J. and R. Greenberg, 1988. *Saving the Tropical Forest*. Earthscan, London.

Gregersen, H., Draper, S., and D. Elz, 1989. *People and Trees*. Washington, D.C.: The World Bank.

Gregory, J., 1896. *The Great Rift Valley*. Nelson, London.

Grosh, B., 1991. *Public Enterprise in Kenya*. Reiner, Boulder.

Guha, R., 1990. *The Unquiet Woods*. University of California Press, Berkeley.

Hallett, R., 1974. *Africa since 1875*. University of Michigan Press, Ann Arbor.

Hardin, G., 1968. The Tragedy of the Commons. *Science* 162: 1243- 48.

Hardin, G., 1985. *Filters Against Folly*. Viking, New York.

Hardin, G. and J. Baden (ed.), 1977. *Managing the Commons*. Freeman, San Francisco.

Haugerud, A., 1989. Land Tenure and Agrarian Change in Kenya. *Africa* 59: 61–90.

Hecht, S. and A. Cockburn, 1989. *The Fate of the Forest*. Verso, London.

Hedberg, O., 1990. Origin, Evolution, and Conservation of the Afroalpine Flora. In: M. Winiger et al. (eds.), *Mount Kenya Area*. Berne, Georaphica Bernensia, pp. 59–64.

Henderson, I. and P. Goodhart, 1958. *The Hunt for Kimathi*. Hamilton, London.

Hobley, C., 1967. *Bantu Beliefs and Magic*. 2nd edn. Cass, London (reprint of 1937 edn).

Hobley, C., 1971. *Ethnology of A-Kamba and Other East African Tribes*. Cass, London (reprint of 1910 edn.).

Houghton, R., 1993. The Role of the World's Forests in Global Warming. In: K. Ramakrishna and G. Woodwell (eds), *World Forests for the Future*. Yale University Press, New Haven, 21–58.

Hutchins, D., 1907. *Report on the Forest of Kenia*. HMSO, London.

Hutchins, D., 1909. *Report on the Forests of British East Africa*. HMSO, London.

Hutchins, D., 1912. Fish Culture in British East Africa. *Journal of East Africa and Uganda Natural History Society* 2.

Huxley, E., 1956. *White Man's Country*, Vol. 1. Chatto and Windus, London (reprint of 1935 edn.).Huxley, E., 1961. *A New Earth*. Chatto and Windus, London.

Huxley, J., 1931. *African View*. Challes and Windus, London.

Hyam, R., 1968. *Elgin and Churchill at the Colonial Office*. Macmillan, London.

Itote, W., 1967. *Mau Mau General*. East African Publishing House, Nairobi.

Jacobs, M., 1988. *The Tropical Rain Forest*. Springer, Berlin.

Jaetzold, R. and H. Schmidt, 1983. *Farm Management Handbook of Kenya*, Vol. II/B. Ministry of Agriculture, Nairobi.

Kaggia, B., 1975. *Roots of Freedom*. East African Publishing House, Nairobi.

Kanogo, T. 1987. *Squatters and the Roots of Mau Mau*. Currey, London.

Kenya Land Commission, 1934. *Evidence*, Vol 1. HMSO, London.

Kenyatta, J., 1938. *Facing Mount Kenya*. Secker and Warburg, London.

Kerkhof, P., 1990. *Agroforestry in Africa*. Panos Institute, London.

Kershaw, G., 1972. The Land Is the People. Unpublished Ph.D. dissertation, University of Chicago.

Kershaw, G., 1991. Mau Mau From Below: Fieldwork and Experience, 1955–57 and 1962. *Canadian Journal of African Studies* 25: 274–97.

Kirinyaga District, 1980. *District Development Plan*. Ministry of Economic Planning and Development, Nairobi.

Kitching, G., 1980. *Class and Economic Change in Kenya*. Yale University Press, New Haven.

Klee, G. (ed.), 1980. *World Systems of Traditional Resource Management*. Winston, New York.

Krapf, J., 1860. *Travels, Researches and Missionary Labours*. Trubner, London.

Kummer, D., 1992. *Deforestation in the Postwar Philippines*. University of Chicago Press, Chicago.

Lamb, G. and L. Muller, 1982. *Control, Accountability, and Incentives in a Successful Development Institution*. World Bank Staff Working Paper, Washington, D.C.

Lambert, H., 1949. *The Systems of Land Tenure in the Kikuyu Land Unit.* School of African Studies, Cape Town.Lambert, H., 1956. *Kikuyu Social and Political Institutions.* Oxford University Press, London.

Leakey, L., 1937. *White African.* Hodder and Stoughton, London.

Leakey, L., 1952. *Mau Mau and the Kikuyu.* Methuen, London.

Leakey, L., 1954. *Defeating Mau Mau.* Methuen, London.

Leakey, L., 1977a. *The Southern Kikuyu before 1903*, Vol. 1. Academic Press, New York.

Leakey, L., 1977b. *The Southern Kikuyu before 1903*, Vol. 2. Academic Press, New York.

Leakey, L., 1977c. *The Southern Kikuyu before 1903*, Vol. 3. Academic Press, New York.

Leo, C., 1984. *Land and Class in Kenya.* University of Toronto Press, Toronto.

Little, P. and M. Horowitz (eds.), 1987. *Lands at Risk in the Third World.* Westview, Boulder.

Logie, J. and W. Dyson. 1962. *Forestry in Kenya.* Government Printers, Nairobi.

Lonsdale, J., 1992a. *The Conquest State of Kenya.* In: B. Berman and J. Lonsdale, *Unhappy Valley.* Currey, London, 13–44.

Lonsdale, J. 1992b. The Moral Economy of Mau Mau: Wealth, Poverty, and Civic Virtue in Kikuyu Political Thought. In: B. Berman and J. Lonsdale, *Unhappy Valley.* Currey, London, 315–504.

Lugard, F., 1893. *The Rise of Our East Africa Empire*, Vol. 1. Blackwood, Edinburgh.

McCay, B. and J. Acheson (ed.) 1987. *The Question of the Commons.* University of Arizona Press, Tucson.

Mackinder, H., 1900. A Journey to the Summit of Mount Kenya. *Geographical Journal*, 15: 453–86.

Madeira, P., 1909. *Hunting in British East Africa.* Lippincott, Philadelphia.

Maher, C., 1938a. *Soil Erosion and Land Utilisation in the Embu Reserve*, Part I. Department of Agriculture, Nairobi.

Maher, C., 1938b. *Soil Erosion and Land Utilisation in the Embu Reserve*, Parts II and III. Department of Agriculture, Nairobi.

Maloba, W., 1993. *Mau Mau and Kenya.* Bloomington: Indiana University Press.

Marris, P. and A. Somerset, 1971. *African Businessmen.* East Africa Publishing House, Nairobi.

Martin, C., 1991. *The Rainforests of West Africa.* Birkhauser, Basel.

Maxon, R. 1993. *Struggle for Kenya.* Fairleigh Dickenson University Press, Rutherford.

Maxwell, G., Fazan, S., and L. Leakey, 1929a. *Native Land Tenure in Kikuyu Province.* Colony and Protectorate of Kenya, Nairobi.

Maxwell, G., Fazan, S., and L. Leakey, 1929b. Record of Evidence Given by Natives at Barazas Held by the Committee. Colonial Office Records (CO 533/398), Public Records Office, London.

Meinertzhagen, R., 1957. *Kenya Diary.* Oliver and Boyd, London.

Merchant, C., 1992. *Radical Ecology.* Routledge, New York.

Messerschmidt, D. (ed.), 1993. *Common Forest Resource Management.* Food and Agriculture Organization, Rome.

Middleton, J. and G. Kershaw, 1965. *The Kikuyu and Kamba.* International African Institute, London.

Milton, K. (ed.), 1993. *Environmentalism.* Routledge, London.

Ministry of Environment and Natural Resources, 1981. Draft Report of the GOK/UNEP/UNDP Project on Environment and Development. Nairobi.

Miracle, M., 1974. Economic Change among the Kikuyu 1895–1905. Working Paper No. 158, Institute of Development Studies, University of Nairobi, Nairobi.

Molnos, A., 1972. *Cultural Source Material for Population Planning in East Africa*, Vol. 2. East African Publishing House, Nairobi.

Moreau, R., 1944. Mount Kenya: A Contribution to the Biology and Bibliography. *Journal of the East Africa Natural History Society* 13: 61–92.

Moris, J., 1970. The Agrarian Revolution in Central Kenya: A Study of Farm Innovation in Embu District. Unpublished Ph.D. dissertation, Northwestern University.

Moris, J., 1973. The Mwea environment. In: R. Chambers and J. Moris (eds), *Mwea*. Weltforum Verlag, Munich, 16–63.

Mungeam, G., 1966. *British Rule in Kenya, 1895–1912*. Clarendon, Oxford.

Munro, J., 1975. *Colonial Rule and the Kamba*. Clarendon, Oxford.

Muriuki, G., 1974. *A History of the Kikuyu, 1500–1900*. Oxford University Press, Nairobi.

Murray, J., 1974. The Kikuyu Female Circumcision Controversy, with Special Reference to the Church Missionary Society's 'Sphere of Influence'. Unpublished Ph.D. dissertation. University of California, Los Angeles.

Mutahi, E., 1983. *Sound Change and the Classification of the Dialects of South Mount Kenya*. Reimer, Berlin.

Mwaniki, H., 1970. Beekeeping: The Dead Industry among the Embu. *Mila* 1: 34–41.

Mwaniki, H., 1973. *The Living History of Embu and Mbeere*. East African Literature Bureau, Nairobi.

Mwaniki, H. 1974. *Embu Historical Text*. East African Literature Bureau, Nairobi.

Myers, N., 1984. *The Primary Source*. Norton, New York.

National Research Council. 1986. *Proceedings of the Conference on Common Property Resource Management*. National Academy Press, Washington, D.C.

Nicholson, J., 1931. *The Future of Forestry in Kenya*. Government Printer, Nairobi.

Nicholson, S., 1985. *African Drought: Monitoring and Prediction*. University Corporation for Atmospheric Research, Boulder.

Oakerson, R., 1986. A Model for the Analysis of Common Property Problems. In: National Research Council, *Proceeedings of the Conference on Common Property Resource Management*. National Academy Press, Washington, D.C, 13–29.

Ochieng', W. and K. Janmohamed (eds), 1977. Some Perspectives on the Mau Mau. *Kenya Historical Review* 5: 170–401.

Ofcansky, T., 1984. Kenya Forestry under British Colonial Administration, 1985–1963. *Journal of Forest History*, 28: 136–43.

Ogallo, L., 1990. Climatic Variations over the Mount Kenya Region and Their Impact on Ecosystems. In: M. Winiger *et al.* (ed.), *Mount Kenya Area*. Berne, Georaphica Bernensia, 137–42.

Ojiambo, J., 1978. *The Trees of Kenya*. Kenya Literature Bureau. Nairobi.

Orde-Browne, G., 1925. *The Vanishing Tribes of Kenya*. Seeley and Service, London.

Ostberg, W., 1987. *Ramblings on Soil Conservation*. Swedish International Development Authority, Stockholm.

Ostrom, E., 1990. *Governing the Commons*. Cambridge University Press, Cambridge.

Peluso, N., 1992. *Rich Forests, Poor People*. Berkeley: University of California Press, Berkeley.

Peters, C., 1891. *New Light on Dark Africa*. Ward and Lock, London.

Phillipson, D., 1985. *African Archaeology*. Cambridge University, Press, Cambridge.

Poffenberger, M., 1990. *Joint Management for Forest Lands*. Ford Foundation.

Poulson, G., 1983. Using Farm Trees for Fuelwood. *Unasylva* 35: 26–9.

Powell-Cotton, P., 1973. *In Unknown Africa*. Kraus, Nendeln (reprint of 1903 edn.).

Presley, C., 1992. *Kikuyu Women, the Mau Mau Rebellion, and Social Change in Kenya*. Westview Press, Boulder.

Richards, J. and R. Tucker (ed.), 1988. *World Deforestation in the Twentieth Century*. Duke University Press, Durham.

Richards, P. (no date). Saving the Rainforest? Contested Futures in Conservation. Unpublished paper.

Riley, B. and Brokensha, D., 1988a. *The Mbeere in Kenya*, Vol. 1. University Press of America, Lanham.

Riley, B. and Brokensha, D., 1988b. *The Mbeere in Kenya*, Vol. 2. University Press of America, Lanham.

Rogers, P., 1979. The British and the Kikuyu 1890–1905: A Reassessment. *Journal of African History* 20: 255–69.

Rosberg, C. and J. Nottingham, 1970. *The Myth of 'Mau Mau'*. Meridian, New York.

Ross, W., 1927. *Kenya from Within*. Allen and Unwin, London.

Routledge, W. and K. Routledge, 1910. *With a Prehistoric People*. Arnold, London.
Saberwal, S., 1967. Historical Notes on the Embu of Central Kenya. *Journal of African History* 8: 29–38.
Saberwal, S., 1970. *The Traditional Political System of the Embu of Central Kenya*. East African Publishing House, Nairobi.
Sandgren, D., 1982, Twentieth Century Religious and Political Divisions among the Kikuyu of Kenya. *African Studies Review* 25: 195–207.
Scheibe, R. and E. Beck, 1990. Ecophysiological Studies on Afroalpine Plants. In: M. Winiger *et al.* (eds), *Mount Kenya Area*. Berne, Georaphica Bernensia, 159–65.
Scott, J., 1985. *Weapons of the Weak*. Yale University Press, New Haven.
Shepherd, G., 1993. Africa: Semi-Arid and Sub-Humid Regions. In: D. Messerschmidt (ed.), *Common Forest Resource Management*. Food and Agriculture Organization, Rome, 99–191.
Shipton, P., 1988. The Kenyan Land Tenure Reform: Misunderstandings in the Public Creation of Private Property. In: R.E. Downs and S.P. Reyna (eds), *Land and Society in Contemporary Africa*. University Press of New England. Hanover, 91–135.
Siiriainen, A., 1971. The Iron Age Site at Gatung'ang'a, Central Kenya. *Azania* 6: 1971.
Simmons, I., 1993. *Interpreting Nature*. Routledge, London.
Sinange, R., 1990. Land Use South and East of Mount Kenya: Present and Future Programmes. In: M. Winiger *et al.* (eds), *Mount Kenya Area*. Berne, Georaphica Bernensia, 167–174.
Sluiter (Kershaw), G., 1956. A Study of Kabare Village in Embu District. Christian Council of Kenya, Nairobi.
Sorrenson, M., 1967. *Land Reform in the Kikuyu Country.* Oxford University Press, Nairobi.
Sorrenson, M., 1968. *Origins of European Settlement in Kenya*. Oxford University Press, Nairobi.
Spear, T., 1981. *Kenya's Past*. Longman, Longman.
The Standard. various dates.
Stichter, S., 1982. *Migrant Labour in Kenya*. Longman, Harlow.
Stigand, C., 1913. *The Land of Zinj*. Constable, London.
Swynnerton, R., 1954. *A Plan to Intensify the Development of African Agriculture in Kenya*. Government Printer, Nairobi.
Thomson, J., 1885. *Through Masailand*. Sampson, London.
Thomson, J., 1992. *A Framework for Analyzing Institutional Incentives in Community Forestry*. Food and Agriculture Organization, Rome.
Throup, D., 1988. *Economic and Social Origins of Mau Mau*. Heinemann, Nairobi.
Tignor, R., 1976. *The Colonial Transformation of Kenya*. Princeton University, Princeton.
Troup, R., 1940. *Colonial Forest Administration*. Oxford University, Oxford.
Trzebinski, E., 1985. *The Kenya Pioneers*. Heinemann, London.
Tucker, R., and J. Richards (eds), 1983. *Global Deforestation in the Nineteenth Century World Economy*. Duke University Press, Durham.
Van Zwanenberg, R., 1975. *Colonial Capitalism and Labour in Kenya, 1919–1939*. East African Literature Bureau, Nairobi.
Veen, J., 1973. The Production System. In: R. Chambers and J. Moris (eds), *Mwea*. Weltforum Verlag, Munich, 99–131.
Von Hohnel, L., 1968. *Discovery of Lakes Rudolf and Stefanie*, Vol. 1. Frank Cass, London (reprint of 1894 edn.).
Wachanga, H., 1975. *The Swords of Kirinyaga*. Kenya Literature Bureau, Nairobi.
Waciuma, C., 1969. *Daughter of Mumbi*. East African Publishing House, Nairobi.
Ward, H. and J. Milligan, 1912. *Handbook of British East Africa 1912–13*. Caxton, Nairobi.
Warner, K., 1992. *Shifting Cultivators*. Food and Agriculture Organization, Rome.
Weekly Review (various dates).
Widner, J., 1992. *The Rise of a Party-State in Kenya*. University of California Press, Berkeley.

William, S.M., (1989). Deforestation: Past and Present. *Progress in Human Geography.* 13: 176–208.

Wimbush, S., 1930. *The Forests of Mount Kenya.* In: E. Dutton (ed.) *Kenya Mountain.* Cape, London, 190–201.

Winiger, M. and J. Rheker, 1990. Mount Kenya: 100 Years of Research -- Its Contribution to the Understanding of Tropical Mountain Ecosystems. In: M. Winiger *et al.* (ed.), *Mount Kenya Area.* Berne, Georaphica Bernensia, 193–6.

Winiger, M., Wiesmann, U., and J. R. Rheker (ed.) 1990. *Mount Kenya Area.* Berne, Georaphica Bernensia.

Wolff, R., 1974. *Britain and Kenya 1870–1930.* Transafrica, Nairobi.

Woodwell, G., 1993. Forests: What in the World Are They For? In: K. Ramakrishna and G. Woodwell (ed.), *World Forests for the Future.* Yale University Press, New Haven, pp. 1–20.

World Bank, 1980. Sociological Aspects of Forestry Project Design. Washington, D.C.

World Bank, 1986a. Kenya Forestry Subsector Review. Eastern and Southern Africa Projects Division, Central Agriculture Division. Washington, D.C.

World Bank, 1986b. Annex I: Forests, Land Use and Environmental Issues. In: Kenya Forestry Subsector Review. Washington, D.C.

World Bank, 1986c. Annex IV: Industrial Forestry. In: Kenya Forestry Subsector Review. Washington, D.C.

Young, T., 1990. Mount Kenya Forest – An Ecological Frontier. In: M. Winiger *et al.* (ed.), *Mount Kenya Area.* Berne, Georaphica Bernensia, 197–201.